Mind

FUNDAMENTALS OF PHILOSOPHY SERIES

Series Editors
John Martin Fischer, University of California, Riverside
John Perry, Stanford University

Mind: A Brief Introduction
John R. Searle

Biomedical Ethics
Walter Glannon

A Contemporary Introduction to Free Will
Robert Kane

Mind

A Brief Introduction

JOHN R. SEARLE

New York ♦ Oxford
OXFORD UNIVERSITY PRESS
2004

Oxford University Press, Inc., publishes works that further Oxford University's
objective of excellence in research, scholarship, and education.

Oxford   New York
Auckland   Cape Town   Dar es Salaam   Hong Kong   Karachi
Kuala Lumpur   Madrid   Melbourne   Mexico City   Nairobi
New Delhi   Shanghai   Taipei   Toronto

With offices in
Argentina   Austria   Brazil   Chile   Czech Republic   France   Greece
Guatemala   Hungary   Italy   Japan   Poland   Portugal   Singapore
South Korea   Switzerland   Thailand   Turkey   Ukraine   Vietnam

Published by Oxford University Press, Inc.
198 Madison Avenue, New York, New York 10016
http://www.oup.com

Library of Congress Cataloging-in-Publication Data

Searle, John R.
Mind: a brief introduction/by John R. Searle
p. cm.—(Fundamentals of Philosophy)
ISBN-13: 978-0-19-515733-8 (alk.paper)—ISBN-13: 978-0-19-515734-5 (pbk.:alk.paper)

1. Philosophy of Mind.
I. Title.
II. Fundamentals of philosophy (Oxford, England).
B.418.3.542004
128'.2—dc22   2004049546

Printing number: 9 8 7 6 5

Printed in the United States of America
on acid-free paper

For Dagmar

Contents

Acknowledgments

Most of the material in this book has been given by me in lectures at Berkeley, and I am indebted to my students for their combination of enthusiasm and skepticism. Two of them, Hua (Linda) Ding and Nadia Taylor, read the entire manuscript and made helpful comments. For help in preparing the electronic text I am also grateful to Maria Francisca Reines, Jessica Samuels, and Jing Fong Williams Ying. I received valuable philosophical advice from Janet Broughton, Josef Moural, Axel Seeman, and Marga Vega. The two readers for Oxford University Press, David Chalmers and an anonymous reader, made many helpful comments. I thank my research assistant, Jennifer Hudin, for assistance throughout, from the early formulation of the ideas to the final preparation of the index. Most of all, I thank my wife Dagmar Searle for her constant advice and support, and I dedicate this book to her.

Mind

Why I Wrote This Book

There are many recent introductory books on the philosophy of mind. Several give a more or less comprehensive survey of the main positions and arguments currently in the field. Some, indeed, are written with great clarity, rigor, intelligence, and scholarship. What then is my excuse for adding another book to this glut? Well, of course, any philosopher who has worked hard on a subject is unlikely to be completely satisfied with somebody else's writings on that same subject, and I suppose that I am a typical philosopher in this respect. But in addition to the usual desire for wanting to state my disagreements, there is an overriding reason for my wanting to write a general introduction to the philosophy of mind. Almost all of the works that I have read accept the same set of historically inherited categories for describing mental phenomena, especially consciousness, and with these categories a certain set of assumptions about how consciousness and other mental phenomena relate to each other and to the rest of the world. It is this set of categories, and the assumptions that the categories carry like heavy baggage, that is completely unchallenged and that keeps the discussion going. The different positions then are all taken within a set of mistaken assumptions. The result is that the philosophy of mind is unique among contemporary philosophical subjects, in that all of the most famous and influential theories are false. By such theories I mean just about anything that has "ism" in its name. I am thinking of dualism, both property dualism and substance dualism, materialism, physicalism, computationalism, functionalism, behaviorism, epiphenomenalism, cognitivism, eliminativism, pan psychism, dual-aspect theory, and emergentism, as it is standardly conceived. To make the whole subject even more poignant, many of these theories, especially dualism and materialism, are trying to say something true. One of my many aims is to try to rescue the truth from the overwhelming urge to falsehood. I have attempted some of this task in other works, especially *The Rediscovery of the Mind*,[1] but this is my only attempt at a comprehensive introduction to the entire subject of the philosophy of mind.

Now what exactly are these assumptions and why are they false? I cannot tell you that just yet. They do not admit of a quick summary without some preliminary work. The first half of this book is in large part about exposing and overcoming those assumptions. It is hard to summarize them because we lack a neutral vocabulary in which to describe mental phenomena. So I have to begin by appealing to your experiences. Suppose you are sitting at a table thinking about the contemporary political situation, about what is going on in Washington, London, and Paris. You turn your attention to this book and you read up to this point. Here I suggest that, to get a feel for the assumptions, you try pinching your left forearm with your right hand. And suppose you do this intentionally. That is, we will suppose your intention causes the movement of your right hand to pinch your left arm. At this point you will experience a mild pain. This pain has the following more or less obvious features. It exists only insofar as it is consciously experienced, and thus it is in one sense of the words entirely "subjective" and not "objective." Furthermore, there is a certain qualitative feel to the pain. So, the conscious pain has at least these two features: subjectivity and qualitativeness.

I want all of this to sound rather innocent, even boring. So far you have had three types of conscious experiences: thinking about something, intentionally doing something, and feeling a sensation. What is the problem? Well, now look at the objects around you, the chairs and tables, houses and trees. These objects are not in any sense "subjective." They exist entirely independent of whether or not they are experienced. Furthermore, we know independently that they are entirely made of the particles described by atomic physics, and that there is no qualitative feel to being a physical particle, or for that matter being a table. They are parts of the world that exist apart from experiences. Now this simple contrast between our experiences and the world that exists independently of our experiences invites a characterization, and in our traditional vocabulary the most natural characterization is to say is that there is a distinction between the mental, on the one hand, and the physical or material, on the other. The mental qua mental is not physical. And the physical qua physical is not mental. It is this simple picture that leads to many of the problems, and our three harmless-looking examples exemplify three of the worst problems. How can conscious experiences like your pain exist in a world that is entirely composed of physical particles and how can some physical particles, presumably in your brain, cause the mental experiences? (This is called the "mind-body problem.") But even if we got a solution to that problem, we still would not be out of the woods because the next obvious question is, How can the subjective, insubstantial, nonphysical mental states of consciousness ever cause anything in the physical world? How can your intention, not a part of the physical world, ever cause the movement of your arm? (This is called the "problem of mental causation.") Finally your thoughts about politics raise a third intractable problem. How can your thoughts, presumably in your head, refer to or be about distant objects and states of affairs, political events occurring in Washington, London, or Paris, for example? (This is called the "problem of intentionality," where "intentionality" means the directedness or aboutness of the mind.)

Our innocent experiences invited a description; and our traditional vocabulary of "mental" and "physical" is hard to resist. This traditional vocabulary assumes the mutual exclusion of the mental and physical; and that assumption creates insoluble problems that have launched a thousand books. People who accept the reality and irreducibility of the mental tend to think of themselves as dualists. But to others, accepting an irreducible mental component in reality seems like giving up on the scientific world-view, so they deny the existence of any such mental reality. They think it can all be reduced to the material or eliminated altogether. They tend to think of themselves as materialists. I think both sides are making the same mistake.

I am going to try to overcome the vocabulary and the assumptions, and in so doing I am going to try to solve or dissolve the traditional problems. But once we do that, the subject, the philosophy of mind, does not end: it gets more interesting. And this is my second reason for wanting to write this book. Most of the general introductions to the subject are just about the Big Questions. They concentrate mainly on the mind-body problem with some attention also devoted to the problem of mental causation and a lesser amount to the problem of intentionality. I do not think these are the only interesting questions in the philosophy of mind. With the big questions out of the way, we can answer the more interesting and neglected set of questions: how does it work in detail?

Specifically, it seems to me we need to investigate questions about the detailed structure of consciousness, and the significance of recent neurobiological research on this subject. I devote an entire chapter to these questions. With the philosophical puzzle about the possibility of intentionality answered, we can then go on to examine the actual structure of human intentionality. Furthermore, there are a series of absolutely fundamental questions that we have to get clear about before we can think that we understand the operation of the mind at all. They are more than I can cover in a single book, but I do devote a chapter each to the problem of the freedom of the will, the actual operation of mental causation, the nature and functioning of the unconscious, the analysis of perception, and the concept of the self. In an introductory book I cannot go into too much detail, but I can at least give you a feel for the richness of the subject matter, a richness that is lost in the usual ways of dealing with this subject in introductory books.

There are two distinctions that I want you to be clear about at the very beginning, because they are essential for the argument and because the failure to understand them has led to massive philosophical confusion. The first is the distinction between those features of a world that are observer independent and those that are observer dependent or observer relative. Think of the things that would exist regardless of what human beings thought or did. Some such things are force, mass, gravitational attraction, the planetary system, photosynthesis, and hydrogen atoms. All of these are observer independent in the sense that their existence does not depend on human attitudes. But there are lots of things that depend for their existence on us and our attitudes. Money, property, government, football games, and cocktail parties are what they are, in large part, because that's what we think they are. All of these are observer relative or observer dependent. In general, the natural sciences deal with observer-independent phenomena, the social sciences with the observer dependent. Observer-dependent facts are created by conscious agents, but the mental states of the conscious agents that create observer-dependent facts are themselves observer-independent mental states. Thus the piece of paper in my hand is only money because I and others regard it as money. Money is observer dependent. But the fact that we regard it as money is not itself observer dependent. It is an observer-independent fact about us that I and others regard this as money.

Where the mind is concerned we also need a distinction between original or intrinsic intentionality on the one hand and derived intentionality on the other. For example I have in my head *information* about how to get to San Jose. I have a set of true *beliefs* about the way to San Jose. This information and these beliefs in me are examples of original or intrinsic intentionality. The map in front of me also contains information about how to get to San Jose, and it contains symbols and expressions that *refer to* or are *about* or *represent* cities, highways, and the like. But the sense in which the map contains intentionality in the form of information, reference, aboutness, and representations is derived from the original intentionality of the map makers and users. Intrinsically the map is just a sheet of cellulose fibers with ink stains on it. Any intentionality it has is imposed on it by the original intentionality of humans.

So there are two distinctions to keep in mind, first between observer-independent and observer-dependent phenomena, and second between original and derived intentionality. They are systematically related: derived intentionality is always observer-dependent.

CHAPTER 1

A Dozen Problems in the Philosophy of Mind

The aim of this book is to introduce the reader to the philosophy of mind. I have three objectives. First, the reader should get an understanding of the most important contemporary issues and discussions in this field, and also get some understanding of their historical background. Second, I want to make clear what I think is the correct way to approach these problems, and I even hope to provide answers to many of the questions I pose. And third, most important of all, I would like the reader to be able to think about these issues for himself or herself after reading the book. I can state all of these aims at once by saying that I am trying to write the book that I wish I had read when I first began to think about these questions. I write out of the conviction that the philosophy of mind is the most important subject in contemporary philosophy and that the standard views—dualism, materialism, behaviorism, functionalism, computationalism, eliminativism, epiphenomenalism—are false.

One agreeable feature of writing about the mind is that it is not necessary to explain why the subject is important. It takes a while to see that illocutionary acts and quantified modal logic are important subjects in philosophy, but everyone can see immediately that the mind is central to our life. The operation of the mind—conscious and unconscious, free and unfree, in perception, action, and thought, in feeling, emotions, reflection, and memory, and in all its other features—is not so much an aspect of our lives, but in a sense, it is our life.

There are risks in writing such a book: among the worst things we can do is to give readers the impression that they understand something they do not really understand, that something has been explained when it has not been explained, and that a problem has been solved when it has not been solved. I am acutely aware of all these risks, and in what follows I will be emphasizing areas of human ignorance—my own as well as others'—as much as areas of human understanding. I think that the philosophy of mind is so important that it is worth taking these risks. For a number of important historical reasons, the philosophy of mind has become the central topic in contemporary philosophy. For most of the twentieth century the philosophy of language was "first philosophy." Other branches of philosophy were seen as derived from the philosophy of language and dependent on results in the philosophy of language for their solution. The center of attention has now moved from language to mind. Why? Well, first, I think many of us working in the philosophy of language see many of the questions of language as special cases of questions about the mind. Our use of language is an expression of our more biologically fundamental mental capacities, and we will not fully understand the functioning of language until we see how it is grounded in our mental abilities. A second reason is that with the growth of knowledge we have seen a movement away from treating the theory of knowledge, epistemology, as central in philosophy and we are now prepared to do a more substantive, theoretical, constructive philosophy, rather than just dealing piecemeal with specific traditional problems. The ideal place to begin that constructive philosophy is to start by examining the nature of the human mind. A third reason for the centrality of the mind is that, for many of us, myself included, the central question in philosophy at the beginning of the twenty-first century is how to give an account of ourselves as apparently conscious, mindful, free, rational, speaking, social, and political agents in a world that science tells us consists entirely of mindless, meaningless, physical particles. Who are we, and how do we fit into the rest of the world? How does the human reality relate to the rest of reality? One special form of this question is, What does it mean to be human? The answers to these questions have to begin with a discussion of the mind, because mental phenomena form the bridge by which we connect with the rest of the world. A fourth reason for the preeminence of the philosophy of mind has been the invention of "cognitive science," a new discipline that attempts to go deeper into the nature of the mind than was customary in traditional empirical psychology. Cognitive science requires a foundation in the philosophy of mind. Finally, more controversially, I think the philosophy of language has reached a period of relative stagnation because of certain common mistakes that surround the doctrine of so-called externalism, the idea that the meanings of words, and by extension the contents of our minds, are not inside our heads, but are matters of causal relations between what is in our heads and the external world. This is not the place to rehearse those issues in detail, but the failures to give an account of language on an externalist premise have led to a fallow period in the philosophy of language; and the philosophy of mind has taken up the slack. I will say more about externalism in chapter 6.

The philosophy of mind has a special feature that distinguishes it from other branches of philosophy. In most philosophical subjects there is no sharp division between what the professionals believe and the opinions of the educated general public. But on the issues discussed in this book, there is an enormous difference between what most people believe and what the professional experts believe. I suppose most people in the Western world today accept some form of dualism. They believe they have both a mind, or a soul, and a body. I have even heard some people tell me they have three parts—a body, a mind, and a soul. But this is definitely not the view of the professionals in philosophy, psychology, cognitive science, neurobiology, or artificial intelligence. Almost without exception, the professional experts in the field accept some version of materialism. A great deal of effort in this book will be devoted to trying to explain these issues and solve the attendant problems.

Let us suppose then that the mind is now the central topic in philosophy and that other questions, such as the nature of language and meaning, the nature of society, and the nature of knowledge are all in one way or another special cases of the more general characteristics of the human mind, How should we proceed to examine the mind?

I. DESCARTES AND OTHER DISASTERS

In philosophy there is no escaping history. Ideally, I sometimes think, I would just like to tell my students the truth about a question and send them home. But such a totally unhistorical approach tends to produce philosophical superficiality. We have to know how it came about historically that we have the questions we do and what sorts of answers our ancestors gave to these questions. The philosophy of mind in the modern era effectively begins with the work of René Descartes (1596-1650). Descartes was not the first person to hold views of the kind he did, but his view of the mind was the most influential of the so-called modern philosophers, the philosophers of the seventeenth century, and after. Many of his views are routinely expounded, and uncritically accepted today by people who cannot even pronounce his name. Descartes' most famous doctrine is dualism, the idea that the world divides into two different kinds of *substances* or entities that can exist on their own. These are mental substances and physical substances. Descartes' form of dualism is sometimes called "substance dualism."[1]

Descartes thought that a substance has to have an essence or an essential trait that makes it the kind of substance that it is (all this jargon about substance and essence, by the way, comes from Aristotle). The essence of mind is consciousness, or as he called it "thinking"; and the essence of body is being extended in three dimensions in physical space, or as he called it "extension." By saying that the essence of the mind is consciousness, Descartes is claiming that we are the sort of beings we are because we are conscious, and that we are always in some conscious state or other and would cease to exist if we ceased to be in some conscious state. For example, right now my mind is concentrating consciously on writing the first chapter of this book, but whatever changes I go through when I stop writing and, for example, start eating dinner, I will still continue to be in some conscious state or other. In saying that the essence of body is extension, Descartes is claiming that bodies have spatial dimensions: the desk in front of me, the planet Earth, and the car in the parking lot are all extended or spread out in space. In Descartes' Latin terminology the distinction is between *res cogitans* and *res extensa*. (Descartes' name, by the way, is a contraction of "Des Cartes," Latin: "Cartesius," meaning of the cards; and the corresponding English adjective is "Cartesian.")

Cartesian dualism was important in the seventeenth century for a number of reasons, not the least of which being that it seemed to divide up the territory between science and religion. In the seventeenth century the new scientific discoveries seemed to pose a threat to traditional religion and there were terrific disputes about the apparent conflict between faith and reason. Descartes partly, although not entirely, defused this conflict by, in effect, giving the material world to the scientists and the mental world to the theologians. Minds were considered to be immortal souls and not a proper topic of scientific investigations, whereas bodies could be investigated by such sciences as biology, physics, and astronomy. Philosophy, by the way, he thought could study both mind and body.

According to Descartes, each essence has different modes or modifications in which it can occur. Bodies are infinitely divisible. That is, they can in principle be divided up indefinitely into smaller pieces, and in this sense each body can be destroyed, though matter in general cannot be destroyed. The amount of matter in the universe is constant. Minds, on the other hand, are indivisible, that is, they cannot be divided into smaller pieces, and thus they cannot be destroyed in the way that bodies can. Each mind is an immortal soul. Bodies, as physical entities, are determined by the laws of physics; but minds have free will. Each of us as a self is identical with his or her mind. As living human beings we are composite entities, comprising both a mind and a body, but for each of us the self, the object referred to by "I," is a mind that is somehow attached to our body. Gilbert Ryle, a twentieth-century philosopher of mind, sneered at this aspect of Descartes' view by calling it the doctrine of "the ghost in the machine." Each of us is a ghost (our mind) inhabiting a machine (our body).[2] We know both the existence and the contents of our minds by a kind of immediate awareness, which Descartes summarizes in the most famous sentence of his philosophy, "*Cogito ergo sum*": I think therefore I exist. This looks like a formal argument with "I think" as premise and "I exist" as conclusion, but I believe that Descartes intended it also to record a kind of inner inspection of the existence and the contents of the mind. I cannot be mistaken about the existence of my own consciousness, hence I cannot be mistaken about my own existence, because it is my essence to be a conscious (that is, thinking) being, a mind. Nor can I be mistaken about the contents of my mind. If it seems to me, for example, that I have a pain, then I do have a pain.

Bodies, on the other hand, cannot be known directly but only indirectly by inferring their existence and features from the contents of the mind. I do not directly perceive the table in front of me; but, strictly speaking, I perceive only my conscious experience of the table, my "idea" of the table; and I infer the existence of the table from the presence of the idea. My present idea of the table is not caused by me, so I have to assume that it is caused by the table.

Descartes' account of the relationship between mind and body can be summarized in the accompanying chart. In addition to having an essence each substance has a series of modifications or properties, and these are the particular forms that the essence takes.

	Substances	
	Mind	Body
Essence	Thinking (consciousness)	Extension (having spatial dimensions)
Properties	Known directly Free Indivisible Indestructible	Known indirectly Determined Infinitely divisible Destructible

Descartes' views have led to endless debates and it is fair to say that he left us with more problems than solutions. The account that I just gave you, brief as it was, of reality as dividing into the mental and the physical, leaves us with a bushel of problems of which here are eight that most concerned Descartes himself and his immediate successors.

1. The Mind-Body Problem

What exactly are the relations between the mental and the physical, and in particular how can there be causal relations between them? It seems impossible that there should be causal relations between two completely different metaphysical realms, the physical realm of extended material objects and the mental or spiritual realm of minds or souls. How does anything in the body cause anything in the mind? How does anything in the mind cause anything in the body? Yet, it seems we know that there are causal relations. We know that if somebody steps on my toe, I feel a pain even though his stepping on my toe is just a physical event in the physical world, and my feeling of pain is a mental event that occurs inside my soul. How can such things happen? Just as bad: it seems there are causal relations going the other way as well. I decide to raise my arm, an event that occurs inside my conscious soul, and, lo and behold, my arm goes up. How are we supposed to think that such a thing could ever happen? How can a decision in my soul cause a movement of a physical object in the world such as my body? This is the most famous problem that Descartes left us, and it is usually called the "mind-body problem." How can there be causal relations between the two? Much of the philosophy of mind after Descartes is concerned with this problem, and it is still, in spite of all of our progress over the centuries, a leading problem in contemporary philosophy. I believe it has a fairly obvious general philosophical solution, which I shall explain later; but I have to tell you in advance that many—maybe most—of my colleagues are strongly in disagreement with my claim that we have a ready solution to Descartes' problem.

There are really two sets of problems. How can anything physical produce an effect inside my soul, which is nonphysical, and how can events in my soul affect the physical world? In the past century and a half the first of these questions has been transformed in a way that Descartes would not have accepted. In its modern version, the question is, How can brain processes produce mental phenomena at all? How can brains cause minds? Descartes did not think such a thing was possible, because on his account minds have an existence completely independent of the brain. The problem for Descartes was not the *general* question of how a mental substance can arise out of neurobiology, because for him it cannot. His question was rather how *specific* mental contents such as feeling a pain can arise from the impact of an injury to my body. We think the very existence of a mind is explained by the operations of the brain. Descartes did not think that was possible. For him the question was only how *specific* thoughts and feelings, such as a sensation of pain, can be caused by events occurring to the body.

It is important to emphasize this point: we tend to think, even the dualists among us, that our bodies with their brains are conscious. Descartes did not think that. He thought bodies and brains could no more be conscious than tables or chairs or houses, or any other hunk of junk. Conscious souls are separate, though somehow attached to human bodies. But no material object, living or dead, is conscious.

2. The Problem of Other Minds

I said that according to Descartes each of us is a mind and that each of us knows the contents of his or her mind directly, but how do I know that other people have minds? What makes me confident, when, for example, I meet you, that you have a mind? After all, all I can observe is your body, including its physical movements and the sounds that come out of its mouth that I interpret as words. But how do I know that there is anything behind all these physical phenomena? How do I know that you have a mind when the only mind that I have direct knowledge of is my own mind?

We might think that I can infer the existence of mental states in you by analogy with myself. Just as I observe in my own case a correlation between input stimulus, inner mental state, and output behavior; so in your case, because I can observe the input stimulus and the output behavior, I infer by analogy that you must have an inner mental state corresponding to mine. Thus, if I hit my thumb with a hammer, the input stimulus causes me to feel a pain, which in turn causes me to cry out. In your case, so the story goes, I observe the input stimulus and the crying out, and I simply plug in the gap by making an analogy between you and me.

This is a famous argument, called the "argument from analogy." But it doesn't work. In general, it is a requirement on inferential knowledge that if the knowledge claim is to be valid, there must be, in principle, some independent or noninferential way to check the inference. Thus, if I think that there is someone in the next room by inferring her presence from sounds that I hear, I can always go in the next room and check on this inference to see if there really is someone in the next room causing the sounds. But if I make an inference from your stimulus and your behavior to your mental state, how can I ever check the inference? How can I ever see that I am correctly inferring and not just making a wild guess? If I take it to be a kind of scientific hypothesis that we test by scientific methods, whether or not you have mental states corresponding to your observable stimulus and response patterns, in the same way that I have mental states corresponding to my stimulus and response patterns, then it seems that what the argument proves is that I am the only person in the world that has any mental states at all. Thus, for example, if I ask everybody in the room to put their thumbs on a desk and I go around pounding each thumb with a hammer to see which ones, if any, hurt; it turns out that as far as I can observe there is only one thumb that hurts: this one, the one I call mine. But when I hit the other thumbs, there is no feeling at all.

The view that I am the only person who has mental states is called "solipsism." Solipsism comes in at least three different grades. One, the most extreme form: I am the only person in the world who has mental states; and indeed in some forms, nothing exists in the world except my mental states. Two, epistemic solipsism: maybe other people have mental states, but I can never know for sure. It is quite possible that they do but I have no way of finding out, because all I can observe is their external behavior. And three: Other people do have mental states, but I can never be sure that they are like mine. For all I know, what I call "seeing red," if you could have that very experience you might call it "seeing green," and if I could have your experience that you call "seeing red" I would call it "seeing green." We both pass the same color blindness tests because we both make the same discriminations in our behavior. If asked to pick out the green pencil from a box of red pencils, we both pick the same pencil. But how do I know that the inner experiences you have that enable you to discriminate are similar to the ones I have that enable me to discriminate?

Solipsism is unusual in the history of philosophy in that there are no famous solipsists. Just about every conceivable crazy philosophical position has been held by some famous philosopher or other, but, as far as I know, no famous historical philosophers have ever been solipsists. Of course, if anyone were a solipsist it would hardly be worth his or her time to tell us that they were solipsists, because on their theory we don't exist.*

Solipsism also involves a peculiar asymmetry in that your solipsism is no threat to me, and my solipsism, if I am tempted to solipsism, cannot be refuted by you. So, for example, if you come to me and say, "I am a solipsist. You don't exist," I do not feel the temptation to think, "Gosh, maybe he's right, maybe I don't exist." But, correspondingly, if I am tempted to solipsism, it is no good my going to you and asking, "Do you exist? Do you really have mental states?" Because anything you say will still be consistent with the hypothesis of solipsism.

3. The Problem of Skepticism about the External World and 4. The Analysis of Perception

The skepticism about other minds that follows from Cartesian dualism is just a special case of a much more general kind of skepticism: skepticism about the existence of the external world. On Descartes' view all I can have certain knowledge of are the contents of my own mind, my actual thoughts, feelings, perceptions,

---

* Bertrand Russell writes:
> As against solipsism it is to be said, in the first place, that it is psychologically impossible to believe, and is rejected in fact even by those who mean to accept it. I once received a letter from an eminent logician, Mrs. Christine Ladd Franklin, saying that she was a solipsist, and was surprised that there were no others.

Human Knowledge: Its Scope and Limits (London: Allen and Unwin, 1948), 180.

and so on. But what about the chairs and tables and mountains and rivers and forests and trees that I see around me? Do I have secure knowledge that they really exist and that I am perceiving them as they really are? It is important to understand that on Descartes' view we do not directly perceive objects and states of affairs in the world. What we directly perceive, that is, perceive without any inferential processes, are the contents of our own minds. So if I hold up my hand in front of my face, what I directly perceive, what I strictly and literally perceive, according to Descartes, is a certain visual experience that I am having. Descartes calls these experiences "ideas." I perceive not the hand in itself, but rather a certain visual representation of the hand, a kind of mental picture of the hand. But then the question arises, How do I know there really is a hand out there on the other side causing me to have this mental picture? Because I do not perceive the hand itself but only a mental representation of the hand, the question arises, How do I know that the representation really represents, or represents accurately? Descartes' view was common in the seventeenth century. It is called the "representative theory of perception," and I am going to tell you more about it later, but I want to point out at this stage that a problem for Descartes is, How can we really be sure? How can we have certain and secure knowledge that there is an object out there that is causing me to have this visual experience, and that the visual experience is in any respect an accurate representation of the real features of the object?

Descartes presents very little by way of an argument to show that we cannot directly perceive tables, chairs, mountains, etc. but can only perceive our ideas of these things. He makes the transition from perceiving real objects to perceiving only the contents of our own minds very casually. Though he was by no means the first philosopher to hold this view, the move from the view that we really perceive real objects to the view that we only perceive our ideas of objects is a move of decisive importance in the history of philosophy. Indeed, I would say it is the greatest single disaster in the history of philosophy over the past four centuries. In contemporary jargon, it is put by saying: we do not perceive material objects, we perceive only "sense data." I will have much more to say about this issue in chapter 10.

There are really two closely related problems. The first is, How do we give an analysis of our perceptual interactions with the world? What exactly is the relationship between our inner perceptual experiences, on the one hand, and material objects and other features of the external world, on the other? The second is, How can we ever be sure that we have knowledge of the external world that is on the other side of our perceptual experiences? The two are closely related because we would like our analysis of perception of the external world to provide us with the tools for answering skepticism about the possibility of having knowledge of the external world.

5. The Problem of Free Will

I have experiences of making up my own mind, of deciding between genuine alternatives, and of doing one thing, when I could easily have done something else. These are manifestations of what I take to be my own freedom of the will. But the question naturally arises, Do I genuinely have free will, or is it only an illusion? The question comes in a very sharp form for Descartes, because if my free will is a feature of my mind, how can it have any effect on the physical world, if the physical world is entirely determined? This problem is an extension of, but not the same as, the mind-body problem. For even if we have a solution to the mind-body problem, even if we can show how my thoughts and feelings can move my body, there is still the question, How is this consistent with the conception of physics of Descartes' time that the physical world is a completely causally closed, deterministic system? Every event that happens in the physical world is determined by preceding physical events. So even if we could prove somehow that we have mental free will, it wouldn't make any difference to the behavior of my body, because the behavior of my body is caused by the preceding states of my body and the rest of the physical universe. The problem of free will seems difficult for anyone, but it raises exceptional problems for someone who accepts dualism.

This problem is still with us today in a form just as acute as that of Descartes' time. Nowadays we think that quantum physics has shown an indeterminacy in the behavior of particles at the subatomic level. Not everything is determined in the way that classical physics supposed. But that seems to be no help with the free will problem, because the form of quantum indeterminacy is randomness, and randomness is not the same as freedom. The fact that particles at the microlevel are not completely determined, and therefore not completely predictable, but only statistically predictable, seems to give no support whatever to the idea that our apparently free actions are really free. Even if our decision making somehow inherited the indeterminacy of the quantum-level events in our brains, that would still not give us free will, but only an unpredictable random element in our decisions and behavior. I will say more about this in chapter 8.

6. The Self and Personal Identity

There is another problem to which Descartes' followers have thought his account provided a conclusive answer, even though Descartes himself did not address the problem directly: the problem of the existence of the self and its identity through time and change. To see what the problem is, consider this example: I am now working on a set of issues while looking out at a lake in Sweden. A month ago I was working on related problems while looking at the ocean off California. The experiences are quite different, but I think of them as both experiences of mine. Why? With what justification? There is really a whole set of questions here, a tangle of philosophy. What fact about these experiences makes them experiences of the same person and what fact about me makes me now the same person as the person who was in California? It is tempting to say that this person is the same as that person because they both have the same body. But is this body really essential to my identity? It seems at least possible to imagine that I might, like Gregor Samsa in the story by Kafka, wake up in a completely different body. But if the same body is not what makes me me, then what does make me me? What is the relation between my personal identity and my bodily identity? In addition to this or that particular experience, do I also have the experience of myself as a self?

The dualist's answer to these questions is swift. My body has nothing whatsoever to do with my identity. My identity consists entirely in the continuation of the same mental substance, the same soul, or *res cogitans*. Material objects may come and go and experiences may come and go, but my identity is guaranteed by the sameness of my mental substance, for I am identical with that substance.

There are two other problems for Descartes that are more in the nature of puzzles that he has to resolve, but his solutions are quite interesting. These are the problem of nonhuman animals and the problem of sleep.

7. Do Animals Have Minds?

If every mind is a spiritual or mental substance, and if minds are indestructible, then it seems that if animals have minds, every animal has an immortal soul. But if it turns out that every dog, cat, mouse, flea, and grasshopper has an immortal soul, then, to put it mildly, heaven is going to be very much overpopulated. Descartes' solution to the problem of animal minds was swift and brutal. He said that animals do not have minds. He was not at all dogmatic about that; he thought that perhaps they have minds, but it seemed to him scientifically unlikely that they had minds. He thought the crucial distinction between us and animals, that enables us to tell for sure that human beings have minds and animals do not, is that human beings have a language in which they express their thoughts and feelings, and animals have no language. Their lack of language he considered to be overwhelming evidence that they have no thoughts or feelings. Descartes agreed that this is a somewhat counterintuitive result. If we see a dog hit by a carriage and we hear the dog howling in apparent pain, it looks like we have to assume that the dog has feelings just as we do. But Descartes says all of that is an illusion. We should no more pity the dog than we pity the carriage when it is involved in a crash. The noise might make it look as if the carriage was suffering pain, but it is not; and likewise with dogs and all other animals. It sounds crazy to deny that dogs and other animals are conscious, but here is how I think Descartes thought of the matter. In the human case, the body is not conscious. It is only the immortal soul, which is attached to the body, that is conscious. But in the dog's case, it seems very unlikely that there is an immortal soul; there is just a body, and bodies cannot be conscious. Therefore, the dog is not conscious. Ditto for all other animals.

8. The Problem of Sleep

The eighth problem for Descartes is the problem of sleep. If every mind is essentially conscious, if consciousness is the essence of mind such that you could not have a mind without being conscious, then it looks like unconsciousness would imply nonexistence. And indeed Descartes' theory implies: if I cease to be conscious, then I cease to exist. But then how do we account for the fact that people, while still alive, nonetheless are often unconscious? They go to sleep, for example. Descartes' answer to that would be that we are never totally 100 percent unconscious. There is always some minimal level of dreaming going on even in the soundest sleep. As long as we continue to exist we necessarily continue to be conscious.

II. FOUR MORE PROBLEMS

There are four other problems arising out of the problems of fitting minds into the rest of the universe, which, however, were either not addressed by Descartes himself or have been transformed in the contemporary era in ways that are quite different from the forms in which Descartes and his immediate followers addressed them.

9. The Problem of Intentionality

Intentionality is a problem that arises not only for dualism, but for the philosophy of mind in general. It was never explicitly faced by Descartes, but in subsequent philosophers it has come to the fore, and indeed in the past hundred years has become one of the central problems in the philosophy of mind.

"Intentionality" is a technical term used by philosophers to refer to that capacity of the mind by which mental states refer to, or are about, or are of objects and states of affairs in the world other than themselves. So, for example, if I have a belief, it must be a belief that something is the case. If I have a desire, it must be a desire to do something or that something should happen. If I have a perception, I must at least take myself to be perceiving some object or state of affairs in the world. All of these are said to be intentional, in the sense that in each case the state refers beyond itself. Intending, in the ordinary sense in which I intend to go to the movies tonight, is just one kind of intentionality among others along with belief, hope, fear, desire, and perception. (The English technical term comes not from the English "intention" but from the German *Intentionalität* and that in turn from Latin.) It is a special technical term, not to be confused with intending in the ordinary sense.

The special philosophical problem of intentionality is this: suppose that I now believe that George W. Bush is in Washington. The question arises, How can my thoughts, which are entirely inside my mind, reach out all the way to Washington, D.C.? If I think the sun is 93 million miles from the earth, how is it, again, that my thoughts can reach out and refer beyond themselves? The problem of how a mental state can refer to or be about something beyond itself is the problem of intentionality.

It is absolutely essential to be clear about the distinction between the intrinsic or original intentionality that I have in my head when I am thinking about something and the derivative intentionality that the marks on paper have when I write my thoughts down. The words on paper really do mean and refer, and thus have intentionality, but their intentionality is derived from mine when I intentionally wrote them down. Also we need to distinguish these two, the original and the derived, from metaphorical ascriptions, or as-if cases of intentionality. If I am now thirsty that is a case of intrinsic or original intentionality. If I write down the sentence, "I am thirsty" that sentence has derived intentionality. If I say, "My car is thirsty for gasoline" that sentence makes a metaphorical or "as-if" ascription of thirst to the car. But the car does not literally have any intentionality, either original or derived. I cannot tell you how much confusion has been generated by the failure to see these elementary distinctions.

In its modern form there are really two problems of intentionality. First there is the problem of how it is possible for events occurring in our brains to refer beyond themselves at all. How is aboutness or directedness possible at all? A second, related, problem is how is it that our brains or minds have the specific intentional contents that they do? So, for example, if I am now thinking about George W. Bush, what fact about me makes my belief have the content that it is about George W. Bush and not, for example, about his brother Jeb or his father George Bush or somebody else named George W. Bush or my dog Gilbert? The two problems are, How is intentionality possible at all? And given that it is possible, How is it that intentional states have the specific contents they do have? I devote chapter 6 to the problems of intentionality.

10. Mental Causation and Epiphenomenalism

I said there were two parts to the mind-body problem, one going in and one going out. How do input stimuli cause mental phenomena, and how do mental phenomena cause output behavior? Each of these deserves separate discussion, so I am going to make the question of how mental states function causally into a separate topic.

Some philosophers who think that we could explain how consciousness is caused by brain processes cannot see how consciousness could have any causal powers of its own. Granted that somehow or other consciousness, and mental phenomena generally, are dependent on brain processes, it is hard to see how they could cause bodily movements or cause anything in the physical world. The view that mental states exist but are causally inert is called "epiphenomenalism." On this view consciousness exists alright, but it is like the froth on the wave or the flash of sunlight reflected off the surface of the water. It is there but it does not really matter. It is an epiphenomenon. But this seems too counter-intuitive. Every time I decide to raise my arm, it goes up. And it is not a random or statistical phenomenon. I do not say, "Well, that's the thing about the old arm. Some days she goes up and some days she doesn't." The problem is to show how something not a part of the physical world could have such effects on the physical world. In the contemporary jargon this problem is posed as follows. It is often said, "The physical world is causally closed." That means that nothing outside the physical world can enter into the physical world and act causally. How then could mental states, which are not physical and thus not part of the physical world, act causally on the physical world?

11. The Unconscious

For Descartes, any mental activity is by definition conscious. The idea of an unconscious mental state is to him a contradiction in terms, an unconscious consciousness. But, in the past century or so, we have come to be quite comfortable with the idea that many of our mental states are unconscious. What can this mean? What is an unconscious mental state and how does it fit in with the rest of our mental life and with the world in general?

The problem of the unconscious is not one just for psychopathology. We do indeed say that people act from motives of which they are unconscious and the presence of which they would sincerely deny. We say that Sam was insulting to his brother Bob because he has an unconscious hostility to his brother. This is the sort of thing that Freudian psychology attempts to deal with. But there is another, more pervasive, use of the notion of the unconscious according to which we think of all sorts of mental processes as going on inside our brains but without any conscious manifestations. On standard theories of perception, we think that people perceive the shapes of objects by unconsciously inferring the real features of the object from the limited features of the physical stimulus with which they are presented. The problem for both of these notions of the unconscious is, What exactly is it supposed to mean in real terms? What facts about brain events could make them both *mental* and at the same time *unconscious*?

12. Psychological and Social Explanation

Explanations of human psychological and social phenomena seem to have a different logical structure from explanations in physics and chemistry. When we explain why we voted the way we did in the last election, or why the First World War broke out, we seem to be using a different sort of explanation from when we explain why plants grow. What are the appropriate forms of explanation for human psychological and social phenomena and what implications does this have for the prospects of the social sciences?

One of the most disappointing features of the intellectual history of the last hundred years was the failure of the social sciences to achieve the rich explanatory power characteristic of the physical and biological sciences. In sociology, or even economics, we do not have the kind of established knowledge structures that we have in physics and chemistry. Why not? Why have the methods of the natural sciences not had the kind of payoff in the study of human behavior and human social relations that they have had in the physical sciences?

III. DESCARTES' SOLUTIONS TO THE PROBLEMS

A large part of this book will be concerned with the 12 problems that I have just outlined. If those problems look interesting to you, you are likely to find this book interesting. If you cannot for the life of you figure out why anybody would be interested in these problems, then this is probably the wrong book for you. The book is not a historical book, and I will not say a great deal about the development of these problems historically. However, since I introduced eight of them by way of Descartes as their origin, I want to tell you, however briefly, what his answers to these eight questions were. I think that, without exception, his answers were inadequate, and to his credit, he was often fully aware that they were inadequate. I think you will understand contemporary philosophy better if you see, at least briefly, how he dealt with these problems.

1. The Mind-Body Problem

Descartes never got an answer to this question that he was satisfied with. He did recognize that the mind caused events in the body and that events in the body caused events in the mental realm. But how exactly was it supposed to work? He never felt he had resolved that.

He studied anatomy and at least once observed the dissection of a cadaver to find out where the point of connection between the mind and the body might be. In the end he came up with the hypothesis that it must be in the pineal gland. This is a small pea-shaped gland at the base of the skull. Descartes thought that this must be where the mental forces and the physical forces come in contact with each other. This is not as crazy as it sounds; he gave a reasonable argument for thinking this. He noticed that everything in the brain has a twin on the opposite side of the brain. Because of the two hemispheres, the anatomy apparently occurs in duplicate. But since all of our mental events occur in a unitary form, there must be some unified point in the brain where the two streams are brought together. The only single unduplicated organ he could find within the brain was the pineal gland, so he assumed that the point of contact between the mental and the physical must be the pineal gland.

(The urge to find the point of contact between the soul and the body is still not dead. I once debated a Nobel Prize-winning neurobiologist, Sir John Eccles, on British television. He argued that the soul attaches to the brain in the supplementary motor area. Here is his argument: If you ask a subject to perform a simple motor task such as touching each of his right fingers with his right thumb, the motor cortex shows a high level of activity. If you now ask the subject to just think the task but not actually perform it, the motor cortex shuts down but the supplementary motor area remains active. The idea that Eccles had is that when the soul alone is active it is stimulating the supplementary motor area.)

In a famous passage Descartes said we should not think of the mind as lodged in the body like a pilot in a ship, but we should really think that it is somehow suffused throughout the body. If I bump into something I do not observe my body banging into another object in a way that the pilot of a ship might observe the ship banging into the wharf, but rather I feel a pain in the part of my body that comes in contact with the object. Descartes says we should think of our mind as if it were somehow suffused throughout the body, but on his own account, that cannot be a correct thing to say, because mental substance cannot be spatially extended. It cannot be spread throughout the body because it cannot be spread out at all.

2. The Problem of Other Minds

Some version of the argument from analogy is often attributed to Descartes, but I have never been able to find it stated explicitly in his writing. According to the argument from analogy, I infer the existence of mental states in other people, by analogy with myself. Just as I observe a correlation of my own behavior with my mental states, so I can infer the presence of appropriate mental states in others when I observe their behavior. I have already pointed out the limitations of this form of argument. The problem is that in general with inferential knowledge there must be some independent check on the inference if the inference is to be valid. Thus for example, I might discover that a container is empty by banging on the container and inferring from the hollow sound that there is nothing in it, but this inferential form of knowledge only makes sense given the assumption that I could open up the container and look inside and thus noninferentially perceive that the container is empty. But in the case of knowledge of other minds there is no noninferential check on my inference from behavior to mental states, no way that I can look inside the container to see if there is something there.

3. Skepticism about the External World and
4. The Correct Analysis of Perception

Descartes has an elaborate argument that we can have certain knowledge about objects and states of affairs in the external world, even though all we directly perceive are the contents of our own minds. The first step in his argument requires that he prove the existence of God. And this is no mean feat in itself. But, assuming that God exists, he argues that God cannot be a deceiver. Because of God's perfection, it would be inconsistent to suppose that he could be a deceiver, for deceit is an imperfection. But if God is not a deceiver, then there must exist an external world, and I must have some sort of correct knowledge when I make observations of the external world. Why? Because God gives me every reason to believe, for example, that there is a desk in front of me, and a chair on which I'm sitting, and no reason to suppose otherwise. Therefore, if I am mistaken, God would be deceiving me, and that is impossible.

This then raises a problem for Descartes: How is error possible? And his answer is that error is possible because my will exceeds my understanding. My will is potentially infinite; my understanding is finite. And I often will to believe things that I do not clearly and distinctly perceive to be true, and consequently, I can be mistaken.

It is important to emphasize that Descartes did not think that our perceptions are in general accurate representations of the world. Objects do not really have colors, tastes, or smells, nor do they give off sounds, even though colors, tastes, smells, and sounds seem to us perceptually to be parts of the world. The point is that we can be certain that there is an external world causing our perceptions and we can get certain sorts of accurate information about it from our perception, even though much of our perceptual experience is illusory.

5. The Problem of Free Will

It seems to me that Descartes has no answer to this question beyond a mere assertion. He says I am free insofar as I feel myself to be free. But the problem, as we will see later, is that it is not at all clear that from the fact that I perceive myself to be free, I really am free.

6. The Self and Personal Identity

Descartes never faced this question explicitly, but Cartesians have generally thought his dualism gives us an automatic solution to this problem. The self just is identical with a mental substance and the identity of the mental substance is simply guaranteed by the fact that it is the same mental substance. But it is hard to see how this is any kind of a solution other than a solution by fiat. How does the mental substance ever acquire all these mysterious powers and properties? And what reason have we to suppose that there is any such mental substance in addition to our physical bodies and our conscious experiences? As we will see, Hume made devastating criticisms of the Cartesian account of the self and personal identity. There is no experience of the self, according to Hume; and the identity that we ascribe to ourselves through the changes in our lives is an entirely fictitious identity. It is a kind of systematic illusion. Many other philosophers follow Hume in supposing that there is no such thing as a self in addition to the sequence of our particular experiences. Lichtenberg thought that the "I" in sentences such as "I think" gives us the illusion that there is an "I" that does the thinking; but he says we should say rather "It thinks," where the "it" is like the "it" in "It's raining." It does not actually refer to an entity.

There is not just one problem of the self but several. I do not think Descartes' account of *res cogitans* is in any way a solution to these problems and I will address the whole bunch of them in chapter 11.

7. Animals and
8. Sleep

I have already criticized Descartes' solutions to these problems so I will be very brief here: it seems to me simply preposterous to claim that animals do not have any conscious states. When I come home from work and my dog rushes out to greet me, wagging his tail and jumping up and down, why exactly is it that I am so confident that he is conscious and indeed that there is a specific content to his consciousness, he is happy to see me? The usual answer given to this question is that because his behavior is so much like that of a happy person I can infer that he is a happy dog. But that seems to me a mistaken argument. To begin with, happy people do not in general wag their tails and try to lick my hands. Furthermore, and more importantly, someone might easily build a robot dog that would wag its tail and jump up and down without having any inner feelings whatever. What is so special about the real dog? I think the answer is that the basis on which I am confident that my dog is conscious and has a specific content to his consciousness is not simply that his behavior is appropriate, but that I can see that the causal underpinnings of the behavior are relatively similar to mine. He has a brain, a perceptual apparatus, and a bodily structure that are relevantly similar to my own: these are his eyes, these are his ears, this is his skin, there is his mouth. It is not just on the basis of his behavior that I conclude that he is conscious, but rather on the basis of the causal structure that mediates the relation between the input stimulus and the output behavior. In the case of humans, the input stimulus causes experiences, which in turn cause output behavior. The underlying physical structure that enables the input stimulus to cause experiences is relevantly similar in humans and higher animals. For that reason we are completely confident that dogs and chimpanzees have conscious states, in many respects like our own. When it comes to snails and termites, we have to leave it up to the experts to tell us whether or not they have a rich enough neurobiological capacity to have conscious life.

Again, just as it seems preposterous to me to suppose that animals are not conscious, it also seems preposterous to me to suppose that we cease to exist if we become completely unconscious during sleep or under anesthesia. However, if Descartes is wrong to suppose that a continuation of consciousness is essential for a continuation of our very existence, then the question is raised, What exactly are the criteria for our continued existence? This is the famous problem of personal identity, which I will discuss further in chapter 11.

The 12 problems I have outlined form the framework for my discussions about the philosophy of mind. But I do not wish to give the impression that the subject is in this way limited. These problems open up into a variety of other problems that we will have to pursue. One thing we will discover is that often there are two sets of problems concerned with each of these issues. There is the overwhelming philosophical problem, the big-deal problem, as it were, then there is a detailed problem or set of problems about how the phenomenon works in real life. So, for example, with consciousness, there is the big-deal problem: How is such a thing possible at all? How *could* the brain cause consciousness? In current discussions this is often called the "hard problem" and the lack of an explanation of how the brain does it is called the "explanatory gap." But there is also, I think, an equally interesting problem: How does consciousness function in actual organisms like ourselves? Similarly with intentionality. There is the huge problem: How is it possible that intentionality could exist at all? But, to me, at least, the more interesting question is: How does it work in detail?

What I have tried to do in this chapter is to present the framework for the discussions that will follow. The problems will not be treated as of equal weight. Not by any means. The next three chapters will be largely devoted to the mind-body problem. I have already said what I will have to say about animals and sleep. Several problems receive a chapter of their own: intentionality, mental causation, free will, the unconscious, perception, and the self. Some of the other problems, though they are of great importance, will receive only rather brief discussion in this book, because they go far beyond the philosophy of mind, especially skepticism and social science explanation. These are both large questions and I will discuss them only briefly in this book, because to give an adequate discussion would require a separate book.

Suggestions for Further Reading

Descartes, R., *The Philosophical Writings of Descartes,* trans. J. Collingham, R. Stoothoff, and D. Murdoch, 2 vols., Cambridge: Cambridge University Press, 1985, vol. II, especially *Meditations on First Philosophy,* Second Meditation 16–23, and Sixth Meditation, 50–62, *Objections and Replies,* especially Author's Replies to the Fourth Set of Objections 154–162.

There are a number of general introductions to the philosophy of mind, among them:

Armstrong, D. M., *The Mind-Body Problem, An Opinionated Introduction*, Boulder, CO: Westview Press, 1999.
Churchland, P. M., *Matter and Consciousness*, Cambridge, MA: MIT Press, 1988.
Heil, J., *Philosophy of Mind*, London and New York: Routledge, 1998.
Jacquette, D., *Philosophy of Mind*, Englewood Cliffs, NJ: Prentice Hall, 1994.
Kim, J., *The Philosophy of Mind*, Boulder, CO: Westview Press, 1998.
Lyons, W., *Matters of the Mind*, New York: Routledge, 2001.

There are also several general collections of articles on the philosophy of mind, among them:

Block, N., ed., *Readings in Philosophy of Psychology*, vol. 1, Cambridge, MA: Harvard University Press, 1980.
Chalmers, D., ed., *Philosophy of Mind, Classical and Contemporary Readings*, New York: Oxford University Press, 2002.
Heil, J., ed., *Philosophy of Mind, A Guide and Anthology*, Oxford: Oxford University Press, 2004.
Lycan, W., ed., *Mind and Cognition: A Reader*, Cambridge, MA: Blackwell 1990.
O'Connor, T., and D. Robb, eds. *Philosophy of Mind, Contemporary Readings*, London and New York: Routledge, 2003.
Rosenthal, D. M., ed., *The Nature of Mind*, New York: Oxford University Press, 1991.

CHAPTER 2

The Turn to Materialism

I. TROUBLES WITH DUALISM

We now skip forward in time to the twentieth and twenty-first centuries. Because of the failures of Cartesian-style dualism, especially the failure to get an adequate or even coherent account of the relationship between the mind and the body, it is widely assumed that substance dualism in any form is out of the question. This is not to say that no serious professionals are substance dualists. But in my experience most substance dualists I know are people who hold this view for some religious reasons, or as part of a religious faith. It is a consequence of substance dualism that when our body is destroyed our soul can continue to survive; and this makes the view appealing to adherents of religions that believe in an afterlife. But among most of the professionals in the field, substance dualism is not regarded as a serious possibility. A prominent exception is the defense of dualism offered by Karl Popper and J. C. Eccles.[1] They claim that there are two quite distinct worlds, World 1 of physical objects and states and World 2 of states of consciousness. Each is a separate and distinct world that interacts with the other. Actually they go Descartes one better and also postulate World 3, a world of "culture in all its manifestations."[2]

All forms of substance dualism inherit Descartes' problem of how to give a coherent account of the causal relations between the soul and the body, but recent versions have an additional problem. It seems impossible to make substance dualism consistent with modern physics. Physics says that the amount of matter/energy in the universe is constant; but substance dualism seems to imply that there is another kind of energy, mental energy or spiritual energy, that is not fixed by physics. So if substance dualism is true then it seems that one of the most fundamental laws of physics, the law of conservation, must be false. Some substance dualists have attempted to cope with this problem by claiming that for each infusion of spiritual energy, there is a diminution of physical energy, thus preserving a constant amount of energy in the universe. Others have said that the mind rearranges the distribution of energy in the universe without adding to it or subtracting from it. Eccles says that the mind can affect the body by altering the probability of neuronal events without any energy input, and that quantum physics enables us to see how this can be done: "The hypothesis of mind-brain interaction is that mental events act by a quantal probability field to alter the probability of emission of vesicles from presynaptic vesicular grids."[3] There is something ad hoc about these maneuvers, in the sense that the authors are convinced in advance of the truth of dualism and are trying to find some way, any way, that will make dualism consistent with physics.

It is important to understand what an extreme doctrine substance dualism is. According to substance dualism our brains and bodies are not really conscious. Your body is just an unconscious machine like your car or your television set. Your body is alive in the way that plants are alive, but there is no consciousness to your body. Rather, your conscious soul is somehow attached to your body and remains attached to it until your body dies, at which time your soul departs. You are identical with your soul and only incidentally and temporarily inhabit this body.

The problem with this view is that, given what we know about how the world works, it is hard to take it seriously as a scientific hypothesis. We know that in humans consciousness cannot exist at all without certain sorts of physical processes going on in the brain. We might, in principle, be able to produce consciousness in some other physical substance, but right now we have no way of knowing how to do this. And the idea that consciousness might be produced apart from any physical substrate whatever, though conceivable, just seems out of the question as a scientific hypothesis.

It is not easy to make the idea that the mind is a separate substance consistent with the rest of what we know about the world. Here are three ways of trying to do it, each with a different conception of the mind.

First, divine intervention. Physical science is incomplete. Our souls are something in addition to the rest of the world. They are created by divine intervention and are not part of the physical world as described by science.

Second, quantum mechanics. The traditional mind-body problem arises only because of an obsolete Newtonian conception of the physical. On one interpretation of quantum measurement, consciousness is required to complete the collapse of the wave function and thus create quantum particles and events. So some form of consciousness is not created by the rest of nature, rather it is essential for the creation of nature in the first place. It is a primitive part of nature required to explain brain processes and everything else.[4]

Third, idealism. The universe is entirely mental. What we think of as the physical world is just one of the forms that the underlying mental reality takes.[5]

I mention these for the sake of completeness. I do not agree with any of them, and I don't think I understand the second; but as none of them is an influential view in the philosophy of mind, and as I am trying to explain the philosophy of mind, I won't discuss them further in this book.

There is a weaker version of dualism called "property dualism," and that view is fairly widespread. The idea is this: Though there are not two kinds of substances in the world, there are two kinds of properties. Most properties, such as having an electrical charge, or having a certain mass, are physical properties; but some properties, such as feeling a pain or thinking about Kansas City, are mental properties. It is characteristic of human beings that though they are not composed of two different kinds of substances, their physical bodies, and in particular their brains, have not only physical properties, but mental properties as well.

Property dualism avoids postulating a separate mental substance, but it inherits some of the difficulties of substance dualism. What are the relationships between the mental and the physical supposed to be? How is it that physical events can ever cause mental properties? And there is a particular problem that property dualists seem to be beset with, and that is the problem of how the mental properties, granted that they exist, can ever function causally to produce anything. How can my conscious states, which on this view are not even parts of an extra substance, but merely nonphysical features of my brain, function to cause any physical events in the world? This difficulty, how mental states can ever function causally to produce physical effects, I described in chapter 1 as the problem of "epiphenomenalism." According to epiphenomenalism, mental states do indeed exist but they are epiphenomena. They just go along for the ride; they do not actually have any causal effects. They are like the froth on the wave that comes up on the shore or the flashes of light that glisten off a lake—they are there all right, but they play no significant causal role in the physical world. Indeed, they are worse than the froth and the flash, because they could not play any causal role. The challenge is, How could they play any causal role in determining physical events when they are not themselves physical? If we assume, as it seems we must, that the physical universe is causally closed, in the sense that nothing outside it could have any effects inside; and if we assume, as it seems we must, that consciousness is not part of the physical universe, then it would seem to follow that consciousness can have no effect in the physical universe.

Property dualism does not force us to postulate the existence of a thing that is attached to the body but not really part of the body. But it still forces us to suppose that there are properties of the body, presumably properties of the brain, that are not ordinary physical properties like the rest of our biological makeup. And the problem with this is that we do not see how to fit an account of these properties into our overall conception of the universe and of how it works. We really do not get out of the postulation of mental entities by calling them properties. We are still postulating nonmaterial mental things. It does not matter whether we say that my conscious pain is a mental property of my brain or that it is an event in my brain. Either way, we are stuck with the traditional difficulties of dualism. One antidualist philosopher characterized these leftover mental phenomena as "nomological danglers" ("nomological" means law-like). They are produced by the brain in a lawlike fashion, but then they do nothing. They just dangle there.[6]

Many, probably most, philosophers have abandoned dualism, but the situation is odd because to many dualists, the arguments I have just presented do not look at all decisive against all forms of dualism. I think a typical property dualist would say, "OK, the mind is not a separate substance but all the same it is just a brute fact of nature that creatures like us do have pains and tickles and itches, as well as thoughts and emotions and these are not in any ordinary sense physical. Nor are they reducible to anything physical." And indeed some dualists bite the bullet and accept epiphenomenalism.

My guess is that dualism, in spite of being out of fashion, will not go away. Indeed in recent years dualism, at least property dualism, has been making something of a comeback, partly due to a renaissance of interest in consciousness. The insight that drives dualism is powerful. Here is the insight, at its most primitive: we all have real conscious experiences and we know that they are not the same sort of thing as the physical objects around us. This primitive insight can be given a more sophisticated formulation: the world consists almost entirely of physical particles and everything else is in some way an illusion (like colors and tastes) or a surface feature (like solidity and liquidity) that can be reduced to the behavior of the physical particles. At the level of molecular structure the table is not really solid. It is, as the physicist Eddington said, a cloud of molecules. It is just that from our point of view it seems solid. But at bottom the physical world consists entirely of microentities, the physical particles. However there is one exception. Consciousness is not just particles. In fact it is not particles at all. Whatever else it is, it is something "over and above" the particles. I believe this is the insight that drives contemporary property dualism.

David Chalmers[7] puts the point by saying that it is not logically possible that the course of the physical universe should be different if the course of microphysical facts is the same. Once you have the microphysics then everything else follows. But that is not true for consciousness. You could imagine the whole physical course of the universe exactly the same, minus consciousness. It is logically possible that the course of the physical universe should be exactly as it is, but with no consciousness.

It is such apparent basic differences between the mental and the physical that drives dualism. I think dualism can be answered and refuted, but we do not yet have the tools to do it. I will do it in chapter 4.

II. THE TURN TO MATERIALISM

The dualists said that there are two kinds of things or properties in the universe, and with the failure of dualism, it is natural to suppose that maybe there is only one kind of thing in the universe. Not surprisingly, this view is called "monism" and it comes in two flavors, mentalist monism and materialist monism. These are called "idealism" and "materialism," respectively. Idealism says that the universe is entirely mental or spiritual; there exists nothing but "ideas" in the technical sense of the word, according to which any mental phenomenon at all is an idea. On some views—for example, Berkeley's—in addition to ideas there are minds that contain the ideas. Idealism had a prodigious influence in philosophy, literally for centuries, but as far as I can tell it has been dead as a doornail among nearly all of the philosophers whose opinions I respect, for many decades, so I will not say much about it. Some of the most famous idealists were Berkeley, Hegel, Bradley, and Royce.

The single most influential family of views in the philosophy of mind throughout the twentieth century and leading into the twenty-first century is one version or another of materialism. Materialism is the view that the only reality that exists is material or physical reality, and consequently if mental states have a real existence, they must in some sense be reducible to, they must be nothing but, physical states of some kind. There is a sense in which materialism is the religion of our time, at least among most of the professional experts in the fields of philosophy, psychology, cognitive science, and other disciplines that study the mind. Like more traditional religions, it is accepted without question and it provides the framework within which other questions can be posed, addressed, and answered. The history of materialism is fascinating, because though the materialists are convinced, with a quasi-religious faith, that their view must be right, they never seem to be able to formulate a version of it that they are completely satisfied with and that can be generally accepted by other philosophers, even by other materialists. I think this is because they are constantly running up against the fact that the different versions of materialism seem to leave out some essential mental feature of the universe, which we know, independently of our philosophical commitments, to exist. The features they generally leave out are consciousness and intentionality. The problem is to give a completely satisfying materialist account of the mind that does not end up denying the obvious fact that we all intrinsically have conscious states and intentional states. In the next few pages I am going to sketch briefly the history of materialism in the twentieth century, up to the point where it finally reached its most sophisticated formulation in the computational theory of the mind, the theory that the brain is a computer and the mind is a computer program. This sketch is necessarily oversimplified. For reasons of space, I can only hit the high points, but I do want you to see those high points and how they relate to each other. There is a natural progression that leads from behaviorism to the computational theory of the mind and I want you to see that progression.

III. THE SAGA OF MATERIALISM: FROM BEHAVIORISM TO STRONG ARTIFICIAL INTELLIGENCE

Behaviorism

The earliest influential form of materialism in the twentieth century was called "behaviorism." In its crudest version, behaviorism says the mind just is the behavior of the body. There is nothing over and above the behavior of the body that is constitutive of the mental. Behaviorism comes in two flavors, "methodological behaviorism" and "logical behaviorism." I will consider each in turn.

Methodological Behaviorism

Methodological behaviorism was a movement in psychology. It attempted to put psychology on a respectable scientific footing, along with other natural sciences, by insisting that psychology should study only objectively observable behavior. The "laws" that such a discipline was supposed to discover were laws that would correlate the input stimulus to the organism with the output response behavior; and for this reason, behaviorist psychology was sometimes called "stimulus-response" psychology. The behaviorists were so influential that for a time they even succeeded in changing the definition of psychology. Psychology was no longer the "science of the mind" but the "science of human behavior." This view was called "methodological behaviorism" because it proposed a method in psychology rather than a substantive claim about the existence or nonexistence of the mind. The real objection to dualism, the methodological behaviorists claimed, was not that it postulates nonexistent entities, but rather that it is scientifically irrelevant. Scientific claims have to be objectively testable, and the only objectively testable claims about the human mind are claims about human behavior.

The big names in methodological behaviorism are John B. Watson (1878–1958) and B. F. Skinner (1904–1990). I think that, in fact, neither of them believed in the existence of any inner qualitative mental phenomena, but for the purposes of a scientific psychology, they only needed to insist on behaviorism as a method rather than as a specific ontological doctrine. It may be unfair to characterize Skinner as a methodological behaviorist, because in fact he objected to something he called "methodological behaviorism." He thought of himself as a "radical behaviorist." Nonetheless, his influences have been mostly methodological; so, I am going to follow the standard textbook account and characterize him as a methodological behaviorist. The only observable psychological phenomena are human behavior, so the right method for psychology has to be the study of human behavior and not the study of any mysterious inner, spiritual, mental entities. Methodological behaviorism was thus a research project in psychology and was surprisingly influential for decades.

Logical Behaviorism

Logical behaviorism was primarily a movement in philosophy, and it made a much stronger claim than methodological behaviorism. The methodological behaviorists said that Cartesian dualism was scientifically irrelevant, but the logical behaviorists said that Descartes was wrong as a matter of logic.[8] A statement about a person's mental state, such as the statement that a person believes that it is going to rain or is feeling a pain in his elbow, just means the same as, it can be translated into, a set of statements about that person's actual and possible behavior. It need not be translatable into statements about presently existing behavior, for a person might have a pain or a belief that he was not then and there manifesting in behavior, but then the statement has to be translatable into a set of hypothetical statements about behavior, what the agent would do or would say under such and such circumstances.

According to a typical behaviorist analysis, to say that Jones believes it is going to rain just means the same as saying an indefinite number of statements such as the following: if the windows in Jones's house are open, he will close them; if the garden tools are left outside, he will put them indoors; if he goes for a walk he will carry an umbrella or wear a raincoat or both; and so forth. The idea was that having a mental state was just being disposed to certain sorts of behavior; and the notion of a disposition was to be analyzed in terms of hypothetical statements, statements of the form "If p then q." As applied to the problem of mental states, these statements would take the form, "If such-and-such conditions obtain, then such-and-such behavior will ensue."

Physicalism and the Identity Theory

By the middle decades of the twentieth century, the difficulties of behaviorism had led to its general weakening and eventual rejection. It was going nowhere as a methodological project in psychology, and indeed was under quite effective attack, especially from the linguist Noam Chomsky. Chomsky claimed that the idea that when we study psychology we are studying behavior is as unintelligent as the idea that when we study physics we are studying meter readings. Of course we use behavior as evidence in psychology, just as we use meter readings as evidence in physics, but it is a mistake to confuse the evidence that we have about a subject matter for the subject matter itself. The subject matter of psychology is the human mind, and human behavior is evidence for the existence and features of the mind, but is not itself the mind.

The difficulties with the logical behaviorists were even more marked. No one had ever given a remotely plausible account of how you could translate statements about minds into statements about behavior. There were various technical difficulties about how to specify the antecedents of the hypotheticals, and especially about how to do it without circularity. I said earlier that the behaviorists would analyze Jones's belief that it is going to rain into sets of statements about his rain-avoidance behavior. But the difficulty with that is that we can only begin to make such a reduction on the assumption that Jones desires to stay dry. So the assumption that Jones will carry an umbrella if he believes that it is going to rain is only plausible if we suppose that Jones does not want to be rained on. But then if we are analyzing belief in terms of desire, it looks like there is a kind of circularity in the reduction. We did not really reduce the belief to behavior; we reduced it to behavior plus desire, which still leaves us with a mental state that needs to be analyzed. Analogous remarks could be made about the reduction of desire. To say that Jones's desire to stay dry consists in such things as his disposition to carry an umbrella will only seem remotely plausible if we suppose that Jones believes it is going to rain.

A second family of difficulties had to do with the causal relations between mental states and behavior. The logical behaviorists had argued that mental states consisted in nothing but behavior and dispositions to behavior, but this runs against our commonsense intuition that there is a causal relation between our inner mental states and our outward behavior. My pain causes me to cry out and to take aspirin; my belief that it is going to rain and my desire to stay dry cause me to take an umbrella, etc., and it seems that this apparent truth is denied by the behaviorists. They cannot account for the causal relations between the inner experience and the external behavior, because they are in effect denying that there is any internal experience in addition to the external behavior.

The real difficulty with behaviorism, though, is that its sheer implausibility became more and more embarrassing. We do have thoughts and feelings and pains and tickles and itches, but it does not seem reasonable to suppose that these are identical with our behavior or even with our dispositions to behavior. The feeling of pain is one thing, pain behavior is something else. Behaviorism is so intuitively implausible that unsympathetic commentators often made fun of it. As early as the 1920s, I. A. Richards pointed out that to be a behaviorist you have to "feign anesthesia."[9] And university lecturers have a stock repertoire of bad jokes about behaviorism. A typical joke: a behaviorist couple just after making love, he says to her "It was great for you. How was it for me?"

The sheer implausibility of behaviorism had become an embarrassment by the 1960s and it was gradually replaced among materialist-minded philosophers by a doctrine called "physicalism," sometimes called the "identity theory." The physicalists said that Descartes was not wrong, as the logical behaviorists had claimed, as a matter of logic, but just as a matter of fact. It might have turned out that we had souls in addition to bodies, but the way that nature in fact turned out, what we think of as minds are just brains, and what we think of as mental states, such as the feeling of pain or having a tickle or an itch, are just states of the brain—and perhaps the rest of the central nervous system. This thesis was sometimes called the "identity thesis" because it asserted an identity between mental states and brain states. The identity theorists were anxious to insist on the contrast between their view and behaviorism. Behaviorism was supposed to be a logical thesis about the definition of mental concepts. The identity thesis was supposed to be a factual claim, not about the analysis of mental concepts, but rather about the mode of existence of mental states. The model for the behaviorists was one of definitional identities. Pains are dispositions to behavior in a way that triangles are three-sided plane figures. In each case it is a matter of definition. The identity theorists said no, the model is not definitions, but rather empirical discoveries of identities in science. We have discovered, as a matter of fact, that a bolt of lightning is identical with an electrical discharge;

we have discovered, as a matter of fact, that water is identical with H_2O, and we are now discovering, and the discovery is proceeding daily, that mental states are really identical with brain states.[10]

Objections to the Identity Theory

There were a number of objections to the identity theory. I find it useful to distinguish between the technical objections and the common-sense objections. The first technical objection was that the theory seemed to violate a principle of logic called "Leibnitz's Law."[11] The law says that if any two things are identical, then they must have all their properties in common. So if you could show that mental states had properties that could not be attributed to brain states, and brain states had properties that could not be attributed to mental states, it looks like you would refute the identity theory. And it did not seem difficult to provide such examples. So I can say, for example, that the brain state that corresponds to my thought that it is raining is 3 cm inside my left ear; but, according to the objectors, it does not make any sense to say that my thought that it is raining is 3 cm inside my left ear. Furthermore, even for conscious states that have a location, such as pain, the pain may be in my toe, but the brain state that corresponds to that pain is not in my toe, but in my brain. So the properties of the brain state are not the same as the properties of the mental state. Therefore, physicalism is false.

The identity theorists thought that they had an easy answer to these objections. The objections, they say, just rest on ignorance. When we come to know more about the brain, we will come to feel perfectly comfortable in attributing spatial location to mental states and attributing so-called mental properties to states of the brain. And, about the location of the pain in the toe, the identity theorists said that what we are interested in is not a putative object, the pain, but rather the total experience of having the pain. And that total experience extends all the way from the stimulation of the peripheral nerve endings in the toe to the brain itself. I think that the identity theorists were successful in answering this objection, but there were other objections that were more serious.

A common-sense objection to the identity theorists was that if the identity was indeed an empirical identity, something that could be discovered as a matter of fact, on the analogy with water and H_2O, or lightning and electrical discharge, then it seems there would have to be two kinds of properties to nail down the two sides of the identity statement.[12] Thus, just as the statement, "lightning is identical with an electrical discharge" has to identify one and the same thing in terms of its lightning properties and in terms of its electrical discharge properties; and "water is identical with H_2O molecules" has to identify one and the same thing in terms of its water properties and in terms of its H_2O properties, so the claim that, for example, "pain is identical with a certain type of brain state" has to identify one and the same thing in terms of its pain properties, and in terms of its brain-state properties. But if there are to be two independent sets of properties in the identity statement, then it looks like we have two different types of properties left over: mental properties and physical properties. It looks, in short, as if in order to make the identity thesis work, we have to fall back into property dualism. If all mental states are brain states, then there are two kinds of brain states, those that are mental and those that are not. What is the difference? The mental states have mental properties. The others have only physical properties. And that view sounds like property dualism.

This was a decisive problem for the identity theorists. The whole point of the theory was to vindicate materialism, to show that mental states were really identical with, were nothing but, were reducible to material states of the brain. But if it turns out that the brain states in question have irreducible mental properties then the project fails. It leaves us with an irreducible mental element. In doing research for this book I found at least one philosopher who thought of himself as an identity theorist who seemed willing to embrace this result at least as a possibility.[13] Grover Maxwell calls his view the identity theory, but he says, "the way is entirely open for speculating that some brain events just are our joys, sorrow, pains, thoughts, etc., in all of their qualitative, and mentalistic richness"(p. 235). This is quite similar to what I think is the correct view and will explain in chapter 4. But it was not a typical view among the identity theorists.

The standard identity theorists' answer to this objection was less plausible than their answer to the Leibnitz Law objections.[14] The answer they gave was that the phenomena in question could be specified without using any mental predicates. They could be specified in a topic-neutral vocabulary. Instead of saying, "There is a yellow-orange afterimage in me," they prefer to say "There is something going on in me that is like what goes on when I see an orange." Such a rephrasing of the identification of the mental states in a "topic-neutral" vocabulary was supposed to answer the objection because it enabled us to specify the mental element in a nonmental, neutral vocabulary: there is this thing going on in me and it can be specified in a way that is neutral between dualism and materialism, but it just turns out that the thing is a brain process. So we can specify the mental feature but in a way that is consistent with materialism.

I think this answer fails. The point that we can talk about mental phenomena without using a mental vocabulary does not change the fact that the mental phenomena continue to have mental properties. My yellow-orange after-image remains qualitative and subjective whether or not we choose to mention those features. If one wanted to refuse to talk about airplanes, one could just say, "some property belonging to United Airlines." But that does not eliminate the existence of airplanes. To put the point succinctly, the fact that one can mention a phenomenon that is intrinsically qualitative and subjective in a vocabulary that does not reveal these features does not remove the features. In the end of course, the identity theorists wanted to deny that there were any such features, but that requires a separate argument.[15]

One slightly more technical objection that really did concern the identity theorists and indeed eventually forced a modification in their views was the accusation of "neuronal chauvinism."[16] If the claim of the identity theorists was that every pain is identical with a certain kind of neuronal stimulation, and every belief is identical with a certain type of brain state, then it seems that a being that did not have neurons or that did not have the right kind of neurons could not have pains and beliefs. But why can't animals that have brain structures different from ours have mental states? And indeed, why couldn't we build a machine that did not have neurons at all, but also had mental states? This objection led to an important shift in the identity theory from what came to be called "type-type identity theory" to "token-token identity theory." In order to explain this distinction I need to say a bit about the type-token distinction. If I write the word "dog" three times: "dog dog dog," have I written one word or three? Well, I have written three instances, or tokens, of one type of word. So we need a distinction between types, which are abstract general entities, and tokens, which are concrete particular objects and events. A token of a type is a particular concrete exemplification of that abstract general type.

Using this distinction we can see how the identity theorists were motivated to move from a type-type identity theory to a token-token identity theory. The type-type identity theory says "Every type of mental state is identical with some type of physical state."

By their own lights this is a bit sloppy, because the identity in question is between actual concrete tokens and not abstract universal types. What they meant is: for every mental-state type there is some brain-state type such that every token of the mental type is a token of the brain type. The token identity theorists simply said: for every token of a certain type of mental state, there is some token of some type of physical state or other with which that mental state token is identical. They, in short, did not require, for example, that all token pains had to exemplify exactly the same type of brain state. They might be tokens of different types of brain states even though they were all tokens of the same mental type, pain. For that reason they were called "token-token" identity theorists as opposed to "type-type" identity theorists. Token-token identity seems much more plausible than type-type identity theory. Suppose I believe that Denver is the capital of Colorado and suppose you believe that Denver is the capital of Colorado. It seems unnecessary to suppose that in order to have the same belief we must be in exactly the same type of neurobiological state. My neurobiological state of believing that Denver is the capital of Colorado might be at a certain point in my brain, and yours might be at another point, without these being different beliefs.

Unfortunately, the identity theorists were often rather feeble at giving examples. One of their favorite examples was to say that pains are identical with C-fiber stimulations. The idea was that according to the type identity theorists, every pain is identical with some C-fiber stimulation and according to the token identity theorists, this particular pain might be identical with this particular C-fiber stimulation, but some other pain might be identical with some other state of a brain or some other state of a machine. Unfortunately, all of this is rather bad neurophysiology. A C-fiber is a type of axon; and it is true that certain types of pain signals, not all, are carried by C-fibers to the brain. But it would be ridiculous, neurophysiologically, to think there is nothing to pains except having your C-fibers stimulated. The C-fiber is just part of a complex pain mechanism in the brain and nervous system. Be that as it may, this was the sort of example that the identity theorists gave, and a good deal of the debate centered on whether or not we would get such type identities or whether token identities were all that we could hope for. In the long run the token identity theorists have been more influential than the type identity theorists.

But now they are faced with an interesting question. What is it that all of these tokens have in common that makes them tokens of the same mental-state type? If you and I both believe that Denver is the capital of Colorado, then what is it exactly that we share if there is nothing there but our brain states and we have different types of brain states? Notice that the two answers that would traditionally be given to this, the dualist answer and the type-type answer, will not do for the token physicalist. The token physicalists cannot say that what they have in common are the same irreducibly mental properties, because their whole idea was to eliminate, or get rid of, such irreducible mental properties. Nor can they say that they are the same type of brain state, because the whole move from type identity theory to token identity theory was to avoid having to say that every token of a particular mental-state type is identical with a token of a certain brain-state type.

Functionalism

At this point the materialists made a move that was crucial for subsequent philosophizing about the mind. They said: what token brain states have that makes them mental states is a certain type of function in the overall behavior of the organism. Not surprisingly, this doctrine was called "functionalism," and when spelled out it developed into views like the following:[17] to say that Jones believes that it is raining is to say that he has a certain event, state, or process going on in him that is caused by certain sorts of external stimuli—for example, he perceives that it is raining; and this phenomenon, in conjunction with certain other factors, such as his desire to stay dry, will cause a certain sort of behavior on his part, the behavior of carrying an umbrella. Mental states, in short, are defined as states that have certain sorts of functions, and the notion of function is explained in terms of causal relations to external stimuli, to other mental states, and to external behavior. We could write this out as follows: Jones's perception that it is raining causes in him the belief that it is raining. The belief that it is raining and the desire to stay dry cause the behavior of carrying the umbrella. What, then, is a belief? A belief is anything that stands in these sorts of causal relations. At that point the identity theorists introduced a beautiful technical device to capture precisely this feature of their theory. The technical device is called a "Ramsey sentence," after its inventor, the British philosopher, Frank Ramsey. In the previous conjunction of sentences we simply knock out the expression "the belief that it is raining" and put in "x." Then we preface the whole sentence with an existential quantifier, which says "there is an x such that." So it now comes out as follows: "there is an x such that the perception that it is raining causes x, and x together with the desire to stay dry causes the behavior of carrying an umbrella." So, on this account, what is a belief really? It is anything, any x, that stands in these (and many of other such) causal relations. Mental states such as beliefs are not defined by any intrinsic features, rather they are defined by their causal relations, and these causal relations constitute their function. Beliefs, for example, are caused by perceptions and together with desires they cause actions. Such causal relations are all that there is to having a belief.

And what about the leftover reference to desires and perceptions? They too will be analyzed functionally. Just as there is an x that is the belief, and is defined by its causal relations, so there is a y that is the desire, and a z that is a perception, and they too are defined by their causal relations.

So several of the objections to behaviorism were met by the functionalist account. One objection was the apparent circularity in behaviorism of having to use desires to explain beliefs, and beliefs to explain desires. This objection is answered by the functionalist in one fell swoop, if we analyze beliefs and desires simultaneously in terms of their causal relations. Furthermore, we have immediately answered the objection that behaviorism left out the causal relations between mental states and external behavior, because we have defined mental states partly in terms of their capacity to cause external behavior. Furthermore, another appeal of the functionalist account of mental states is that it seemed to assimilate the mental realm to a very familiar realm of human functional entities. Thus if we ask, What is a carburetor? What is a thermostat? What is a clock?—all of these questions are answered causally, by describing the causal functions performed by carburetors, thermostats, and clocks. None of these things are defined by their physical structure. A clock, for example, can be made out of gears and wheels, it can be made out of an hourglass with sand in it, it can be made out of quartz oscillators, it can be made out of any number of physical materials, but the defining feature of a clock is that it is any physical mechanism that enables us to tell the time. Analogous remarks could be made about carburetors and thermostats. Mental states are like carburetors, thermostats, and clocks. They are defined not by their physical structure and not by any Cartesian mental essence; rather, they are defined by their causal relations. A belief is just any entity that, standing in certain relationships to input stimuli and to other mental states, will cause external behavior.

The underlying impulse of functionalism was to answer the question, Why do we attribute mental states to people at all? And the answer was, we say they have such things as beliefs and desires because we want to explain their behavior. Functionalism seems to have captured all of these intuitions.

The functionalists naturally wanted to know what was the nature of the inner mental brain states that enabled them to cause behavior. How did the mental states differ from other sorts of brain states? One answer was to say that this is not really a suitable question for philosophy at all; it should be left to psychologists and neurobiologists. We can treat the brain as just a "black box," which produces behavior in response to stimuli, and we need not, as philosophers, worry about the mechanism inside the black box. This view was sometimes called "black-box functionalism."

But black-box functionalism is intellectually unsatisfying in that it does not answer our natural intellectual curiosity. We want to know, really, how does the system work?

Computer Functionalism (= Strong Artificial Intelligence)

At this point there occurred one of the most exciting developments in the entire history of the philosophy of mind in the twentieth century. To many of us who participated in the developments (though not to me), it seemed like not merely an exciting development, but at long last a solution to problems that had beset philosophers for more than 2,000 years. The idea was based on a convergence of work in philosophy, cognitive psychology, linguistics, computer science, and artificial intelligence. It seemed that we knew the answer to the question that faced us: the way the system works is that the brain is a digital computer and what we call the "mind" is a digital computer program or set of programs. We had made the greatest breakthrough in the history of philosophy of mind: mental states are computational states of the brain. The brain is a computer and the mind is a program or set of programs. A principle that formed the foundation for any number of textbooks was this: the mind is to the brain as the program is to the hardware.[18]

$$\frac{\text{Mind}}{\text{Brain}} = \frac{\text{Program}}{\text{Hardware}}$$

This view is sometimes called "computer functionalism," though I have also baptized it "Strong Artificial Intelligence" to distinguish it from Weak Artificial Intelligence, which aims to study the mind by doing computer simulations as opposed to purporting to create a mind. On the Strong AI view, the appropriately programmed digital computer does not just simulate having a mind; it literally has a mind.

With the advent of the computer model of the mind, it seemed that at long last we had the solution to the problems that had bothered Descartes, and indeed to problems that go back 2,500 years to the early Greek philosophers. In particular, it seemed we had a perfect solution to the traditional mind-body problem. The relation of mind and body seemed mysterious, but the relation of program to computer hardware, the relation of the software to its physical implementation, is not the least bit mysterious. It is a relation that is understood in every Computer Science department in the world, and this understanding is routinely employed on a daily basis to program computers.

IV. COMPUTATION AND MENTAL PROCESSES

So far I have criticized materialist views as they came up. But now I am going to set out the computer theory of the mind and save criticisms of it and other versions of functionalism till the next chapter. Before explaining in detail how the computer theory of the mind is supposed to solve our problems, I want to introduce several crucial notions. These notions are important not only for their relevance to contemporary philosophy but, indeed, for intellectual life in general. The notions I hope to explain briefly are those of an algorithm, a Turing machine, Church's thesis, Turing's theorem, the Turing test, levels of description, multiple realizability, and recursive decomposition. These notions lie at the heart of what was until recently, and in some quarters still is, the single most influential view of the nature of the mind in cognitive science and related disciplines. Furthermore, several of these ideas are so important that it is essential to your general education, quite apart from philosophy, that you should be fully familiar with these concepts.

Algorithms. An algorithm is a method for solving a problem by going through a precise series of steps. The steps must be finite in number, and if carried out correctly, they guarantee a solution to the problem. For this reason algorithms are also called "effective procedures." Good examples are the methods used to solve problems in arithmetic, such as addition and subtraction. If you follow the steps exactly, you will get the correct solution.

Turing Machines. A Turing machine is a device that carries out calculations using only two types of symbols. These are usually thought of as zeros and ones, but any symbols will do. The idea of the Turing machine was invented by Alan Turing, the great British logician and mathematician. The striking feature of the Turing machine is its simplicity: it has an endless tape on which the symbols are written. It has a head that reads symbols on the tape. The Turing machine head will move to the left or to the right, it can erase a zero, it can print a one, it can erase a one, it can print a zero. It does all of these things in accordance with a program, which consists of a set of rules. The rules always have the same form; under condition C, perform act A: C → A. For example, a rule might be of the form, if you are scanning a zero, replace it with a one and move one square to the left.

A Turing machine is not a machine in the ordinary sense. You cannot go into a store and buy a Turing machine. It is an abstract mathematical concept. For example, the Turing machine has an infinite tape and thus an infinite amount of storage capacity. No real machine has that. Real machines break down, get rusty, or have beer poured on them. Turing machines have none of these defects because they are purely abstract. However, though the concept of a Turing machine is the concept of something formal and abstract, for practical purposes the kind of computer you buy in a store is a Turing machine. Ordinary commercial computers implement algorithms by manipulating two sorts of symbols. Contemporary electronics is so sophisticated that the modern computer can carry out these symbolic operations at the rate of millions per second.

Church's Thesis. Due originally to Alonzo Church (arrived at independently by Turing, so sometimes called the Church-Turing Thesis), this thesis states that any problem that has an algorithmic solution can be solved on a Turing machine. Or another way to say the same thing is that any algorithm at all can be carried out on a Turing machine. The idea of a machine that just uses binary symbols, zeros and ones, is sufficient to carry out any algorithm whatever. This is a very important thesis because it says in mathematical terms that any problem that is computable can be computed on a Turing machine. Any computable function is Turing computable.

Turing machines can come in many different kinds, states, and varieties. In my car there are specialized computers for detecting the rate of fuel consumption, for example. But in addition to the idea of these special-purpose computers, or Turing machines, there is the idea of a general-purpose computer, something that can implement any program at all. And Turing, in an important mathematical result known as Turing's Theorem, proved that there is a Universal Turing machine that can simulate the behavior of any other Turing machine. More precisely, Turing proved that there is a Universal Turing machine, UTM, such that for any Turing machine carrying out a specific program, TP, UTM can carry out TP.

What made these ideas so exciting was the following thought: Suppose the human brain is a Universal Turing machine? I cannot exaggerate the excitement that this idea generated, because it gave us at long last not just a solution to the philosophical problems that beset us, but it gave us a research program. We can study the mind, we can find out how the mind really works, by discovering which programs are implemented in the brain. An immensely appealing feature of this research program is that we do not actually have to know how the brain works as a physical system in order to do a complete and strict science of the mind. The specifics of the brain are really irrelevant to the mind, because any other physical system would do as well, provided only that it was stable enough and rich enough to carry the programs. On this view, the neurobiological details of brain operation are irrelevant to the mind. We just happen, by a kind of evolutionary accident, to be implemented in neurons, but any sufficiently complex hardware system would do as well as what we have in our skulls. To get a really adequate scientific account of the mind we need only to discover the Turing machine programs that we are all using when we engage in cognition.

The Turing Test. However, we need a test. We need a test that will tell us when a machine is genuinely behaving intelligently, and when it is not. This test was also invented by Alan Turing, and is called the Turing test. There are different versions of it, but the basic idea is this: we can side-step all the great debates about the other minds problem, about whether or not there really is any thinking going on in the machine, whether the machine is really intelligent, by simply asking ourselves, Can the machine perform in such a way that an expert cannot distinguish its performance from a human performance? If the machine responds to questions put to it in Chinese as well as a native Chinese speaker, so that other native Chinese speakers could not tell the difference between the machine and a native Chinese speaker, then we would have to say that the machine understood Chinese. The Turing test, as you will have noticed, expresses a kind of behaviorism. It says that the behavioral test is conclusive for the presence of mental states.

Levels of Description. Any complex system can be described in different ways. Thus, for example, a car engine can be characterized in terms of its molecular structure, in terms of its gross physical shape, in terms of its component parts, etc. It is tempting to describe this variability of descriptive possibilities in terms of the metaphor of "levels," and this terminology has become generally accepted. We think of the microlevel of molecules as a lower level of description than the level of gross physical structure or physical components, which are higher levels of description. Most of the interest of this distinction is that it applies in a dramatic fashion to computers. At a lower level of description your computer and mine might be quite different. Yours may have a different type of processor than mine, for example. But at a higher level of description they may be implementing exactly the same algorithm. They may be carrying out the same program.

Multiple Realizability. The notion of different levels of description already implicitly contains another notion that is crucial to the computational theory of mind, and that is the idea of multiple realizability. The point is that a higher-level feature, such as being the Word program or being a carburetor, may be physically realized in different systems, thus one and the same higher-level feature can be said to be multiply realizable in different lower-level hardwares. Multiple realizability seems to be a natural feature of token identity theories. The different tokens of different types at the lower level may be different forms of realization of some common higher level mental feature. Just as the same computer program may be implemented in different sorts of hardware and thus is multiply realizable; so the same mental state, such as the belief that it is going to rain, might be implemented in different sorts of hardware, and thus also be multiply realizable.

This diagram illustrates the distinction between levels of description and the multiple realizability of the higher level in lower levels:

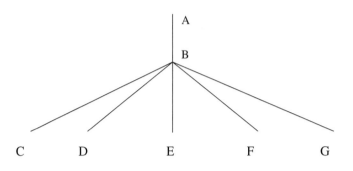

One and the same system represented by the line AB can be realized in different lower level systems, represented by lines BC, BD, BE, BF, and BG.

Recursive Decomposition. Yet another important idea, already implicit in what I have said, is that big complex problems can be broken down into little simple problems, which can be broken down into even simpler problems, until we reach the level of ultimate simplicity. Doing multiplication with several digits, for example multiplying 28×71, may seem to us a complex operation, but the beauty of the idea of a Turing machine is that at bottom, all such problems break down into simple maneuvers with zeros and ones. You print a one, you erase a zero, you move one square to the left or one square to the right. That is all the machine needs to know how to do in order to carry out not only arithmetic but the most incredibly complex algorithms for other sorts of tasks. The complex tasks can be broken down (decomposed) into simple tasks by repeated application (recursively) of the same procedures until all that is left are simple binary operations with two symbols, the zeroes and ones. In the early heady days, some people even said that the fact that neurons were either firing or not firing was an indication that the brain was a binary system, just like any other digital computer. Again, the idea of recursive decomposition seemed to give us an important clue to understanding human intelligence. Complex intelligent human tasks are recursively decomposable into simple tasks, and that is how we are so intelligent.

The collection of ideas that I have just explained contains the tools necessary to articulate the single most influential and powerful theory of the mind in the last decades of the twentieth century. The brain is a digital computer, in all probability a Universal Turing machine. As such it carries out algorithms by implementing programs, and what we call the mind is a program or a set of such programs. To understand human cognitive capacities it is only necessary to discover the programs that human beings are actually implementing when they activate such cognitive capacities as perception, memory, etc. Because the mental level of description is a program level, we do not need to understand the details of how the brain works in order to understand human cognition. Indeed, because the level of description is at a higher level than neuronal structures, we are not forced to any type-type identity theory of the mind. Rather, mental states are multiply realizable in different sorts of physical structures, which just happen to be implemented in brains but could equally well have been implemented in an indefinite range of computer hardwares. Any hardware implementation will do for the human mind provided only that it is stable enough and rich enough to carry the programs. Because we are Turing machines we will be able to understand cognition by reducing complex operations into the ultimately simplest operations, the manipulation of zeros and ones. Furthermore, we have a test that will enable us to tell when we have actually duplicated human cognition, the Turing test. The Turing test gives us a conclusive proof of the presence of cognitive capacities. To find out whether or not we have actually invented an intelligent machine we need only apply the Turing test. And we now have a research project; indeed, it is the research project of cognitive science.

We try to discover the programs that are implemented in the brain by designing programs for our commercial machines that will pass the Turing test, and then we ask the psychologists to perform experiments on humans to see if they are following the same program as the program on our computer. For example, in one famous experiment involving the memory of numbers, the reaction times of the subjects seemed to vary in the same way as the processing time of a computer. This seemed to a lot of cognitive scientists good evidence that the humans were using the algorithmic procedures of the computer.

Such was the appeal of the computational theory of the mind in the early days of cognitive science. If I have not made it sound appealing to you, then I have not done a good job of exposition, because to many it was immensely exciting at the time. It spawned a thousand research projects and it garnered a nearly equal number of research grants. But, alas, it is hopelessly mistaken. I thought so at the time, and nothing since the early days has changed my opinion. In the next chapter, I will explain why it is mistaken. For now, I want you to appreciate its appeal.

With some hesitation (because it oversimplifies) I present a chart that shows the relations between the theories we have so far discussed.

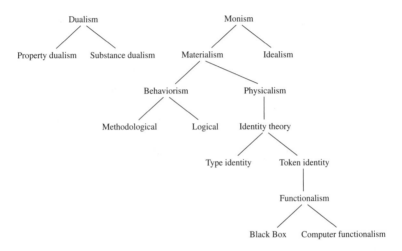

V. OTHER VERSIONS OF MATERIALISM

One of the interesting features of materialism is that just about every conceivable materialist position has been taken by some philosopher or other. And to complete the story of modern materialism, I want to mention two other versions: eliminative materialism, the idea that mental states do not exist at all, and anomalous monism, Donald Davidson's idea, which is a version of the token-identity theory.

The eliminative materialists argued as follows.[19] Why do we say that people have beliefs and desires and other sorts of mental states? We say these things because we wish to be able to explain their behavior. Our postulation, therefore, of beliefs and desires, etc., is the postulation of a kind of theoretical entity, much as the postulations of electrons or electromagnetic force in physics are postulations of theoretical entities. It is characteristic of such postulations that if the theory proves to be false, that is sufficient to establish that the entity does not exist. The now-obsolete theory of phlogiston, that the burning of an object consisted in the release of a substance called "phlogiston," has been refuted and with the refutation of the theory, we no longer believe in the existence of phlogiston. What then is the theory that postulates beliefs, desires, etc.? Well, it is common sense, or grandmother psychology, and, in the literature it is usually called "folk psychology." But now, so the story goes, folk psychology is almost certain to be shown to be an inadequate, indeed, a false theory. Why? Well, for one thing, folk theories have always been refuted by scientific progress. Furthermore, folk psychology is going nowhere as a research program. Our folk theories of rationality, for example, are not much of an improvement on Aristotle's. But if the theory that postulates beliefs, desires, etc., is a false theory, then these entities do not exist. So eliminative materialism simply is a version of materialism that eliminates mental states altogether. They are shown to be illusions in the way that sunsets and phlogiston are illusions.

Another and related argument against the entities of folk psychology was one that appealed to the absence of type-type reductions of the folk-psychological notions to neurobiological phenomena. A mature neuroscience is very unlikely to make much use of notions such as belief and desire, because these notions do not match the categories of neurobiology. With the absence of a type-type reduction of beliefs and desires, it seems reasonable to suppose that such entities do not exist.

Anomalous monism is a view put forward by Donald Davidson[20] for which he advances the following argument:

Step 1:   There are causal relations between mental phenomena and physical phenomena.

Step 2:   Wherever there are events related as cause and effect they must fall under strict, deterministic causal laws.

Step 3:   But there are no such strict deterministic causal laws relating the mental and the physical. In Davidson's terms, there are no psycho-physical laws.

Therefore,

Step 4:   Conclusion. All so-called mental events are physical events.

They have to be physical events to instantiate physical laws, and when we describe them as mental, we are just picking out a category of physical events that satisfy a certain mental vocabulary. They are mental under one description, but the same events are also physical under another description. The result, then, is a kind of materialism, a materialism that says that the subject matter of the psychological sciences will never be describable by the kinds of universal laws that we get in physics, not because they are a mysterious kind of spiritual or mental entity, but rather because the descriptions we use to pick them out, the mental descriptions, do not relate in a lawlike fashion to physical phenomena picked out under physical descriptions. The only argument that Davidson gives for this point is that mental phenomena, like beliefs and desires, are subject to constraints of rationality, and rationality has "no echo in physics."

I have tried to be as fair as I can in laying out the standard versions of materialism over the past century. If I have not made them seem the least bit appealing then I have failed in my task of expounding other people's views. I have to confess, however, that I think all of these theories are hopelessly inadequate. In subsequent chapters I am going to discuss their inadequacies. For the purposes of the immediate discussion I will assume that behaviorism is not a plausible form of materialism and that we need to examine the different forms of physicalism, especially functionalism.

Most of the discussion in the next chapter will be about the historical tradition of functionalism culminating in Strong Artificial Intelligence. I will not say anything about anomalous monism, because it turns out that it falls under the general heading of token identity theories. I will now be brief about, but I hope not unfair to, eliminative materialism. I mentioned three arguments for eliminative materialism. The first argument says that the entities of folk psychology are postulated as part of a theoretical structure. But in general, that is not true. My actual conscious thought processes of making up my mind to try to get something because I desire it are all directly experienced by me.

The second argument is that the propositions of folk psychology are in all likelihood going to prove to be false. But the problem is, if you look at the authors who hold this view, they are extremely implausible in their specification of the propositions of folk psychology. Sometimes they attribute to us beliefs that we obviously do not hold. For example, one author attributes to us the belief that if we believe that p and if we believe that if p then q we will believe that q.[21] This is an incredible claim. It would imply, for example, that anyone who believes each member of a complicated set of propositions, a, b, c, etc., that occur in the premises of a proof, where the other premises occur in conditionals of the form, if a then d, if b then e, if c then f, etc., would automatically believe all of the logical consequences. If this were true, such complex logical and mathematical proofs could never surprise us, because we believed the conclusion all along! The absurdity derives from confusing our logical commitment to the truth of a proposition with actually believing the proposition before becoming aware of our commitment. Complex logical and mathematical proofs show what our belief in the premises commits us to believing in the conclusion. They do not show that we really believed the conclusion all along.

And indeed, eliminative materialists are extremely hesitant to state the propositions of folk psychology. I believe there is a reason for this. Many of the propositions of so-called folk psychology are not in fact empirical propositions. They are in a sense, constitutive principles, they are analytic principles of our mental contents. So, for example, here is a proposition of folk psychology: beliefs can typically be either true or false. Now, the problem with treating that as if it were a hypothesis that might turn out to be false is that it is part of the definition of belief, it is a constitutive principle. It is like saying that touchdowns in American football count six points. The difficulty with the eliminative materialists is that they treat the propositions of so-called folk psychology as if they were empirical hypotheses, but in many cases they are not. If you read in the newspaper that investigators at MIT using the latest computer technology have discovered that touchdowns do not in fact count six points, but count only 5.99999 points, then you know that they have made a stupid mistake. The proposition that touchdowns count six points is part of the definition of a touchdown, as it is currently defined by the rules of American football. You cannot discover that it is false the way that you can discover that ordinary empirical propositions are false. Some of Churchland's examples are like this. He says that it is a proposition of folk psychology that someone who fears that p does not want p to happen. But if you add an "other things being equal" clause, that is part of the definition of fear. If I am afraid of something then, other things equal, I do not want the thing I am afraid of to happen. So you can't show that folk-psychological entities do not exist by first showing that our beliefs about them are false because many of the basic propositions of folk psychology are similarly definitional, or analytical, or constitutive principles of the entities of folk psychology. This is why the enemies of folk psychology are so inadequate in their efforts to formulate refutations of it. This does not prove that the entities of folk psychology exist, but that one argument to show they do not exist does not get off the ground.

The last argument against folk psychology is even worse. The idea is that because we cannot do a smooth type-type reduction of beliefs, desires, etc., to neurobiology, that therefore somehow or other these entities do not exist. But compare a similar proposition: we cannot do a smooth type-type reduction of sports utility vehicles, tennis rackets, or split-level ranch houses to the entities of atomic physics. We cannot do a type-type reduction for reasons implicit in this chapter: tennis rackets, etc., are multiply realizable in physics. Indeed, atomic physics really has no use for the notion of a sports utility vehicle, a split-level ranch house, or a tennis racket. But does anyone in his right mind think that it follows from this that these entities do not exist? As a general formal argument, the fact that we do not get type-type reductions of some entity into more basic sciences does not show that the irreducible entities do not exist. Quite the contrary.

There is an interesting irony in all of this discussion. Reductionists and eliminativists tend to think their positions are quite different. Reductionists think mental entities exist but can be reduced to physical events. Eliminativists think mental entities do not exist at all. But these amount to very much the same conclusion. Reductionists say there is nothing there but brain processes materialistically described. Eliminativists say there is nothing there but brain processes materialistically described. The apparent difference is a difference in vocabulary. The earlier materialists wanted to show that mental states did not exist as such by showing that they could undergo a type-type reduction to the entities of neurobiology. The later eliminative materialists wanted to show that the entities of common-sense psychology do not exist at all by showing that they cannot undergo a type-type reduction to the entities of neurobiology. Neither argument is any good, but what they suggest is that these people are determined to try to show that our ordinary common-sense notions of the mental do not name anything in the real world, and they are willing to advance any argument that they can think of for this conclusion.

Suggestions for Further Reading

The following selections give most of the basic arguments discussed in this chapter:

Armstrong, D. M., *A Materialist Theory of the Mind*, London: Routledge, 1993.

Block, N., "Troubles with Functionalism," in *Minnesota Studies in the Philosophy of Science*, vol. IX, ed. C. Wade Savage, Minneapolis: University of Minnesota Press, 1978, 261–325, reprinted in Block, ed., *Readings in Philosophy of Psychology*, vol. 1, Cambridge, MA: Harvard University Press, 1980.

Borst, C., ed., *The Mind/Brain Identity Theory*, New York: St. Martin's Press, 1970.

Churchland, P. M., "Eliminative Materialism and the Propositional Attitudes," in Rosenthal, D., ed., *The Nature of Mind*, New York: Oxford University Press, 1991, 601–612.

Crane, T., *The Mechanical Mind*, 2nd ed., London: Routledge, 2003.

Davidson, D., "Mental Events," in *Essays on Actions and Events*, Oxford: Oxford University Press, 1980, 207–227.

Feigl, H., "The 'Mental' and the 'Physical,'" in *Minnesota Studies in the Philosophy of Science*, vol. 2, eds. H. Feigl, M. Scriven, and G. Maxwell, Minneapolis: University of Minnesota Press, 1958.

Haugeland, J., ed., *Mind Design: Philosophy, Psychology, Artificial Intelligence*, Cambridge, MA: A Bradford Book, MIT Press, 1982.

Hempel, C., "The Logical Analysis of Psychology" in Block ed., *Readings in Philosophy of Psychology*, vol. 1, Cambridge, MA: Harvard University Press, 1980.

Lewis, D., "Psychophysical and Theoretical Identifications" and "Mad Pain and Martian Pain" both in Block, ed., *Readings in Philosophy of Psychology*, vol. 1, Cambridge, MA: Harvard University Press, 1980.

McDermott, D. V., *Mind and Mechanism*, Cambridge, MA: MIT Press, 2001.

Nagel, T., "Armstrong on the Mind," in Block, ed., *Readings in Philosophy of Psychology*, vol. 1, Cambridge, MA: Harvard University Press, 1980.

Place, U. T., "Is Consciousness a Brain Process?" *British Journal of Psychology*, vol. 47, pt. 1 (1956) 44–50.

Putnam, P., "The Nature of Mental States" in Block, ed., *Readings in Philosophy of Psychology*, vol. 1, Cambridge, MA: Harvard University Press, 1980.

Ryle, G., *The Concept of Mind*, London: Hutchinson, 1949.

Smart, J. J. C., "Sensations and Brain Processes," in Rosenthal, D., ed., *The Nature of Mind*, New York: Oxford University Press, 1991, 169–176.

Searle, J. R., *The Rediscovery of the Mind*, Cambridge, MA: MIT Press, 1992.

Turing, A., "Computing Machinery and Intelligence," *Mind*, vol. 59 (1950): 433–460.

CHAPTER 3

Arguments against Materialism

In the last chapter I presented some of the history of recent materialism, and I considered arguments against some versions, especially against behaviorism, type identity theory, and eliminative materialism. In this chapter I will present the most common arguments against materialism, concentrating on functionalism, because it is currently the most influential version of materialism. In general, these attacks have the same logical structure: the materialist account leaves out some essential feature of the mind such as consciousness or intentionality. In the jargon of philosophers, the materialist analysis fails to give *sufficient* conditions for mental phenomena, because it is possible to satisfy the materialist analysis and not have the appropriate mental phenomena. Strictly speaking, functionalism does not require materialism. The functionalist defines mental states in terms of causal relations and the causal relations could in principle be in anything. It just happens, as the world turned out, that they are in physical brains, physical computers, and other physical systems. The functionalist analysis is supposed to be a conceptual truth that analyzes mental concepts in causal terms. The fact that these causal relations are realized in human brains is an empirical discovery, not a conceptual truth. But the driving motivation for functionalism was a materialist rejection of dualism. Functionalists want to analyze mental phenomena in a way that avoids any reference to anything intrinsically subjective and nonphysical.

I. EIGHT (AND ONE HALF) ARGUMENTS AGAINST MATERIALISM

1. Absent Qualia

Conscious experiences have a qualitative aspect. There is a qualitative feel to drinking beer, which is quite different from the qualitative feel of listening to Beethoven's Ninth Symphony. Several philosophers have found it useful to introduce a technical term to describe this qualitative aspect of consciousness. The term for qualitative states is "qualia," of which the singular is "quale." Each conscious state is a quale, because there is a certain qualitative feel to each state. Now, say the anti-functionalists, the problem with functionalism is that it leaves out qualia. It leaves out the qualitative aspect of our conscious experiences, and thus qualia are absent from the functionalist account. Qualia really exist, so any theory like functionalism that denies their existence, either explicitly or implicitly, is false.

2. Spectrum Inversion

A related argument was advanced by a number of philosophers, and it relies on an old thought experiment, which has occurred to many people in the history of the subject, and to many people outside of philosophy as well.

Let us suppose that neither you nor I is color blind. We both make exactly the same color discriminations. If asked to pick out the red pencils from the green pencils, you and I will both pick out the red pencils. When the traffic light changes from red to green, we both go at once. But let us suppose that, in fact, the inner experiences we have are quite different. If I could have the experience you call "seeing green," I would call it "seeing red." And similarly, if you could have the experience I call "seeing green," you would call it "seeing red." We have, in short, a red-green inversion. This is totally undetectable by any behavioral tests, because the tests identify powers to make discriminations among objects in the world, and not the power to label inner experiences. The inner experiences might be different, even though the external behavior is exactly the same. But if that is possible, then functionalism cannot be giving an account of inner experience, for the inner experience is left out of any functionalist account. The functionalist would give exactly the same account of my experience described by "I see something green" and your experience described by "I see something green," but the experiences are different, so functionalism is false.

3. Thomas Nagel: What Is It Like to Be a Bat?

One of the earliest well-known arguments against functionalist types of materialism was advanced in an article by Thomas Nagel called, "What It Is Like to Be a Bat?"[1] According to Nagel, the really difficult part of the mind-body problem is the problem of consciousness. Suppose we had a fully satisfactory functionalist, materialist, neurobiological account of various mental states: beliefs, desires, hopes, fears, etc. All the same, such an account would not explain consciousness. Nagel illustrates this with the example of a bat. Bats have a different lifestyle from ours. They sleep all day long, hanging upside down from rafters, and then they fly around at night, navigating by detecting echoes from sonar they bounce off of solid objects. Now, says Nagel, someone might have a complete knowledge of a bat's neurophysiology; he might have a complete knowledge of all the functional mechanisms that enable bats to live and navigate; but all the same, there would be something left out of this person's knowledge: What is it like to be a bat? What does it feel like? And this is the essence of consciousness. For any conscious being, there is a what-it-is-like aspect to his existence. And this is left out of any objective account of consciousness because an objective account cannot explain the subjective character of consciousness.

4. Frank Jackson: What Mary Didn't Know

A similar argument was advanced by the Australian philosopher, Frank Jackson.[2] Jackson imagines a neurobiologist, Mary, who knows all there is to know about color perception. She has a total and complete knowledge of the neurophysiology of our color-perceiving apparatus, and she also has a complete knowledge of the physics of light and of the color spectrum. But, says Jackson, let us imagine that she has been brought up entirely in a black and white environment. She has never seen anything colored, only black, white, and shades of gray. Now, says Jackson, it seems clear that there is something left out of her knowledge. What is left out, for example, is what the color red actually looks like. But, then, it seems that a functionalist or a materialist account of the mind would leave something out, because a person might have the complete knowledge of all there was to know on a functionalist or materialist account, without knowing what colors look like. And the problem with colors is only a special case of the problem of qualitative experiences generally. Any account of the mind that leaves out these qualitative experiences is inadequate.

5. Ned Block: The Chinese Nation

A fifth argument for the same general antifunctionalist view was advanced by Ned Block.[3] Block says that we might imagine a large population carrying out the steps in a functionalist program of the sort that is presumably carried out by the brain. So, for example, imagine that there are a billion neurons in the brain, and imagine that there are a billion citizens of China. (The figure of a billion neurons is, of course, ludicrously small for the brain, but it does not matter for this argument.) Now we might imagine that just as the brain carries out certain functionalist steps, so we could get the population of China to carry out exactly those steps. But, all the same, the population of China does not thereby have any mental states as a total population in the way that the brain *does* have mental states.

6. Saul Kripke: Rigid Designators

A purely logical argument was advanced by Saul Kripke[4] against any version of the identity theory. Kripke's argument appeals to the concept of a "rigid designator." A rigid designator is defined as an expression that always refers to the same object in any possible state of affairs. Thus, the expression, "Benjamin Franklin," is a rigid designator because in the usage that I am now invoking, it always refers to the same man. This is not to say, of course, that I cannot name my dog "Benjamin Franklin," but, then, that is a different usage, a different meaning of the expression. On the standard meaning, "Benjamin Franklin" is a rigid designator. But the expression, "The inventor of daylight saving time," though it also refers to Benjamin Franklin, is not a rigid designator because it is easy to imagine a world in which Benjamin Franklin was not the inventor of daylight saving time. It makes sense to say that someone else, other than the actual inventor, might have been the inventor of daylight saving time, but it makes no sense to say that someone else, other than Benjamin Franklin, might have been Benjamin Franklin. For these reasons, "Benjamin Franklin" is a rigid designator, but "the inventor of daylight saving time" is nonrigid.

With the notion of rigid designators in hand, Kripke then proceeds to examine identity statements. His claim is that identity
statements, where one term is rigid and the other not rigid, are in
general not necessarily true; they might turn out to be false. Thus,
the sentence, "Benjamin Franklin is identical with the inventor of
daylight saving time," is true, but only contingently true. We can
imagine a world in which it is false. But, says Kripke, where both
sides of the identity statement are rigid, the statement, if true, must
be necessarily true. Thus, the statement, "Samuel Clemens is identical with Mark Twain," is necessarily true because there cannot be
a world in which Samuel Clemens exists, and Mark Twain exists,
but they are two different people. Similarly with words naming
kinds of things. Water is identical with H_2O, and because both
expressions are rigid, the identity must be necessary. And here is
the relevance to the mind-body problem: if we have on the left
hand side of our identity statement an expression referring to a
type of mental state rigidly, and on the right hand side, an expression referring to a type of brain state rigidly, then the statement, if
true, would have to be necessarily true. Thus, if pains really were
identical with C-fiber stimulations, then the statement, "Pain =
C-fiber stimulation," would have to be necessarily true, if it were
to be true at all. But, it is clearly not necessarily true. For even if
there is a strict correlation between pains and C-fiber stimulations,
all the same, it is easy to imagine that a pain might exist without a
C-fiber stimulation existing, and a C-fiber stimulation might exist
without a corresponding pain. But, if that is so, then the identity
statement is not necessarily true, and if it is not necessarily true, it
cannot be true at all. Therefore, it is false. And what goes for the
identification of pains with neurobiological events goes for any
identification of conscious mental states with physical events.

7. John Searle: The Chinese Room

An argument explicitly directed against Strong AI was put forth by
the present author.[5] The strategy of the argument is to appeal to
one's first person experiences in testing any theory of the mind. If
Strong AI were true, then anybody should be able to acquire any
cognitive capacity just by implementing the computer program simulating that cognitive capacity. Let us try this with Chinese. I do not,
as a matter of fact, understand any Chinese at all. I cannot even tell
Chinese writing from Japanese writing. But, we imagine that I am
locked in a room with boxes full of Chinese symbols, and I have a

rule book, in effect, a computer program, that enables me to answer questions put to me in Chinese. I receive symbols that, unknown to me, are questions; I look up in the rule book what I am supposed to do; I pick up symbols from the boxes, manipulate them according to the rules in the program, and hand out the required symbols, which are interpreted as answers. We can suppose that I pass the Turing test for understanding Chinese, but, all the same, I do not understand a word of Chinese. And if I do not understand Chinese on the basis of implementing the right computer program, then neither does any other computer just on the basis of implementing the program, because no computer has anything that I do not have.

You can see the difference between computation and real understanding if you imagine what it is like for me also to answer questions in English. Imagine that in the same room I am given questions in English, which I then answer. From the outside my answers to the English and the Chinese questions are equally good. I pass the Turing test for both. But from the inside, there is a tremendous difference. What is the difference exactly? In English, I understand what the words mean; in Chinese, I understand nothing. In Chinese, I am just a computer.

The Chinese Room Argument struck at the heart of the Strong AI project. Prior to its publication, attacks on artificial intelligence usually took the form of saying that the human mind has certain abilities that the computer does not have and could not acquire.[6] This is always a dangerous strategy, because as soon as someone says that there is a certain sort of task that computers cannot do, the temptation is very strong to design a program that performs precisely that task. And this has often happened. When it happens, the critics of artificial intelligence usually say that the task was not all that important anyway and the computer successes do not really count. The defenders of artificial intelligence feel, with some justice, that the goal posts are being constantly moved. The Chinese Room Argument adopted a totally different strategy. It assumes complete success on the part of artificial intelligence in simulating human cognition. It assumes that AI researchers can design a program that passes the Turing test for understanding Chinese or anything else. All the same, as far as human cognition is concerned, such achievements are simply irrelevant. And they are irrelevant for a deep reason: the computer operates by manipulating symbols. Its processes are defined purely syntactically, whereas the human mind has more than just uninterpreted symbols, it attaches meanings to the symbols.

There is a further development of the argument that seems to me more powerful though it received much less attention than the original Chinese Room Argument. In the original argument I assumed that the attribution of syntax and computation to the system was unproblematic. But if you think about it you will see that *computation and syntax are observer relative.* Except for cases where a person is actually computing in his own mind there are no intrinsic or original computations in nature. When I add two plus two to get four, that computation is not observer relative. I am doing that regardless of what anybody thinks. But when I punch "2+2 =" on my pocket calculator and it prints out "4" it knows nothing of computation, arithmetic, or symbols, because it knows nothing about anything. Intrinsically it is a complex electronic circuit that we *use* to compute with. The electrical state transitions are intrinsic to the machine, but the computation is in the eye of the beholder. What goes for the calculator goes for any commercial computer. The sense in which computation is in the machine is the sense in which information is in a book. It is there alright, but it is observer relative and not intrinsic. For this reason you could not discover that the brain is a digital computer, because computation is not discovered in nature, it is assigned to it. So the question, Is the brain a digital computer? is ill defined. If it asks, Is the brain intrinsically a digital computer? the answer is that nothing is intrinsically a digital computer except for conscious agents thinking through computations. If it asks, Could we assign a computational interpretation to the brain? the answer is that we can assign a computational interpretation to anything.

I do not develop the argument here but I want you to know at least the bare bones of the argument. For a fuller statement of it see *The Rediscovery of the Mind*, chapter 9.[7]

8. The Conceivability of Zombies

One of the oldest arguments, and in a way the underlying argument in several of the others, is this: it is conceivable that there could be a being who was physically exactly like me in every respect but who was totally without any mental life at all. On one version of this argument it is logically possible that there might be a zombie who was exactly like me, molecule for molecule, but who had no mental life at all. In philosophy a zombie is a system that behaves just like humans but has no mental life, no consciousness or real intentionality; and this argument claims that zombies are logically possible. And if zombies are even logically possible, that is, if it is logically possible that a system might have all the right behavior and all the right functional mechanisms and even the right physical structure while still having no mental life, then the behaviorist and functionalist analyses are mistaken. They do not state logically sufficient conditions for having a mind.

This argument occurs in various forms. One of the earliest contemporary statements is by Thomas Nagel.[8] Nagel argues, "I can conceive of my body doing precisely what it is doing now, inside and out, with complete physical causation of its behavior (including typically self-conscious behavior), but without any of the mental states which I am now experiencing, or any others, for that matter. If that is really conceivable, then the mental states must be distinct from the body's physical state." This is a kind of mirror image of Descartes' argument. Descartes argued that it is conceivable that my mind could exist without my body, therefore my mind cannot be identical with my body. And this argument says it is conceivable that my body could exist and be exactly as it is, but without my mind, therefore my mind is not identical with my body, or any part of, or any functioning of my body.

9. The Aspectual Shape of Intentionality

The final argument I can present only in an abbreviated form (hence I call it half an argument) because I haven't yet explained intentionality in enough detail to spell it out fully. But I think I can give you a clear enough idea of how it goes. Intentional states, like beliefs and desires, represent the world under some aspects and not others. For example, the desire for water is not the same as the desire for H_2O, because a person might desire water without knowing that it is H_2O and even believing that it is not H_2O. Because all intentional states represent under aspects we might say that all intentional states have an aspectual shape. But a causal account of intentionality such as the one given by functionalists cannot capture differences in aspectual shape because causation does not have this kind of aspectual shape. Whatever water causes, H_2O causes; and whatever causes water, causes H_2O. The functionalist analysis of my belief that this stuff is water and my desire for water given in causal terms can't distinguish this belief and desire from my belief that this stuff is H_2O and my desire for H_2O. But they are clearly distinct, so functionalism fails.

And you cannot answer this argument by saying that we could ask the person, "Do you believe that this stuff is water? Do you believe that this stuff is H_2O?" because the problem we had about belief and desire now arises for *meaning*. How do we know that the person means by "H_2O" what we mean by "H_2O," and by "water" what we mean by "water"? If all we have to go on is behavior and causal relations, they are not enough to distinguish different meanings in the head of the agent. In short, alternative and inconsistent translations will be consistent with all the causal and behavioral facts.[9]

I have not seen this argument stated before and it only occurred to me when writing this book. To summarize it in the jargon I will explain in chapter 6, intentionality essentially involves aspectual shape. All mental representation is under representational aspects. Causation also has aspects but they are not representational aspects. You can't analyze mental concepts in causal terms because the representational aspectual shape of the intentional gets lost in the translation. This is why statements about intentionality are intensional-with-an-s, but statements about causation, of the form A caused B, are extensional. (Don't worry if you don't understand this paragraph. We will get there in chapter 6.)

II. MATERIALIST ANSWERS TO THE FOREGOING ARGUMENTS

Not surprisingly, the defenders of functionalism, the identity theory, and Strong AI, in general, felt that they could answer the foregoing arguments (except the last that is published here for the first time). There is a huge literature on this subject, and I will not attempt to review it in this book. (I know of over 100 published attacks on the Chinese Room Argument in English alone, and I assume there must be dozens more that I do not know about, in English and other languages.) But some of the arguments defending materialism are quite common and have received wide acceptance, so are worth discussing here.

Answers to Nagel and Jackson

Against Nagel and Jackson, a standard answer given by the materialists was this: both arguments rest on what is known, either what someone might know about the physiology of a bat, or what Mary might know about the physiology of color perception. Thus, both arguments make the claim that even a perfect knowledge of the third-person functional or physiological phenomena would leave something out. It would leave out the subjective, qualitative, first-person, experiential phenomena. The answer to this is that any argument based on what is known under one description, and not known under another description, is insufficient to establish that there is no identity between the things described by the two descriptions. Thus, to take an obvious example, suppose Sam knows that water is wet, and suppose that Sam does not know that H_2O is wet. Suppose someone argues that water cannot be identical with H_2O because there is something about H_2O that Sam does not know, that he does know about water. I think everybody can see that that is a bad argument. From the fact that one might know something about a substance under one description, for example, as water, and not know that very same thing about it under another description, for example, as H_2O, does not imply that water is not H_2O.

Will this argument work against Nagel and Jackson? To make the parallel case, one would have to argue as follows. Mary knows, for example, that neuron process X437B is caused by red objects. Mary does not know that this type of color experience of red is caused by red objects. She does not know that because she has never had the color experience of red. And the conclusion is supposed to be that this color experience cannot be identical with processes X437B. This argument is just as fallacious as the argument we considered about water and H_2O. And if Nagel and Jackson intended their arguments to be interpreted in this way they would be subject to the charge that they are similarly fallacious.

Does this refute Nagel and Jackson? I do not think so. It is possible to state the argument as an argument about knowledge, and they typically do state it in this form (indeed Jackson's argument is often called the "knowledge argument"), but it is not in its import subject to the charge that it commits the fallacy of supposing that if something is known about an entity under one description and not known about an entity under another description, the first entity cannot be identical with the second entity. The point of the argument is not to appeal to the ignorance of the bat specialist or Mary. The point of the argument is that there exist real phenomena that are necessarily left out of the scope of their knowledge, as long as their knowledge is only of objective, third-person, physical facts. The real phenomena are color experiences and the bat's feelings, respectively; and these are subjective, first-person, conscious phenomena. The problem in Mary's case is not just that she lacks *information* about some other phenomenon; rather, there is a certain type of *experience* that she has not yet had. And that experience, a first-person subjective phenomenon, cannot be identical with the third-person, objective neuronal and functional correlates. The point about the epistemology, the information, is just a way of getting at the underlying ontological difference. Similar remarks apply to Nagel's example of the bat. The problem is not that the bat investigator lacks information; he may indeed have perfect third-person information. What he lacks is the experience that the bat has; he lacks the kind of phenomena that occur in the bat's consciousness. So, though both arguments are stated as if they were epistemic, in fact I think that properly construed they are ontological, and thus they are not subject to the objection we considered.

The logical form of the arguments is this: I stand in a relation to a certain entities, my experiences of colors. And the bat stands in a relation to certain entities, its experiences of what it feels like to be a bat. A complete third-person description of the world leaves out these entities, therefore the description is incomplete. The examples of Mary and the bat expert are ways of illustrating the incompleteness.

The real problem with all forms of reductionism, as we will see, is that they are confronted with the question, Are there two phenomena there or only one? In the case of water, there is really only one phenomenon. Water consists entirely of H_2O molecules. There are not two different things, water and H_2O molecules; there is only one thing, water, consisting entirely of H_2O molecules. But when it comes to identifying features of the mind, such as consciousness and intentionality, with features of the brain, such as computational states or neurobiological states, it looks like there have to be two features, because the mental phenomena have a first-person ontology, in the sense that they exist only insofar as they are experienced by some human or animal subject, some "I" that has the experience. And this makes them irreducible to any third-person ontology, any mode of existence that is independent of any experiencing agent. Calling attention to the difference between the first-person ontology and the third person is really the point of all these arguments against this sort of reductionism.

Answers to Kripke on Rigid Designators

A common answer to Kripke's argument concerning rigid designators is that it did not refute token identity claims.[10] The idea was that it might be valid against type identities but would not be valid against token identities. So, even if, in general, we might imagine a C-fiber firing without a pain, and a pain without a C-fiber firing, for this particular instance, this particular token of a C-fiber firing, I could not have this very C-fiber firing without it being painful, and I could not have had this very pain without these C-fiber firings. Does this answer Kripke's argument? I do not see that it does. If you grant me that there are really two features to this experience, the feeling of pain and the firing of C-fibers, then it looks like Kripke's argument will go through. I could have had this very feeling without there being any correlated C-fiber firings, and I could have had these very C-fiber firings without any correlated feelings. Now, of course, it is always possible to patch things up by simply making a criterion for the identity of the feeling and the C-fiber firings, the co-occurrence between the two. So, if part of what makes this pain the very pain that it is, is that it co-occurs with these C-fiber firings, and part of what makes these very C-fiber firings the C-fiber firings that they are, is that they co-occur with this very pain, then we do get a necessary identity between this pain and these C-fiber firings. However, we still have not achieved the aim of token identity because now we have a version of property dualism. What we are saying is that one and the same entity has both objective C-fiber firing properties and subjective painful properties. I will come back to this point in chapter 4.

Actually, it is not really clear to what extent we use correlations, even causal correlations, as identity conditions for sensations. Suppose I feel a pain, and suppose it has a specific cause. Suppose however, while I am feeling that very pain, the experience continues but the initial cause ceases and another cause takes over. Shall we say that I had two different pains because, though there was a continuous sensation, it had two different causes? Or shall we say that I had a continuous single pain, but that the first portion of it had one cause and the second portion had another cause? I do not think that ordinary language will settle this issue for us. We have to make a decision. The important thing to see, however, is that in the case of pains, we need to distinguish between the actual experience on the one hand and the neurobiological substrate on the other. I cannot tell you how much resistance this obvious point encounters from materialist philosophers.

Answers to Searle's Chinese Room Argument

I am reluctant to resume discussion of the Chinese Room because I have discussed it in so many places already. But, for the purposes of this book, it is worthwhile to point out the inadequacies of the standard arguments against it. To my surprise, the standard argument against the Chinese Room is what I call the "Systems Reply." The idea of the Systems Reply is that though the man in the room does not understand Chinese, the man is only part of a larger system, consisting of room, rule books, windows, boxes, program, etc., and it is not the man, but the whole system, that understands Chinese. As one person put it to me, the whole room understands Chinese. It is important to say exactly why this reply is inadequate. If you ask, why do I not understand Chinese in the room? the answer is because I have no way of knowing what any of the Chinese symbols mean. I have the syntax but no semantics. But, then, if I have no way of getting from the syntax to the semantics, neither does the whole room. The room has no resources for attaching meaning to symbols that I do not have. I illustrated this with an extension of the thought experiment. Imagine that I get rid of the room and work outdoors. I do all the calculations in my head, memorize the program, and memorize the database. We can even imagine that I work in the middle of an open field. All the same, there is still no way that I will understand Chinese, nor is there any subsystem in me that will understand Chinese, nor is there any feature of me that will understand Chinese, because there is nothing in me, nor in any subsystem of me, nor in any larger system of which I am a part, that will enable the system to attach any meanings to the symbols. Manipulating the symbols is one thing, knowing their meanings is another. Computers are defined in terms of symbol manipulation, and symbol manipulation by itself is neither constitutive of nor sufficient for meaning.

The distinction between syntax and semantics is so important for the rest of the argument of this book that I want to say a little more about it here. In order that there can be human linguistic communication at all, there has to be a language. A language consists of symbols, typically words, combined into sentences. These elements, symbols, words, sentences, are all syntactical. But language only works if these elements are meaningful—if they carry meaning. But what is meaning? There are many different accounts of meaning in the philosophical, linguistic, and psychological literature. I have definite opinions about which are right and which are wrong, but for the purposes of this argument those disputes do not matter. Any sane account of meaning has to recognize the distinction between the symbols, construed as purely abstract syntactical entities, and the meanings attached to those symbols. The symbols have to be distinguished from their meanings. For example, if I write down a sentence in German, *"Es regnet,"* you will see words on the page and thus see the syntactical objects, but if you do not know German, you will be aware only of the syntax, not of the semantics. You will be in the situation that I am in in the Chinese Room, where I am aware of the syntax of the computational system, but I do not know what any of it means.

Answers to the Conceivability of Zombies

There are many discussions of the zombie argument. One answer is just to deny that zombies who behave exactly like us but with no mental life are conceivable. This does not seem a very promising strategy, because intuitively it seems very easy to imagine a machine that is exactly like me but without consciousness. Daniel Dennett[11] supports the strategy with the following analogy. Suppose someone said there are iron bars that behave in all respects exactly like magnets but are not magnets, they are zagnets. Such a thing is inconceivable, because, says Dennett, zagnets would just be magnets. Analogously a machine that behaves in all respects like a conscious agent is a conscious agent. Zagnets are magnets and zombies are conscious agents.

This analogy does not work. A suitable description of a zagnet will *entail* that it is a magnet, but no third-person description of a physical system will entail that it has conscious states because there are two different phenomena, the third-person behavioral, functional, neurobiological structures and the first-person conscious experience.

Another answer to the zombie argument one sometimes hears is that if it were right, then consciousness would become epiphenomenal. If you could have the same behavior without consciousness, then consciousness would not be doing any work. This answer rests on a misunderstanding. The point of the zombie argument is to show that consciousness, on the one hand, and behavior and causal relations, on the other, are different phenomena by showing that it is logically possible to have one without the other. But this logical possibility does not imply that consciousness does not do any work in the real world. Analogously: Gasoline combustion is not the same thing as car movement, because it is conceivable to have one without the other. But the fact that it is logically possible for cars to move without gasoline, or indeed without any fuel at all, does not show that gasoline and other fuels are epiphenomenal.

III. CONCLUSION

What should we say about these arguments? It is important in philosophy always to step back and look at the issues from a broader intellectual and historical perspective. Why are so many philosophers driven to deny certain common-sense claims, such as, that we really do have conscious thoughts and feelings; that we do have real intentional states such as beliefs, hopes, fears, and desires; and that these are caused by processes in the brain and do themselves function causally; and that they are real intrinsic parts of the real world and as much a part of our biological life as digestion, or growth, or the secretion of bile? The answer has to be found historically. The failures of dualism and the success of the physical sciences, together, give us the impression that, somehow or other, we must be able to give an account of all there is to be said about the real world in completely materialist terms. The existence of some irreducible *mental* phenomena does not fit in and seems intellectually repulsive. It is indigestible. Notice that people do not have these problems where other parts of our biological life are concerned. Nobody feels the necessity of reducing other biological phenomena to something else. Nobody thinks there is, for example, a problem about the existence of thumbs, that we should do a functionalist analysis of thumbs to show that they can be entirely defined in terms of their grasping behavior. The reason that philosophers are worried about pains, and not about thumbs, is that pains, on the common-sense view, have a kind of irreducible private, subjective, qualitative component, and the aim is always to get rid of that.

In the history that we have been examining, a distinction was made between consciousness and intentionality. Many philosophers would have been willing to agree that there was no functionalist account of consciousness, but they wanted to maintain that intentionality was subject to a functionalist reduction and that the computational account of the mind gave us a beautiful and scientifically impeccable reduction. Forget about consciousness, which is scientifically irrelevant anyway. What matters about the mind is its capacity for information processing, and the modern computer at long last gives us the right model for understanding the information processing capacities of the mind. This conception in modern materialism that consciousness could be set on one side, while we concentrated on intentionality, is why there were so many more attacks on the Chinese Room than on the other arguments. It threatened the very citadel of the functionalist-computationalist account, which is the idea that if you had the right input-output relations, and if you had the right program mediating those relations, then you would have all there is to intentionality. The Chinese Room Argument shows that there are two things going on in the human being, one is the actual symbols that the human is aware of when he or she thinks, and second, there is the meaning, or interpretation, or sense that attaches to those symbols.

Now, this is always the problem with reduction. Are there two phenomena or only one? If there are two real phenomena, then there is no way to deny the existence of one without producing a falsehood, no way to do an ontological reduction of one to the other.

So where does that leave us? Are we forced to go back to dualism? If materialism has failed to state a convincing alternative to the traditional dualism it was designed to supplant, then why not revert to dualism? And, indeed, are we not tacitly conceding dualism when we say that consciousness and intentionality are irreducible?

I think our real problems have to do with a tangle of conceptual confusions that I will try to sort out in the next chapter.

We end this chapter in a depressing intellectual state: neither dualism nor materialism is acceptable and yet they are presented to us as the only possibilities. Furthermore we know independently that both what dualism is trying to say and what materialism is trying to say are true. Materialism is trying to say that the world consists entirely of physical particles in fields of force. Dualism is trying to say that there are irreducible and ineliminable mental features to the world, consciousness and intentionality, in particular. But if both views are true, there must be a way of stating them that renders them consistent. Given the traditional categories, it is not easy to see how they could be consistent; for materialism so stated seems to imply that there cannot be any irreducible nonphysical phenomena; and dualism so stated seems to imply that there must, in addition to material phenomena, be irreducible nonphysical mental phenomena. We will explore these issues in more detail in the next chapter and see that in order to render these views consistent, we have to abandon the assumptions behind the traditional vocabulary.

Suggestions for Further Reading

Block, N., "Troubles with Functionalism," in *Minnesota Studies in the Philosophy of Science*, Minneapolis: University of Minnesota Press, vol. 9 (1978): 261–325. Reprinted in Block, ed., *Readings in Philosophy of Psychology*, vol. 1, Cambridge, MA: Harvard University Press, 1980, 268–305.

Jackson, F., "What Mary Didn't Know," *Journal of Philosophy*, vol. 83 (1986): 291–295; also "Epiphenomenal Qualia," in *Philosophical Quarterly*, vol. 32 (1986): 127–136.

Kripke, S. A., *Naming and Necessity*, Cambridge MA: Harvard University Press, 1980, excerpts in Chalmers, D. ed., *Philosophy of Mind, Classical and Contemporary Readings*, New York: Oxford University Press, 2002, 329–332.

McGinn, C., "Anomalous Monism and Kripke's Cartesian Intuitions," in Block, ed., *Readings in Philosophy of Psychology*, vol. 1, Cambridge, MA: Harvard University Press, 1980, 156–158.

Nagel, T., "Armstrong on the Mind," in Block, ed., *Readings in Philosophy of Psychology*, vol. 1, Cambridge, MA: Harvard University Press, 1980, 200–206.

Nagel, T., *The View from Nowhere*, New York: Oxford University Press, 1986.

Nagel, T., "What Is It Like to be a Bat?," in *Philosophical Review*, vol. 83 (1974): 435–450, reprinted in Chalmers, ed., *The Philosophy of Mind: Classical and Contemporary Readings*, New York: Oxford University Press, 2002.

Searle, J. R., "Minds, Brains and Programs," in *Behavioral and Brain Sciences*, 3 (1980), 417–424, reprinted in O'Connor, T. and D. Robb, *Philosophy of Mind, Contemporary Readings*, London: Routledge, 2003, 332–352.

Searle, J. R., *Minds, Brains and Science*, Cambridge, MA: Harvard University Press, 1984.

Searle, J. R., *The Rediscovery of the Mind*, Cambridge, MA: MIT Press, 1992.

CHAPTER 4

Consciousness Part I

Consciousness and the Mind-Body Problem

We ended the last chapter with an apparent contradiction of the sort that is typical in philosophy. On the one hand we accept a view that seems overwhelmingly convincing—the universe is material—but that seems inconsistent with another view that we cannot give up—minds exist. This pattern occurs over and over in philosophy. We will see in chapter 7 that the free-will problem exhibits the same sort of conflict or contradiction: we think all events must be causally determined, but we experience freedom. In other branches of philosophy, similar inconsistencies arise. In ethics we feel there must be an objective moral truth but at the same time we feel there cannot be that kind of objectivity in morals. Some people find these contradictions in philosophy exasperating. Others, like me, find them fun and challenging.

In this chapter I am going to attempt to resolve the contradiction about mind and matter.

I. FOUR MISTAKEN ASSUMPTIONS

So far, in this book, I have mostly been concerned with the opinions of other people. I have tried to describe the lay of the land, inserting my own opinion only when it seemed part of the lay of the land. And I have even used the accepted terminology, though I find it inadequate. In this chapter I will tell you what I actually think about the "mind-body problem." As the very first step I want to suggest that we should not accept the traditional terminology and the assumptions that go with the terminology. Expressions like "mind" and "body," "mental" and "material" or "physical," as well as "reduction," "causation," and "identity," as they are used in discussions of the mind-body problem, are the source of our difficulty and not tools for its resolution. As my solution to the mind-body problem runs counter to these assumptions, I want to lay them out explicitly (with preliminary comments in parentheses). There are four assumptions we need to question.

Assumption 1. The Distinction between the Mental and the Physical

It is assumed that "mental" and "physical" name mutually exclusive ontological categories. If it is mental then it cannot be in that very respect physical. And if it is physical, then it cannot be in that very respect mental. Mental qua mental excludes physical qua physical.

(This is the basic assumption and gets the whole discussion going. If we think of the world as at bottom physical, then how are we supposed to think of the mental as fitting in? A standard move of people who think they are denying this assumption is to say that we can *reduce* the mental to the physical. The mental is nothing but the physical. They think that somehow or other they are overcoming the dualist dichotomy, but they are accepting its worst feature. When they say that the mental is physical, they are not saying that the mental qua mental is physical qua physical. They are saying that the mental qua mental does not exist, that there is nothing there but the physical. This is a crucial point and I will come back to it later.)

Assumption 2. The Notion of Reduction

It is generally assumed that the notion of reduction, where one kind of phenomenon is reduced to another kind, is clear, unambiguous, and unproblematic. When you reduce A's to B's you show that A's are nothing but B's. For example material objects can be reduced to molecules because material objects are nothing but collections of molecules. Similarly, if consciousness can be reduced to brain processes then consciousness is nothing but a brain process.

(The model of reduction comes from the natural sciences. Just as science has shown that material objects are nothing but collections of particles, so science would show that consciousness is nothing but something else—neuron firings or computer programs are the favorite candidates. Later on we will see that the notion of reduction is multiply ambiguous. We will need a distinction between those reductions that eliminate the reduced phenomenon by showing it to be an illusion—sunsets, for example are eliminated by showing that they are an illusion generated by the earth's rotation—and those reductions that show how a real phenomenon is realized in the world—material objects, for example, are reduced to molecules, but that does not show that the objects do not exist. We will also need a distinction between causal reductions and ontological reductions.)

Assumption 3. Causation and Events

It is almost universally assumed that causation is always a relation between discrete events ordered in time, where the cause precedes the effect. One event, the cause, comes before another event, the effect. Specific examples of cause-and-effect relations must instantiate a universal causal law.

(It is an immediate consequence of assumptions 1 and 3 that if brain events cause mental events, then dualism follows. The brain event is one [physical] thing. The mental event is another [mental] thing.)

Assumption 4. The Transparency of Identity

Identity, like reduction, is assumed to be unproblematic. Everything is identical with itself and not with anything else. Paradigms of identity are object identities and identities of composition. An example of the first: the object, the Evening Star, is identical with the object, the Morning Star. An example of identity of composition: water is identical with H_2O molecules because any body of water is composed of H_2O.

(The idea of introducing the concept of identity into this discussion is that we just might discover that a mental state is identical with a neurophysiological state of the brain in the way that we have discovered that the Evening Star is the Morning Star, or that water is H_2O.)

I think these assumptions contain massive confusions. My method will not be to attack them head-on, at least not just yet. First, I want to approach the relation of consciousness to brain processes naïvely, as if we did not have many centuries of motivated confusion. Then, after I have explained the relations of mind and body, I will go back and explain why these assumptions, as they stand, have prevented us from getting a clear picture of the facts and need serious amendment and revision.

II. THE SOLUTION TO THE MIND-BODY PROBLEM

My method in philosophy is to try to forget about the history of a problem and the traditional ways of thinking about it and just try to state the facts as far as we know them. Let us try this method with a fairly simple case. We will concentrate on consciousness and take up intentionality in a later chapter. Here goes: I now feel thirsty. Not a desperate thirst, just a conscious, medium-strength desire to drink some water. Such a feeling, like all conscious states, only exists as experienced by a human or animal subject, and in that sense it has a subjective or first-person ontology. In order for feelings like my thirst to exist they have to be experienced by a subject, by an "I" that is thirsty. But how do these subjective feelings of thirst fit into the rest of the world? The first thing we have to insist on is that my thirst is a real phenomenon, a part of the real world, and that it functions causally in my behavior. If I now drink, it is because I am thirsty. The next thing to notice is that my feelings of thirst are entirely caused by neurobiological processes in the brain. If I do not have enough water in my system, this shortage triggers a complex series of neurobiological phenomena and all of that causes my feelings of thirst. (There is, by the way, a strange reluctance to admit that our conscious states are caused by brain processes. Some authors fudge and say that the brain "gives rise" to consciousness;[1] others say that the brain is the "seat" of consciousness.[2] One who grants that consciousness is dependent on the brain says the relation is "not happily construed as causal."[3]) But what are these feelings of thirst exactly? Where and how do they exist? They are conscious processes going on in the brain, and in that sense they are features of the brain, though at a level higher than that of neurons and synapses. The conscious feeling of thirst is a process going on in my brain system.

Just so it does not sound like I am vaguely talking about how things might be as opposed to how they are in fact, let me nail the whole issue down to reality by summarizing some of what we know about how brain processes cause feelings of thirst. Suppose an animal gets a shortage of water in its system. The shortage of water will cause "saline imbalances" in the system, because the ratio of salt to water is excessive in favor of salt. This triggers certain activities in the kidneys. The kidneys secrete rennin, and the rennin synthesizes a substance called angiotensin 2. This substance gets inside the hypothalamus and affects the rate of neuron firings. As far as we know the differential rates of neuron firings cause the animal to feel thirsty. Now, of course, we do not know all of the details and no doubt as we come to understand more, this brief sketch I have given will seem quaint. But that is the sort of explanation of how the existence of conscious feelings of thirst fits into our overall world-view. All forms of consciousness are caused by the behavior of neurons and are realized in the brain system, which is itself composed of neurons. What goes for thirst goes for all forms of our conscious life whatever, from wanting to throw up to wondering how to translate the poems of Stéphane Mallarmé into colloquial English. All conscious states are caused by lower-level neuronal processes in the brain. We have conscious thoughts and feelings; they are caused by neurobiological processes in the brain; and they exist as biological features of the brain system.

I believe that this brief account provides the germ of a solution to the "mind-body problem": I am suspicious of isms, but it is sometimes helpful to have a name, just to distinguish clearly between one view and another. I call my view "biological naturalism," because it provides a naturalistic solution to the traditional "mind-body problem," one that emphasizes the biological character of mental states, and avoids both materialism and dualism.

I will state biological naturalism about consciousness as a set of four theses:

1. Conscious states, with their subjective, first-person ontology, are real phenomena in the real world. We cannot do an eliminative reduction of consciousness, showing that it is just an illusion. Nor can we reduce consciousness to its neurobiological basis, because such a third-person reduction would leave out the first-person ontology of consciousness.

2. Conscious states are entirely caused by lower level neurobiological processes in the brain. Conscious states are thus *causally reducible* to neurobiological processes. They have absolutely no life of their own, independent of the neurobiology. Causally speaking, they are not something "over and above" neurobiological processes.

3. Conscious states are realized in the brain as features of the brain system, and thus exist at a level higher than that of neurons and synapses. Individual neurons are not conscious, but portions of the brain system composed of neurons are conscious.

4. Because conscious states are real features of the real world, they function causally. My conscious thirst causes me to drink water for example. I will explain in detail how this works in chapter 7, Mental Causation.

Can the solution to the famous "mind-body problem" really be that simple? If we can just get out of the traditional categories I really think it is that simple. We know for a fact that all of our mental processes are caused by neurobiological processes and we also know that they are going on in the brain and perhaps in the rest of the central nervous system. We know that they function causally, though they have no causal powers in addition to those of the underlying neurobiology, and we know that they are not ontologically reducible to third-person phenomena, because they have a first person ontology. Why then does this apparently obvious solution encounter so much resistance? Many philosophers do not see how these apparently mysterious mental entities can exist at all, and if they do exist how they can be caused by brute physical processes in the brain, and if they do exist and are caused by physical processes how they can exist in the physical system of the brain. But notice that this way of posing the difficulties and questions already accepts the dualism of the mental and the physical. If we state the thesis without employing the traditional Cartesian vocabulary, it does not sound mysterious at all. My conscious feelings of thirst really do exist and function causally in my behavior (does anyone who has ever been thirsty really doubt their existence and causal power?). We know for a fact that they are caused by neuronal processes and the feelings themselves are processes going on inside the brain.

III. OVERCOMING THE MISTAKEN ASSUMPTIONS

To see why it is so hard to accept these points let us now go back and examine the four assumptions that I said made it impossible to get a solution to the so-called mind-body problem.

Assumption 1. *The Distinction between the Mental and the Physical*

The worst mistake is to suppose that the common-sense distinction between mental states naïvely construed and physical states naïvely construed is an expression of some deep metaphysical distinction. On the view that I am presenting, it is not. Consciousness is a system-level, biological feature in much the same way that digestion, or growth, or the secretion of bile are system level, biological features. As such, consciousness is a feature of the brain and thus a part of the physical world. The tradition that I am militating against says that because mental states are intrinsically mental, they cannot be in that very respect, physical. I am in effect saying that because they are intrinsically mental, they are a certain type of biological state, and therefore *a fortiori* they are physical. However, the whole terminology of mental and physical was designed to try to make an absolute opposition between the *mental* and the *physical*, so maybe it is better not to use that terminology at all and just say that consciousness is a biological feature of the brain in the same way that digestion is a biological feature of the digestive tract. We are in both cases talking about natural processes. There is no metaphysical gulf.

The problem we face with the terminology is that the terms have traditionally been defined so as to be mutually exclusive. "Mental" is defined as qualitative, subjective, first personal, and therefore immaterial. "Physical" is defined as quantitative, objective, third personal, and therefore material. I am suggesting that these definitions are inadequate to capture the fact that the world works in such a way that some biological processes are qualitative, subjective, and first personal. If we are going to keep this terminology at all, we need an expanded notion of the physical to allow for its intrinsic, subjective mental component. So let's do it. Let us make a list of the traditional features of the mental and the physical that are supposed to render them mutually exclusive and then revise the list as necessary to fit the facts.

On the traditional conception if anything is mental it has the left-hand features, if physical, the right hand features.[4]

Mental	Physical
Subjective	Objective
Qualitative	Quantitative
Intentional	Nonintentional
Not spatially located & Nonextended in space	Spatially located & Spatially extended
Not explainable by physical processes	Causally explainable by microphysics
Incapable of acting causally on the physical	Acts causally and as a system is causally closed

The features of the mental that we need to account for in a unified theory of everything are consciousness and intentionality. The relevant features of consciousness are that it is qualitative and subjective (these together imply "first personal," so we do not need to list that as a special feature). The question is, How do qualitative, subjective, and intentional phenomena fit into the physical world? Well what are the features of the physical world that they need to fit into? The contemporary concept of the physical is much more complex than the Cartesian tradition allows. For example, if electrons are points of mass/energy, they are not physical on Descartes' definition because they are not extended. But at least these formal features are required by any reasonable conception of the physical: First, real physical phenomena are located in space-time. (Thus electrons are physical and numbers are not.) Second, their features and behavior are causally explainable by microphysics. (Thus, solidity and liquidity meet this test. Ghosts, if they existed, would not.) Third, where real, physical phenomena function causally. (Thus solidity is a real physical phenomenon. Rainbows, under the description "rainbow," are not real physical arches in the sky. They do not cause anything.) And the physical universe is causally closed in the trivial sense that anything that functions causally in it must be part of it.

Now look at the lists. The first three features on the mental list are perfectly consistent with the last four features on the physical list. That is, qualitativeness, subjectivity, and intentionality are physical by the last four criteria. They are located in the space of the brain at certain periods of time, causally explicable by lower-level processes and capable of acting causally. What about the other features? The last four features on the mental list are just mistaken. It is not a condition of being a mental phenomenon that it be nonspatial, nonexplicable by microprocesses, and causally inert. Nor are these implied by the first three. On the contrary, all my mental life occurs in the space of my brain, is caused by microprocesses there, and acts causally from there. Well, what about the first three on the physical list? These are not necessary conditions for being part of the physical universe. *There is no reason why a physical system such as a human or animal organism should not have states that are qualitative, subjective, and intentional.* In fact, in real life, studies of the perceptual and cognitive systems are precisely cases of treating qualitativeness, subjectivity, and original intentionality as part of the domain of natural science and thus as part of the physical world. The distinction between quantity and quality, by the way, is probably bogus. There is no metaphysical reason why you could not have measurements of the degrees of pain or conscious awareness, for example.

This is one of the most important messages of this book. Once you revise the traditional categories to fit the facts, there is no problem in recognizing that the mental qua mental is physical qua physical. You have to revise the traditional Cartesian definitions of both "mental" and "physical," but those definitions were inadequate to the facts in any case.

Assumption 2. *Reduction*

The notions of reduction and reducibility are among the most confused in philosophy, because they are multiply ambiguous. First we need to distinguish between causal reductions and ontological reductions. We can say that phenomena of type A are *causally reducible* to phenomena of type B, if and only if the behavior of A's is entirely causally explained by the behavior of B's, and A's have no causal powers in addition to the powers of B's. So, for example, solidity is causally reducible to molecular behavior. The features of solid objects—impenetrability, the ability to support other solid objects, etc.—are causally explained by molecular behavior, and solidity has no causal powers in addition to the causal powers of the molecules. Phenomena of type A are *ontologically* reducible to phenomena of type B if and only if A's are nothing but B's. So, for example, material objects are nothing but collections of molecules; and sunsets are nothing but appearances generated by the rotation of the earth on its axis relative to the sun.

Often, indeed typically, in the history of science we make an *ontological reduction* on the basis of a *causal reduction*. We say: solidity is nothing but a certain sort of molecular behavior. We carve off the surface features of solidity such as the fact that solid objects have a certain feel, resist pressure, and are impenetrable by other objects, and we redefine the notion in terms of the underlying causes. Solidity is now defined not in terms of surface features but in terms of molecular behavior. And here is the point for our present discussion: *in the case of consciousness we can make a causal reduction but we cannot make an ontological reduction without losing the point of having the concept.* Consciousness is entirely causally explained by neuronal behavior but it is not thereby shown to be nothing but neuronal behavior. Why couldn't we make an ontological reduction and say that consciousness was nothing but neuronal behavior? Well, we could, and we might for medical or other scientific purposes redefine consciousness in terms of microsubstrates, as we have redefined solidity and liquidity. We would then be able to say, for example, "This guy is really in pain, but he can't feel it yet. Our brainoscope shows the presence of pain in the thalamocortical system." Analogously we can now say, "Glass is really liquid, though it looks and feels solid." But the main point of having the concept of consciousness is to capture the first-person, subjective features of the phenomenon and this point is lost if we redefine consciousness in third-person, objective terms. We would still need a name for the first-person ontology. So consciousness differs from other phenomena such as liquidity and solidity that have surface features, in that we are reluctant to carve off the surface feature and redefine the notion in terms of the causes of the surface feature, because the point of the concept is to identify the surface features. There are lots of concepts where the surface features of the phenomena are more interesting than the microstructure. Consider mud or Beethoven's Ninth Symphony. Mud behavior is molecular behavior but that is not the interesting thing about mud, so few people are anxious to insist: "Mud can be reduced to molecular behavior," though they could if they really wanted to. Similarly with Beethoven. Performances of the Ninth can be reduced to wave motions in the air, but that is not what is interesting to us about the performance. The music critic who writes, "All I could hear were wave motions," has missed the point of the performance. Analogously you could do a reduction of consciousness and intentionality, but you would still need a vocabulary to talk about the surface features. Consciousness and intentionality are unique only in that they have a first-person ontology.

In an earlier version of this argument (*The Rediscovery of the Mind*), I said that the irreducibility of consciousness was a trivial consequence of our definitional practices. This remark was widely misunderstood, so let me clarify it here. Grant me that the real "physical" world contains both entities with a third-person ontology (trees and mushrooms, for example) and entities with a first-person ontology (pains and color experiences, for example). All of these first-person entities are causally reducible to their third-person causal bases. But there is an asymmetry. Where color is concerned we are willing (or at least some of us are willing) to carve off the conscious experiences, the color experiences with their first-person ontology, to set them on one side, and then redefine the color words in third-person terms. Colors, on one view, are not essentially defined in terms of color experiences, but in terms of light reflectances that cause color experiences. But we are not willing to do that in the case of consciousness and in the case of concepts of consciousness such as pain. Why not? Why not carve off the first-person experiences of consciousness and of pain, set them on one side, and redefine the concepts in terms of their causes, as we did with color?

Well, we could, and if we knew a lot more about the causes, for certain purpose, we might. But there is an asymmetry between colors on the one hand and pains and consciousness on the other, because we would lose the point of having the concepts of consciousness if we carved off the first-person ontology and redefined the words in third-person terms. In that sense the irreducibility of consciousness does not reveal a deep metaphysical asymmetry between, for example, the way color experiences relate to their causes and the way pain experiences relate to their causes, but rather an asymmetry in our definitional practices. For the definition of "pain" we care more about how pains feel to us than we do for the definition of "color."

Some of my critics thought I was trying to claim that the very existence of consciousness was a trivial consequence of our definitional practices. But I make no such claim. I hope this clears up the misunderstanding.

But don't reductions get rid of the reduced phenomenon by showing it is really something else? No, and this leads to the second confusion in the notion of reduction. We need to distinguish between those reductions that are *eliminative* and those that are not. Eliminative reductions show that the reduced phenomenon did not really exist. Thus the reduction of sunsets to the earth's rotation is eliminative because it shows that the sunset was a mere appearance. But the reduction of solidity is not in that way eliminative because it does not show that objects do not really resist other objects, for example. You cannot do an eliminative reduction on something that really exists.

But why couldn't we show that consciousness was an illusion like sunsets and thus do an eliminative reduction? Eliminative reductions rest on the distinction between appearance and reality. But we cannot show that the very existence of consciousness is an illusion like sunsets, because where consciousness is concerned the appearance is the reality. The sun appears to set over Mt. Tamalpais though it does not really do so. But if it consciously seems to me that I am conscious, then I am conscious. I can make all sorts of mistakes about the contents of my conscious states, but not in that way about their very existence.

To summarize this brief discussion of reduction: you can't do an eliminative reduction of consciousness because it really exists; and its real existence is not subject to the usual epistemic doubts, because those doubts rest on a distinction between appearance and reality and you can't make that distinction for the very existence of your own conscious states. You can do a causal reduction of consciousness to its neuronal substrate, but that reduction does not lead to an ontological reduction because consciousness has a first-person ontology, and you lose the point of having the concept if you redefine it in third-person terms.

Assumption 3. *Causation and Events*

Lots of causal relations are between discrete events ordered in time. A paradigm case, much loved by philosophers, is the case of billiard ball one striking billiard ball two and stopping, while billiard ball two moves away. But not all causation is like that. In lots of cases of causation the cause is simultaneous with the effect. Look at the objects around you and notice that they are exerting pressure on the floor of the room you are in. What is the causal explanation of this pressure? It is caused by the force of gravity. But the force of gravity is not a separate event. It is a continuous force operating in nature. Furthermore, there are lots of cases of simultaneous causation that are, so to speak, bottom up, in the sense that lower-level microphenomena cause higher-level macro-features. Again look at the objects around you. The table supports books. The fact that the table supports books is causally explained by the behavior of the molecules. For solidity, as I mentioned earlier, we do an ontological reduction on the basis of the causal reduction. But the terminology could have gone either way. We could have said solidity is a matter of how things resist pressure, are impenetrable by other objects, and support other objects. And this is causally explained by the behavior of the molecules. We have not gone that way because we think the microstructure gives us a deeper explanation. We say, solidity just is the vibratory movement of molecules in lattice structures, and that explains the fact that one object supports another. The point, however, is that we are discussing the causal order of nature, and that order is often not a matter of discrete events sequential in time, but of microphenomena causally explaining macrofeatures of systems.

Assumption 4. *Identity*

Criteria of identity for material objects like planets, and types of compounds like water, are reasonably clear. But for events, like the Great Depression, or my birthday party, the criteria are not so clear. When we consider mental events, like my having a certain experience, we have to decide how large we want the event to be. Is consciousness identical with a brain process or not? Well, obviously and trivially, as I have said, consciousness is just a brain process. It is a qualitative, subjective, first-person process going on in the nervous system. Yes, but that is not what the identity theorists wanted. What they wanted was to identify a conscious state with a neurobiological process, neurobiologically described. Here it seems to me we are looking for a decision and not for a discovery. It seems to me we can treat one and the same event as having both neurobiological features and phenomenological features. One and the same event is a sequence of neuron firings and is also painful. But this type of identity does not give the materialists what they wanted. The case is a bit like Jaegwon Kim's[5] example of token identities. Every token colored object is identical with a token shaped object. That is no doubt true, but it does not show that being colored and being shaped are the same thing. In the same way, we can have a notion of neurobiological processes big enough so that every token pain process is a token neurobiological process in the brain, but it does not follow that the first-person painful feeling is the same thing as the third-person neurobiological process. The concept of identity is not much help with the mind-body problem because we can make our events big enough to include both the phenomenological and the neurobiological. The right move, as usual, is to forget about these great categories and try to describe the facts. Then go back and see how you have to adjust the preconceptions you may have of the other categories in order to accommodate the facts.

But if we defined our event so that it had both phenomenological and neurobiological features, would the resulting identity not be subject to Kripke's objection about necessary identities? No. In the case of the necessary identity between water and H_2O, the necessity is achieved by redefinition. Once we discover that the stuff we have been calling water is composed of H_2O molecules, we then include "H_2O" in the definition of "water." It then becomes a necessary truth that water is H_2O. Similarly, we can readjust our definitions so that part of what makes this type of pain the pain that it is, is that it is caused by and realized in this type of neurobiological process. Part of what makes this very neurobiological process the process that it is, is that it causes and realizes this very pain. Defining sensations in terms of their causes, by the way, is very common. Consider "sciatica." Sciatica is defined as a type of pain caused by the stimulation of the sciatic nerve.

IV. NEITHER MATERIALISM NOR DUALISM

It is worth emphasizing that the view that I am expounding differs from both materialism and dualism. Because I think that both materialism and dualism are trying to say something true, it is important to carve off the true parts in each from the false parts. To do that I need to state exactly the differences between my view and these traditional views. Materialism tries to say truly that the universe is entirely made up of physical particles that exist in fields of force and are often organized into systems. But it ends up saying falsely that there are no ontologically irreducible mental phenomena. Dualism tries to say truly that there are irreducible mental phenomena. But it ends up saying falsely that these are something apart from the ordinary physical world we all live in, that they are something over and above their physical substrate. The challenge is to state the true part of each view and deny the false part. If you stick with the traditional vocabulary it seems impossible to do that, because you end up saying that the irreducible (subjective, qualitative) mental is just an ordinary part of the physical world, and that sounds self-contradictory. So in the end I have tried to challenge the traditional vocabulary.

Notice that if we try to state my position in the traditional vocabulary the words end up meaning something totally different from the way they are defined by the tradition. The materialist says, "Consciousness is just a brain process." I say, "Consciousness is just a brain process." But the materialist means: consciousness as an irreducibly qualitative, subjective, first-personal, airy-fairy, and touchy-feely phenomenon does not really exist. There exist only third-person, objective phenomena. But what I mean is that consciousness precisely as an irreducibly qualitative, subjective, first-personal, airy-fairy, and touchy-feely phenomenon is a process going on in the brain. The dualist says, "Consciousness is irreducible to third-person neurobiological processes." I say, "Consciousness is irreducible to third-person neurobiological processes." But the dualist takes this to imply that consciousness is not part of the ordinary physical world but is something over and above it. What I mean is that consciousness is causally reducible but not ontologically reducible. It is part of the ordinary physical world and is not something over and above it.

Let us now zero in on precisely this feature of dualism. On the dualist's conception, consciousness is definitely something over and above its material substrate. Indeed the dualist supposes that the irreducibility of consciousness already implies that consciousness is something over and above its neurobiological base. I deny that implication. This point is so crucial for the entire argument of this book that I am going to spell it out in some detail. The fact that the causal powers of consciousness and the causal powers of its neuronal base are exactly the same shows that we are not talking about two independent things, consciousness and neuronal processes. If two things in the real empirical world have an independent existence they must have different causal powers. But the causal powers of consciousness are exactly the same as those of the neuronal substrate. This situation is exactly like the causal powers of solid objects and the causal powers of their molecular constituents. We are not talking about two different entities but about the same system at different levels. Consciousness differs from solidity, liquidity, etc., in that the causal reduction does not lead to an ontological reduction. This, as we have seen, is so for an obvious, and indeed trivial, reason. Consciousness has a first-person ontology; neuronal processes have a third-person ontology. For that reason you cannot ontologically reduce the former to the latter. Consciousness is thus an aspect of the brain, the aspect that consists of ontologically subjective experiences. But there are not two different metaphysical realms in your skull, one "physical" and one "mental." Rather, there are just processes going on in your brain and some of them are conscious experiences.

I said in chapter 3 that dualists think they are possessed of a deep insight that justifies dualism. Now is the time to answer that claim. Here is the insight: there must be a distinction between the mental and physical because once the existence and the trajectories of all the microparticles in the universe are set, then the entire physical history of the universe is determined by the behavior of the microparticles. But it is still conceivable that there could be no conscious states at all. That is, it is logically possible that the physical universe could be exactly as it is, atom for atom, but without consciousness. But in fact it is not logically possible that the physical universe should be exactly as it is, atom for atom, without all of its physical features being exactly as they are. Notice that this argument is an extension of the zombie argument I presented against materialism in the chapter 3.

The argument is correct in pointing out that a description of the third-person facts does not entail the existence of the first-person facts, and this for the trivial reason that the first-person ontology cannot be reduced to the third-person ontology. But the dualist then wants to conclude that consciousness is in a different ontological realm, that it is something over and above the brain. But that conclusion does not follow. What the dualist leaves out of this thought experiment are the laws of nature. When we imagined the trajectory of the microparticles, we were holding all laws of nature constant. But if we try to imagine the trajectory of the microparticles being the same but minus consciousness then we are cheating in the thought experiment, because we are imagining the microparticles *not* behaving in precisely the way they would behave if they were acting in accordance with all the laws of nature, i.e., in such a way as to cause and realize (first-personal, subjective) conscious states. Once the laws of nature are included in the description of the physical universe, and they must be included because they are partly constitutive of the physical universe, then the existence of consciousness follows, as a logical consequence of those laws.

Whether or not a state of affairs is logically possible depends on how it is described. Is it logically possible that there should be physical particles without any consciousness in the universe? The answer is yes. But is it possible that there should be the trajectories of physical particles as they have in fact occurred together with the laws of nature that, among lots of other things, determine those trajectories to cause and realize consciousness, but minus any consciousness? Then the answer is no. Described in one way the absence of consciousness is logically possible; described in another way it is not. The picture the dualists have is that the microphysical particles are like tiny grains of sand affected by independent forces, and they can imagine the movement of the sand without any consciousness. But that is a false picture. At the most fundamental level points of mass/energy are constituted by the forces that are described by the laws of nature. From those laws the existence of consciousness follows as a logical consequence, just as does the existence of any other biological phenomena, such as growth, digestion, or reproduction.

Once again it seems to me the illusion of dualism is generated by misunderstanding a very real distinction. There really is a distinction between those irreducible features of the world that have a first-person or subjective ontology and those that do not. But it is a deep mistake to suppose that that real distinction is the same as the old-time distinction between the mental and the physical, between *res cogitans* and *res extensa*, or that the subjective phenomena are something over and above the systems in which they are realized.

The dualist thinks "irreducibility" already implies that the irreducible phenomenon is something over and above its physical basis. This poses an impossible problem for the property dualist: either consciousness functions causally or it does not. If it does, then we appear to have causal over determination: if I intentionally raise my arm it appears that my arm going up has two causes, one physical, one mental. But if consciousness does not function causally then we have epiphenomenalism. No such problem arises for biological naturalism, because the causal functioning of consciousness is just a form of brain functioning described at a level higher than that of neurons and synapses. Think of it this way: roughly speaking, consciousness is to neurons as the solidity of the piston is to the metal molecules. Both consciousness and solidity function causally. But neither is "over and above" the systems of which they are a part.

V. SUMMARY OF THE REFUTATION OF MATERIALISM AND DUALISM

I promised in chapter 3 a refutation of dualism. In the interests of even-handedness, let us add a bottom line statement of the refutation of materialism.

Let us define materialism as the view that there is nothing in the universe except material phenomena as traditionally defined. There are no irreducible intrinsic, subjective states of consciousness or awareness or anything else that is intrinsically mental. Every apparent case can be eliminated or reduced to something physical.

This is a rather easy view to refute, because it denies the existence of the things we all know to exist. It asserts that there are no ontologically subjective phenomena, and we know this is false because we experience them all the time. As philosophers we find this sort of refutation unsatisfying because it is too simple, so we invent more complex arguments to make the same point, about bats and colors and inverted spectra and qualia and Chinese Rooms and so on. But this is the point they, in their different ways, are making.

The refutation of dualism is harder. Let us define dualism as the view that there are two distinct metaphysical ontological realms in the universe, one mental the other physical. This is harder to refute, because whereas materialism postulated the nonexistence of something we know to exist, this view postulates the existence of something, and to refute it formally you would have to prove a universal negative. Rather than give a formal "refutation," I will give what I take to be conclusive arguments against dualism.

1. No one has ever succeeded in giving an intelligible account of the relationships between these two realms.

2. The postulation is unnecessary. It is possible to account for all of the first-person facts and all the third-person facts without the postulation of separate realms.
3. The postulation creates intolerable difficulties. It becomes impossible on this view to explain how mental states and events can cause physical states and events. In short, it is impossible to avoid epiphenomenalism.

Notice that these arguments still leave dualism as a logical possibility. It is a logical possibility, though I think extremely unlikely, that when our bodies are destroyed, our souls will go marching on. I have not tried to show that this is an impossibility (indeed, I wish it were true), but rather that it is inconsistent with just about everything else we know about how the universe works and therefore it is irrational to believe in it.

Suggestions for Further Reading

There is a flood of recent work on consciousness, including some by the present author. I will list a representative sample.

Chalmers, D., *The Conscious Mind*, Oxford: Oxford University Press, 1996.
Dennett, D., *Consciousness Explained*, Boston: Little Brown, 1991.
McGinn, C., *The Problem of Consciousness: Essays toward a Resolution*, Cambridge MA: Basil Blackwell, 1991.
Nagel, T., *The View from Nowhere*, Oxford: Oxford University Press, 1986.
O'Shaughnessy, B., *Consciousness and the World*, Oxford: Oxford University Press, 2000.
Searle, J. R., *The Mystery of Consciousness*, New York: New York Review of Books, 1997.
Searle, J. R., *The Rediscovery of the Mind*, Cambridge, MA: MIT Press, 1992.
Siewert, C., *The Significance of Consciousness*, Princeton: Princeton University Press, 1998.
Tye, M., *Ten Problems of Consciousness*, Cambridge, MA: MIT Press, 1995.

There is also a huge (over 800 pages) collection of articles on consciousness: Block, N., O. Flanagan, and G. Guzeldere, eds., *The Nature of Consciousness: Philosophical Debates*, Cambridge, MA: MIT Press, 1997.

More neurobiologically oriented readings will be listed at the end of Consciousness Part II.

CHAPTER 5

Consciousness Part II

The Structure of Consciousness and Neurobiology

In the last chapter I described a certain basic ontology. We need to keep this ontology in mind, with all its simplicity and even crudity, while we now explore the remarkable complexity and uniqueness of consciousness. Though the basic ontology is simple, the resulting phenomena are complicated and the details of their neurobiological relations to the brain are difficult to understand and at present largely unknown. Once we have solved the relatively easy philosophical problem, we have very difficult neurobiological problems left over.

In this chapter I will first describe the structure of consciousness, then state accounts that disagree with the account I have proposed, and finally I will conclude with a discussion of some of the neurobiological problems of consciousness.

I. FEATURES OF CONSCIOUSNESS

What are the features of consciousness that any philosophical-scientific theory should hope to explain? I think that the best way for me to proceed is to simply list several of the central features of human, and presumably animal, consciousness. Here goes.

1. Qualitativeness

As I remarked in the earlier chapters, every conscious state has a qualitative feel to it. Conscious states are in that sense always qualitative. I mentioned that some philosophers introduce the word "qualia" to describe this feature, but I think that the term is, at best, misleading because its usage suggests that some conscious states are not qualitative. Apparently the idea is that some conscious states, such as feeling a pain or tasting ice cream, are qualitative but some others, such as thinking about arithmetic problems, have no special qualitative feel. I think this is a mistake. If you think there is no qualitative feel to thinking two plus two equals four, try thinking it in French or German. To me it feels completely different to think *"zwei und zwei sind vier,"* even though the intentional content is the same in German as it is in English. Because the notion of consciousness and the notion of qualia are completely coextensive, I will not use the notion of "qualia" as something distinct from consciousness but will just assume that when I say "consciousness," the reader knows that I am discussing states that have this qualitative character.

2. Subjectivity

Because of the qualitative character of consciousness, conscious states exist only when they are experienced by a human or animal subject. They have a type of subjectivity that I call ontological subjectivity. Another way to make this same point is to say that consciousness has a first-person ontology. It exists only as experienced by a human or animal subject and in that sense it exists only from a first-person point of view. When I know about your consciousness, I have knowledge that is quite different from the kind of knowledge I have of my own consciousness.

The fact that conscious states are ontologically subjective, in the sense that they exist only as experienced by a human or animal subject, does not imply that there cannot be a scientifically objective study of conscious states. "Objective" and "subjective" are systematically ambiguous between an ontological and an epistemic sense. In the epistemic sense, there is a distinction between those statements that can be ascertained as true or false independently of the feelings and attitudes of the speakers or hearers and those statements whose truth or falsity depends on those feelings and attitudes. Thus the statement "Jones is six feet tall" is epistemically objective because its truth or falsity has nothing to do with the feelings and attitudes of the speaker and hearer. But the statement "Jones is a nicer person than Smith" is epistemically subjective because its truth or falsity cannot be settled independently of the feelings and attitudes of the participants in the discussion. In addition to this epistemic sense, there is a distinction between two modes of existence. Conscious states have a subjective mode of existence in the sense that they exist only when they are experienced by a human or animal subject. In this respect they differ from nearly all the rest of the universe, such as mountains, molecules, and tectonic plates, which have an objective mode of existence. The mode of existence of conscious states is indeed ontologically subjective, but *ontological subjectivity of the subject matter does not preclude an epistemically objective science of that very subject matter.* Indeed, the whole science of neurology requires that we try to seek an epistemically objective scientific account of pains, anxieties, and other afflictions that patients suffer from in order that we can treat these with medical techniques. Whenever I hear philosophers and neurobiologists say that science cannot deal with subjective experiences I always want to show them textbooks in neurology where the scientists and doctors who write and use the books have no choice but to try to give a scientific account of people's subjective feelings, because they are trying to help actual patients who are suffering.[1]

3. Unity

At present, I do not just experience the feelings in my fingertips, the pressure of the shirt against my neck, and the sight of the falling autumn leaves outside, but I experience all of these as part of a single, unified, conscious field. Consciousness of the normal, nonpathological kind, comes to us with a unified structure. Kant called this unity of the conscious field the "transcendental unity of apperception," and he made a great deal out of it. He was right to do so. It is immensely important, as we will see.

I used to think that these three features, qualitativeness, subjectivity, and unity, could be described as distinct features of consciousness. It now seems to me that that is a mistake; they are all aspects of the same phenomenon. Consciousness is by its very essence qualitative, subjective, and unified. There is no way that a state could be qualitative, in the sense that I have introduced, without it also being subjective in the sense that I have explained. But there is no way that the state could be both qualitative and subjective, without having the kind of unity that I have been describing. You can see this last point if you try to imagine your present state of consciousness broken into 17 independent bits. If this occurred, you would not have one conscious state with 17 parts; rather, there would be 17 independent consciousnesses, 17 different loci of consciousness. It is absolutely essential to understand that consciousness is not divisible in the way that physical objects typically are; rather, consciousness always comes in discrete units of unified conscious fields.

A good illustration of this feature of unity is provided by the so-called split brain experiments, and I will digress briefly to describe these. One of the ways to study consciousness is to study the pathological or degenerate forms of consciousness, and this is a method that I will use several times in this book. The split-brain patients suffered from terrible forms of epilepsy that could not be treated by the normal methods. In desperation, the doctors cut the corpus callosum, the body of tissue that connects the two brain hemispheres. This did, in fact, cure many of the patients of epilepsy, but it had some other interesting effects. Most strikingly, it caused the patient to behave in certain circumstances as if he had two independent centers of consciousness. In a typical experiment the following occurs: the patient is shown a spoon, but the spoon is put in a portion of his left visual field so that the visual stimulus only goes to the right side of his brain. Language is on the left side of his brain. He is then asked, "What do you see?" Since he has no visual perception of the spoon on the left side of the brain where he has language; and since, because of the severed corpus callosum, there is only very imperfect communication between the two hemispheres, the patient in such a case says, "I do not see anything." However, he then reaches out with his left hand, which is controlled by his right hemisphere, where the visual experience of the spoon does occur, and grabs the spoon. There is a large number of experiments of this kind conducted by Roger Sperry and Michael Gazzaniga.[2] Does the patient have one or two centers of consciousness? At present, we just do not know for sure. But, at least, we have to consider the possibility that there are, in fact, two conscious fields inside one brain, one corresponding to each hemisphere and that in the normal case the two fields of consciousness coalesce into a single unified conscious field.

4. Intentionality

I have been talking about intentionality and consciousness as if they were independent phenomena, but, of course, many conscious states are intrinsically intentional. My present visual perception, for example, could not be the visual experience it is if it did not seem to me that I was seeing chairs and tables in my immediate vicinity. This feature, whereby many of my experiences seem to refer to things beyond themselves, is the feature that philosophers have come to label "intentionality." Not all consciousness is intentional, and not all intentionality is conscious, but there is a very serious and important overlap between consciousness and intentionality, and later we will see that there are, in fact, logical connections between the two: mental states that are in fact unconscious have to be the kind of thing that could in principle become conscious. For a number of reasons, ranging from brain damage to psychological repression, they may be in fact inaccessible to consciousness, but they have to be the sort of thing that could be part of a conscious mental state. An example of a conscious state that is not intentional is the sense of anxiety that one sometimes gets when one is not anxious about anything in particular but just has a feeling of anxiousness. Examples of intentional states that are not conscious are too numerous to mention, but obvious cases are those that exist even when one is sound asleep. For example, when asleep, it is still true to say that I believe that Bush is president, that two plus two equals four, and so on with a very large number of other beliefs that are not then and there present to my consciousness.

5. Mood

All of my conscious states come to me in some sort of mood or other. I am always in some kind of mood, even if it is not a mood that has a specific name. I need not be especially elated, nor especially depressed, nor even just blah; but all the same, there is what one might call a certain flavor to consciousness, a certain tone to one's conscious experiences. One way to become aware of this is to observe dramatic changes. If you suddenly receive some very bad news, you will find that your mood changes. If you receive good news, it will change in the opposite direction. Mood is not the same as emotion, because, for one thing, emotions are always intentional. They always have some intentional content, whereas mood need not have an intentional content. But moods predispose us to emotions. If you are in an irritable mood, you will be more likely to experience the emotion of anger, for example.

Moods seem to be more susceptible to artificial pharmacological control than most other aspects of consciousness. Like pains, which we can control through anesthetics and analgesics, we can affect moods such as depression with drugs such as Prozac and lithium. It seems likely that pharmacological advances will enable us to get even greater therapeutic control of debilitating moods, as we did of pains.

6. The Distinction between the Center and the Periphery

Within the conscious field, one is always paying more attention to some things than others. I am, right now, concentrating my attention on writing down ideas about the philosophy of mind, and not on the sounds coming from outside, or the light streaming in through the window. Some things are at the center of my conscious field, others are at the periphery. A good mark of this is that one can shift one's attention at will. I can focus my attention on the glass of water in front of me, or on the trees outside the window, without even altering my position, and indeed without even moving my eyes. In some sense, the conscious field remains the same, but I focus on different features of it. This ability to redirect attention and the distinction between those features in the conscious field that we are paying attention to, and those we are not paying attention to, is already a subject of important research in neurobiology.

In addition to our capacity to shift our attention at will, typically the brain plays small tricks to cover for certain deficits. We do not see our blind spot, though we do have a blind spot; and we see color at the periphery of our visual field even though there is no color receptivity there.

7. Pleasure / Unpleasure

Related to, but not identical with, mood is the phenomenon that for any conscious state there is some degree of pleasure or unpleasure. Or rather, one might say, there is some position on a scale that includes the ordinary notions of pleasure and unpleasure. So, for any conscious experience you have, it makes sense to ask, Did you enjoy it? Was it fun? Did you have a good time, bad time, boring time, amusing time? Was it disgusting, delightful, or depressing? The pleasure/unpleasure dimension is pervasive where consciousness is concerned.

8. Situatedness

All of our conscious experiences come to us with a sense of what one might call the background situation in which one experiences the conscious field. The sense of one's situation need not be, and generally is not, a part of the conscious field. But, normally I am in some sense cognizant of where I am on the surface of the earth, what time of day it is, what time of year it is, whether or not I have had lunch, what country I am a citizen of, and so on with a range of features that I take for granted as the situation in which my conscious field finds itself. One becomes aware of the sense of situatedness when it is lost or disrupted. A characteristic experience, as one gets older, is the sense of vertigo that sometimes comes over one when one suddenly wonders, what month are we in? Is this the spring semester or the fall semester? More spectacular cases are illustrated by the sense of bewilderment that one gets on waking up in the middle of the night in a strange location. Where on earth am I?

9. Active and Passive Consciousness

To anyone who reflects on his conscious experiences, there is an obvious distinction between the experience of voluntary intentional activity on the one hand and the experience of passive perception on the other. I do not suggest that this is a sharp distinction, because there is a voluntaristic element of perception and there are passive components of voluntary action. But there is clearly a difference, for example, between voluntarily raising your arm as part of a conscious act, and having your arm raised by someone who triggers your nerve connections. This distinction is well illustrated by the researches of the Canadian neurosurgeon Wilder Penfield. Penfield found that by stimulating the motor cortex of his patients, he could cause their limbs to move. The patient invariably said, "I didn't do that, you did it."[3] In this case, the patient has the perception of his arm moving but he does not have the experience of voluntary action. The basic distinction is this: in the case of perception (seeing the glass in front of me, feeling the shirt against my neck) one has the feeling, I am perceiving this, and in that sense, this is happening to me. In the case of action (raising my arm, walking across the room) one has the feeling, I am doing this, and in that sense, I am making this happen.

It is experience of voluntary action, more than anything else, that gives us the conviction of our own free will, and any account of the mind has to confront this experience. I will have more to say about free will in chapter 8.

10. The Gestalt Structure

Our conscious experiences do not just come to us as a disorganized mess; rather they typically come to us with well-defined, and sometimes even precise, structures. We do not, for example, in normal vision see undifferentiated blurs and fragments; rather, we see tables, chairs, people, cars, etc., even though only fragments of those objects are reflecting photons at the retina, and the retinal image is in various ways distorted. The Gestalt psychologists investigated these structures and found certain interesting facts. One is, the brain has a capacity to take degenerate stimuli and organize them into coherent wholes. Furthermore, it is able to take a constant stimulus and treat it now as one perception, now as another. So in the famous "duck-rabbit" example there is a constant perceptual input but I perceive it now as a duck, now as a rabbit.

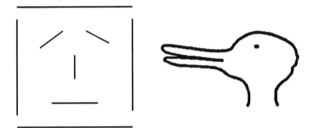

In these drawings, the left-hand figure does not actually physically resemble a human face, but nonetheless, you will perceive it as a face because your brain organizes the degernate stimulus into a coherent whole. The right-hand figure is the famous duck-rabbit, which can be seen either as a duck or as a rabbit.

Furthermore, the Gestalt structure is not only a matter of organizing our perceptions into coherent wholes, but within the entire conscious field, we make a distinction between the figures that we are perceiving and the ground on which they are perceived. So, for example, I see the pen against the background of the book, the book against the background of the desk, the desk against the background of the floor, and the floor against the rest of the room, until I reach the horizon of my entire perceptual field.

There are thus two aspects, at least, to the Gestalt structure of consciousness. First, the capacity that the brain has to organize perceptions into coherent wholes, and second, the capacity that the brain has to discriminate figures from backgrounds.

11. The Sense of Self

There is one other feature of normal conscious experiences that I cannot forbear to mention. It is typical of normal conscious experiences that I have a certain sense of who I am, a sense of myself as a self. But what can this possibly mean? I do not experience my "self" in the way that I experience the shoes on my feet or the beer that I am drinking. I am reluctant even to raise this issue, first, because the whole discussion of the self has such a sordid history in philosophy, but second, worse yet, the problem of the self poses such hard questions that I am reluctant to attempt to tackle them in this book. However, I will have to face them eventually, so I reserve a separate chapter, 11, for an account of the self.

One could continue the list of these features, but I hope to have succeeded in conveying the complexity of our conscious experiences. In what follows we will find reasons to emphasize the essential feature of consciousness, namely, qualitative unified subjectivity, and we will have to explore its relation to intentionality.

II. SOME OTHER PHILOSOPHICAL APPROACHES TO THE PROBLEM OF CONSCIOUSNESS

In the course of this book I have already discussed a number of approaches to the philosophy of mind, ranging all the way from eliminative materialism to substance dualism. These approaches are implicitly or explicitly theories of consciousness. For example, the computationalist theory of the mind simply says that consciousness is a computational process in the brain. It is important to emphasize that such a theory, along with other forms of reductionism, is not saying, for example, that if you had the right computer program, the machine would, *in addition*, be conscious. But rather, they are saying that is all there is to consciousness. There is nothing in addition to the right computer program with the right inputs and outputs.[4] However, despite the many philosophies I have covered there are still a number of influential views of consciousness that I have not yet mentioned. So, in the interest of thoroughness, I am going to discuss some views that we have not so far considered.

1. Mysterians

Mysterians think that consciousness is a mystery that cannot be solved by our existing scientific methods; and some mysterians think we will never be able to understand how consciousness could be explained by brain processes. Thomas Nagel[5] thinks it might be possible one day to understand how brain causes consciousness but it would require a total revolution in our way of thinking about reality and in our conception of scientific explanation, because given our present apparatus we cannot conceive how subjective, qualitative inner experiences could arise from third-person neuronal phenomena. Colin McGinn,[6] an extreme mysterian, thinks it is impossible in principle that human beings should ever come to be able to understand how the brain causes consciousness.

I think the mysterians are too pessimistic. They may be right, of course, that we will never find a scientific account of consciousness. But it would be defeatism to give up in advance. Suppose we actually found the various neuronal correlates for the unified conscious field. Suppose we could then, as a second step, show that these correlated elements were in fact causes. That is, suppose we could—so to speak—turn on consciousness by turning these neurobiological processes on, and turn off consciousness by turning them off. Suppose, as a third step, we then developed a theory as to how the whole system worked. Suppose, that is, that we could embed the statements of causal correlations in statements of general laws or principles. It seems to me that this is precisely the sort of theoretical structure that we have accepted elsewhere in science. The germ theory of disease is a good example: first, find a correlation; second, test to see that it is a causal correlation; third, get a theory. Nagel objects to any such project on the ground that even if we got such a correlation, and even if we could make general statements about it, it would not have the kind of necessity that we would expect from causal explanations. When we explain, for example, why the table is solid, we can understand that given that molecular behavior, the table *must* resist pressure from other objects and *must* be impenetrable by other objects. This "must," thinks Nagel, is typical of scientific explanations.

I think this sense of necessity is largely an illusion generated by analogies we draw between molecular behavior and familiar objects around us. We think that the table must support objects because we think of the molecular movements as forming a kind of lattice of the sort that we are familiar with. But it is not a general feature of explanations in science that they should convey some intuitive sense that this is how things must necessarily occur. On the contrary, nature is radically contingent. Many of the most important explanatory principles in science are by no means intuitive or obvious. Think of the Schroedinger equation or Planck's constant or for that matter, Einstein's famous $e=mc^2$. In each case, this is just how nature turned out. It did not have to turn out that way, but that is in fact how it did turn out. I am with Hume in thinking that the conviction that nature must *necessarily* be the way it is, is an illusion. So, for example, even when the billiard ball strikes the other billiard ball, it is just a fact of nature that the second will move. But it could equally well be a fact of nature that they both move backward or that the first would swallow the second. It is just that nature turned out one way and not another way. Nature is full of surprises. We should never forget, for example, that liquid helium 3 placed in a container will climb up its side. So, I do not regard Nagel's objection as in anyway conclusive against the possibility of a neurobiological explanation of consciousness.

2. Supervenience

To say that a phenomenon A is supervenient on a phenomenon B is to say that A is totally dependent on B in such a way that any change in the A property has to be correlated with a change in the B property. It is commonly said that consciousness is supervenient on brain processes. The basic idea is that there can be no changes in mental states without corresponding changes in a brain states. For example, if I go from a state where I am thirsty to a state where I am not thirsty, there must be some corresponding change in my brain. And this is true generally, so conscious states are totally dependent, or supervenient, on brain states. A number of philosophers have articulated this view, perhaps most prominently Jaegwon Kim.[7] This view leads to a view that is sometimes described as "nonreductive materialism." The idea of supervenience is to give a completely materialistic account without in any sense trying to eliminate consciousness. It just says consciousness is entirely supervenient on brain processes. Some people have thought that supervenience solves the mind-body problem or at least provides the first step in its solution.

It is certainly true that consciousness is supervenient on the brain. But this principle is of rather limited usefulness in understanding mind-brain relations. And the reason is that there are two different kinds of supervenience: constitutive supervenience and causal supervenience. The concept of supervenience in philosophy was traditionally used to describe ethical and other evaluative properties. It was said that two acts could not differ solely in their goodness. It could not be the case that one act was good and another act was bad, but they had no other difference. Goodness and badness must be supervenient on some other features of the act. This is what I call "constitutive supervenience." The features that make an act good do *not cause* it to be good; rather, they *constitute* its goodness. But this analogy does not carry over into the mind in a way that the supervenience philosophers of mind thought that it would. The supervenience of consciousness on brain processes is a causal supervenience. The brain processes are causally responsible for the supervenient feature. The brain processes do not, at the level of neuron firings, constitute consciousness; rather, the neuron firings at the lower level cause the higher-level or system feature of consciousness. But if that is right, and everything we know about the brain suggests that it is right, then the concept of supervenience adds nothing to the concepts that we already have, such concepts as causation, including bottom-up causation, higher and lower levels of description, and higher-order features being realized in the system composed of the lower-level elements. Yes, consciousness is supervenient on brain processes, but now you still have to tell us how it works.

3. Pan-Psychism

Pan-psychism is the view that consciousness is everywhere. This view is seldom stated explicitly, but it is implicit in several authors particularly among the mysterians who think that if we are going to explain consciousness in terms of microprocesses, then, somehow or other, some form of consciousness must already be present in the microprocesses. At one time Thomas Nagel flirted with this view, and David Chalmers[8] explores it and supports it, though he does not explicitly endorse it. On this view, everything is conscious to some degree. In giving an example of the ubiquity of consciousness, Chalmers eloquently describes what it might be like to be a conscious thermostat.

Aside from its inherent implausibility, pan-psychism has the additional demerit of being incoherent. I do not see any way that it can cope with the problem of the unity of consciousness.

Consciousness is not spread out like jam on a piece of bread, but rather, it comes in discrete units. If the thermostat is conscious, how about the parts of the thermostat? Is there a separate consciousness to each screw? Each molecule? If so, how does their consciousness relate to the consciousness of the whole thermostat? And if not, what is the principle that makes the thermostat the unit of consciousness and not the parts of the thermostat or the whole heating system of which the thermostat is a part or the building in which the heating system exists?

4. Neurobiology

A fourth set of approaches to consciousness that I have not so far discussed is the neurobiological attempts to solve the scientific problem of consciousness. By now, it will be no secret to the reader that I think this is exactly the right approach. The research is so important I will devote the next section to it.

III. CURRENT NEUROBIOLOGICAL APPROACHES TO CONSCIOUSNESS

For a long time, most neurobiologists were reluctant to approach the problem of consciousness at all, and indeed many are still reluctant. The reasons vary. Some people feel that we are "not ready" to study consciousness, that we need to know more about brain functions in nonconscious phenomena first. Others feel that the problem of consciousness is not really a scientific problem at all: it should be left to theologians and philosophers, but it is not properly construed as a scientific question. Others feel that we cannot give a biological account of consciousness, that there is no way that science could ever explain why warm feels warm or why red looks red. Notice the connection between this type of skepticism and the view of the mysterians that I mentioned earlier.

Nonetheless, our present era is remarkable in that there is a large number of very able neurobiologists attempting to figure out exactly how brain processes cause conscious states. Ideally, such a research project proceeds in the three stages I mentioned earlier. First, find the neuronal correlate of consciousness, called the NCC; second, test to see if the correlation is causal; third, get a theory.

I think that we can divide this research for the purpose of our analysis into two different camps that I call respectively the "building-block approach" and the "unified-field approach." On the building-block approach, we treat the entire conscious field as made up of more-or-less independent conscious units that I call "building blocks." The experience of red, the taste of the beer, the sound of middle C, would be examples of the sorts of building blocks I have in mind. The idea of the building-block approach is this: if we could figure out exactly how the brain causes even one building block, say the perception of red, then we might use that knowledge to crack the whole problem of consciousness. Presumably, if we can figure out how the brain gets us over the hump from the input stimulus of the red rose to the actual conscious visual experience of redness, then we could apply those lessons to other colors, as well as to sounds, tastes, smells, and consciousness generally. The building block approach seems ideally suited to the three-stage research project I just described, and much of the most interesting current research consists of an effort to find the NCC's of specific conscious experiences.

I think it is fair to say that most neurobiologists working on the problem of consciousness today have some version of the building-block approach. And certainly it is very tempting to think that we ought to take an atomistic approach to consciousness, to break the whole problem of consciousness into a whole lot of much smaller problems and try to solve individual smaller problems. Do not try to ask how in general, does the brain produce consciousness; but ask, how does the brain produce the specific conscious experience of the redness of the rose. This atomistic approach has worked so well in the rest of science that it seems natural to suppose that it would work for consciousness.

Three lines of research are commonly employed in the building block approach. First, the investigation of so-called blind sight seems to give us an ideal entering wedge into the problem of consciousness. Blind-sight patients have damage to Visual Area 1, at the back of the brain. They are able to see normally in most of the visual field, but in a certain portion they are blind. However, the blind-sight patients are often able to answer questions about events occurring in the portion of the visual field in which they are blind. (Hence the use of the apparently oxymoronic expression "blind sight.") Thus, for example, the patient can report that there is an X or an O on the screen, though he also reports that he does not, in fact, see it. He just, as he says, "makes a guess." But the guesses tend to be right an overwhelming percentage of the time, and thus they are not a matter of chance. In such a case, it seems that if we could find the point in the brain at which the conscious experience of an X differs from the blind-sight experience, we might discover the NCC for that visual experience.

A second line of research has to do with so-called binocular rivalry and Gestalt switching. If you present one eye with a series of horizontal lines and the other eye with a series of vertical lines, the subject does not typically have the visual experience of a grid. Rather, the subject will switch from seeing horizontal lines to seeing vertical lines. Now, because the perceptual stimulus is constant and the experience differs, it seems that we should be able to find the point in the brain at which the same constant stimulus switched from producing the experience of horizontal lines to producing the experience of vertical lines. That, so it seems, would give us the NCC's for those forms of consciousness.

Similar remarks can be made about the Gestalt phenomena. In the case of the duck-rabbit, the constant stimulus on the paper produces now the experience of a rabbit, now the experience of a duck. If we could find the point in the brain where the experience switches from duck to rabbit and vice versa, it looks like we would have the NCC's for those experiences.

Finally, a very influential line of research is simply to follow perceptual stimulus inputs into the brain and try to locate the point at which they cause conscious visual experiences. There is now an enormous amount of research being done on vision, and to many researchers it seems that this is a plausible research project for discovering how the brain causes consciousness.[9]

The second approach to the problem of consciousness, the unified-field approach, begins by taking seriously the feature of qualitative subjective unity that I mentioned earlier. For this approach, the paradigm of consciousness, the initial target of the investigation, is not such things as the experience of the color red, but rather the whole conscious field of qualitative, unified subjectivity. For this approach the basic question is not, How does the brain produce this specific building block in the conscious field? but How does it produce the whole conscious field in the first place? What is the difference between the conscious brain and the unconscious brain, and how does that difference causally explain consciousness?

Think of it this way: Imagine that you wake in a dark room. You may become completely awake and alert though you have minimal sensory inputs. Imagine that there are no visual stimuli and no sounds. You see and hear nothing. The only perceptual input you have is the weight of your body against the bed and the weight of the covers against your body. But, and this is the important thing, you may become totally conscious and alert in the situation of minimal perceptual input. Now, at this point, your brain has produced a complete conscious field, and what we need to understand is how the brain produces this conscious field and how the field exists in the brain. Now, let us imagine that in this dark room you get up, turn on the lights, and move about. Are you creating consciousness? Well, in a sense you are, because you now have conscious states that you did not have before. But I like to think of it this way: you are not creating a new consciousness; you are modifying the preexisting conscious field. On the unified-field model we should think of perceptual inputs not as creating building blocks of consciousness but as producing bumps and valleys in the conscious field that has to exist prior to our having the perceptions.

I think the unified-field approach is more likely to succeed in solving the problem of consciousness than the building-block approach. Why? The building-block approach might succeed, and it is certainly the approach most commonly favored by existing researchers in the field. However, it has some worrisome features that make it seem to me unlikely to succeed. This approach would predict that in an otherwise totally unconscious subject, if you could produce the NCC for even one building block, say the NCC for experiencing red, then the unconscious subject would suddenly have a conscious experience of red and nothing else. He would have a conscious flash of redness and then lapse immediately into unconsciousness. Now that is of course logically possible, but it does not seem at all likely, given what we know about the brain. To put the point very crudely, a conscious experience of red can only occur in a brain that is already conscious. *We should think of perception not as creating consciousness but as modifying a preexisting conscious field.* Again, consider dreams. Like many people, I dream in color. When I see the color red in a dream, I do not have a perceptual input that creates a building block of red. Rather the mechanisms in the brain that create the whole unified field of dream consciousness create my experience of red as part of the field.

As I said earlier, most researchers adopt the building-block approach, and I think this is at least in part because it gives them an easier research project. It seems very difficult to try to study massive amounts of synchronized neuron firings that might produce consciousness in large portions of the brain such as the thalamocortical system. It seems much easier to try to study particular forms of consciousness, such as color experiences.

This issue is very much in doubt. In the coming years, we will see more research on consciousness. I am betting on the unified-field approach, but I am prepared to be proven wrong.

IV. CONSCIOUSNESS, MEMORY, AND THE SELF

I said that in the study of consciousness it is useful to look at the clinical or pathological cases because they remind us of features of the ordinary cases that we might overlook if we did not contrast them with the pathological. Two examples I have mentioned already are the split-brain cases and blind sight. Here is a case that is close to home. On January 4, 1999, I was skiing fast on an icy run on KT 22 in Squaw Valley, California. From my inner, subjective point of view I remember thinking that the light was very flat and that it was hard to see the bumps. The next thing I remember is that I was sitting in the Funitel lift wondering what day it was. Have we had Christmas yet? Is it after New Year? I looked at a woman sitting opposite me who had on a three-day lift ticket dated January 4th to January 6th. I knew it was January 4th. (Why the 4th and not the 5th or the 6th? I just knew.)

People who saw me fall say that my skis stopped but my body kept going and I landed on my head. I managed to get up, find my goggles and glasses in the snow, put my skis back on, and I skied down the rest of the mountain very cautiously. But I was unresponsive to questions and conversation. I made it to the bottom of the mountain and got back on the ski lift before I "came to."

There was a 15-minute period of my life of which I have no recollection whatever. During that period, I behaved as if I were fully conscious though not completely normal. The interest of the case derives from the following question, Was I conscious during that 15-minute period? The case is very much like the Penfield cases in which patients during a *petit mal* epileptic seizure, continued in the course of activity they had been engaged in, such as driving home or playing the piano, even though they were unconscious. I used to believe Penfield's account but now after my own experiences I am not so sure. I am convinced in my own case that I was conscious during that period but was simply unable to register my conscious experiences in my memory. I have absolutely no recollection, but I believe I behaved in a way I could not have behaved if I had not been conscious, though I was not 100-percent normal. What we have in this case is a lower level of consciousness not registered in memory. (By the way, the medical exams revealed that I had a concussion and subdural hematoma. I recovered completely. I now wear a helmet when skiing.)

V. CONCLUSION

Of all the subjects discussed in this book, this is the one where I feel the greatest sense of inadequacy. Consciousness is such a stunning and mysterious phenomenon that one always feels that the very effort to describe it in ordinary words somehow is not only bound to fail, but the very effort reveals a failure of sensibility. The general character of the relation of consciousness to the brain, and thus the general solution of the mind-body problem is not hard to state: consciousness is caused by microlevel processes in the brain and realized in the brain as higher-level or system feature. But the complexity of the structure itself, and the precise nature of the brain processes involved remains unanalyzed by this characterization. We are tempted to trivialize consciousness by thinking of it as just one aspect of our lives; and of course, biologically speaking, it is just one aspect, but as far as our actual life experiences are concerned, consciousness is the very essence of our meaningful existence. If Descartes had not already destroyed the meaning of the sentence we could say "the essence of mind is consciousness." If I try to describe the varieties of your consciousness you will find that I am describing the varieties of your life. One of the weird features of recent intellectual life was the idea that consciousness—in the literal sense of qualitative, subjective states and processes— was not important, that somehow it did not matter. One reason this is so preposterous is that consciousness is itself the condition of anything having importance. Only to a conscious being can there be any such thing as importance.

Suggestions for Further Reading

There are a number of neurobiological approaches to consciousness. Among them:

Crick, F., *The Astonishing Hypothesis*, New York: Scribner's, 1994.
Damasio, A. R., *The Feeling of What Happens: Body and Emotion in the Making of Consciousness*, New York: Harcourt Brace & Co., 1999.

Edelman, G., *The Remembered Present*, New York: Basic Books, 1989.

Llinas, R., *I of the Vortex: From Neurons to Self*, Cambridge, MA: MIT Press, 2001.

Searle, J. R., "Consciousness," in *Annual Review of Neuroscience*, vol. 23, 2000, reprinted in Searle, J. R., *Consciousness and Language*, Cambridge: Cambridge University Press, 2002. (This article contains an extensive bibliography of current neurobiological research on consciousness.)

Kock, C., *The Quest for Consciousness: A Neurobiological Approach*, Englewood, CO: Roberts and Co., 2004.

CHAPTER 6

Intentionality

The problem of intentionality is second only to the problem of consciousness as a supposedly difficult, perhaps impossibly difficult, problem in the philosophy of mind. Indeed, the problem of intentionality is something of a mirror image of the problem of consciousness. Just as it is supposed to be extremely difficult to fathom how mere bits of matter inside the skull could be conscious, or could through their interactions create consciousness, so it is difficult to imagine how mere bits of matter inside the skull could "refer to" or be about something in the world beyond themselves, or could through their interactions create such a reference. To take an example, I am now thinking that the sun is 93 million miles from the Earth. My thoughts definitely refer to, or are about, the sun. They are not about the moon, my car in the garage, my dog Gilbert, or my next-door neighbor. Now what is it about the thought that enables it to reach as far as the sun? Do I send mental rays all the way to the sun, just as the sun sends light rays all the way to the Earth? Unless there is some sort of connection between me and the sun, it is hard to imagine how my thoughts could reach the sun. And what goes for the sun, goes for just about any object that I can represent in my beliefs, desires, and other intentional states. So for example, if I think that Caesar crossed the Rubicon, then my thought is about Caesar, and it has the content that he crossed the Rubicon. But now, what fact about the stuff inside my skull makes it refer all the way back in history to a specific individual, and a specific river, and ascribe the specific action of the individual crossing the river?

In addition to the problem of how such a thing is possible, there is a related problem about how I can be so confident that it is happening right. When I refer to Julius Caesar how can I be so smugly confident that my thoughts are actually hitting Julius Caesar and not, for example, Mark Anthony or Caesar Augustus or my dog Gilbert? If I throw a stone into the dark, I may not have the faintest idea what it is hitting, but when I throw my reference into the unseen I am often completely confident about what it is hitting.

To make matters even worse, it seems that I can sometimes think about objects that do not even exist. When I was a small child I believed that Santa Claus comes on Christmas Eve. Was my belief about Santa Claus? It certainly seems so, but how is that possible, since Santa Claus does not even exist?

Notice that these are questions that only a philosopher would ask. Philosophy begins with a sense of mystery and wonder at what any sane person regards as too obvious to worry about.

Notice also that we cannot explain the intentionality of the mind by saying it is just like the intentionality of language. In the case of language, the utterance "Caesar crossed the Rubicon" is about Caesar and says of him that he crossed the Rubicon. I cannot say that a mental representation derives its intentional capacity from language, because of course the same problem arises for language. How is it possible that a mere sentence, sounds that come out of my mouth or marks that I write on paper, can refer to, be about, or describe objects and states of affairs that are 2,000 years in the past and 10,000 miles away? The intentionality of language has to be explained in terms of the intentionality of the mind and not conversely. For it is only in virtue of the fact that the mind has imposed intentionality on these sounds and marks that they refer to the objects and events that I have mentioned. The meaning of language is derived intentionality and it has to be derived from the original intentionality of the mind.

There are three problems about intentionality we need to address. First, how is intentionality possible at all; second, given that intentional states are possible, how is their content determined; and third, how does the whole system of intentionality work? Most of the philosophical literature is about the first two questions. I find the third question the most interesting. In this chapter I am going to first deal with the question about how intentionality is possible, and I will use my usual method of trying to demystify the whole phenomenon by bringing it down to earth. Then I will go to the third topic and describe the structure of intentionality; and I will include a section on the differences between intentionality-with-a-t and intensionality-with-an-s. Finally, I will conclude with the second question, how the contents of intentional states are determined. Readers familiar with cognitive science will recognize that when we talk about intentionality we are discussing what in cognitive science is known as "information." I prefer "intentionality" because "information" is systematically ambiguous between a genuinely observer-independent mental sense (for example, by looking out the window now I have information about the weather) and a nonmental observer-relative sense (for example, the rings in the tree stump contain information about the age of the tree). This ambiguity can also arise for "intentionality," but it is easier to avoid and confusion is less likely.

I. HOW IS INTENTIONALITY POSSIBLE AT ALL?

This problem is supposed to be as difficult as the problem of consciousness, so the sorts of solutions that are supposed to solve it are much like the solutions proposed for the problem of consciousness.

The dualistic solution is to say that as there are two different realms, the mental and the physical, so the mental realm has its own sorts of powers not possessed by the physical realm. The physical realm is incapable of referring, but the mental realm is essentially capable of thinking, and thinking involves reference. I hope it is obvious that this dualistic solution is no solution at all. To explain the mystery of intentionality it appeals to the mystery of the mental in general.

I think that the most common contemporary philosophical solution to the problem of intentionality is some form of functionalism. The idea is that intentionality is to be analyzed entirely in terms of causal relations. These causal relations exist between the environment and the agent and between various events going on inside the agent. On this view there is nothing mysterious about intentionality. It is just a form of causation. The only special feature is that intentional relations exist between the agent's cerebral innards and the external world. And, by this time, I do not need to tell the reader that the most influential version of functionalism is computer functionalism, or Strong Artificial Intelligence.

Finally, there is the eliminativist view of intentionality: there really are no intentional states. The belief that there are such things is just a residue of a primitive folk psychology, one that a mature science of the brain will enable us to overcome. A variant of the eliminativist view is what we might call "interpretativism." The idea here is that attributions of intentionality are always forms of interpretation made by some outside observer. An extreme version of this view is Daniel Dennett's conception that we sometimes adopt the "intentional stance" and that we should not think of people as literally having beliefs and desires, but rather that this is a useful stance to adopt about them for the purpose of predicting their behavior.[1]

I will not spend much time criticizing these various accounts of intentionality because I have already criticized the general thrusts of these arguments in earlier chapters. What I want to do, as I did with the problem of consciousness, is bring the whole issue down to earth. If you ask, how is it possible that anything as ethereal and abstract as a thought process can reach out to the sun, to the moon, to Caesar, and to the Rubicon, it must seem like a very difficult problem. But if you pose the problem in a much simpler form, How can an animal be hungry or thirsty? How can an animal see anything or fear anything? then it seems much easier to fathom. We are speaking, as we did about consciousness, of a certain set of biological capacities of the mind. And it is best to start with the biological capacities that are primitive—for instance, hunger, thirst, the sex drive, perception, and intentional action. In the last chapter I described some of the neurobiological details about how brain processes cause conscious feelings of thirst. But in explaining how brain processes can cause feelings of thirst, we have already explained how brain processes can cause forms of intentionality, because thirst is an intentional phenomenon. To be thirsty is to have a desire to drink. When the angiotensin 2 gets inside the hypothalamus and triggers the neuronal activity that eventually results in the feeling of thirst it has *eo ipso* resulted in an intentional feeling. The basic forms of consciousness and intentionality are caused by the behavior of neurons and are realized in the brain system, that is itself composed of neurons. What goes for thirst goes for hunger and fear and perception and desire and all the rest.

Once we demystify the problem of intentionality by removing it from the abstract, spiritual level down to the concrete level of real animal biology, I do not believe that any unsolvable mystery remains about how it is possible for animals to have intentional states. If you start with such simple and obvious cases as hunger and thirst, intentionality is not at all difficult to explain. Of course, beliefs, desires, and sophisticated forms of thought processes are more complex and more removed from the immediate stimulation of the brain by the impact of the environment than are perceptions or feelings of hunger and thirst. But even they are caused by brain processes and realized in the brain system.

When it seems mysterious to us that intentional relations can exist at all, when we pose such questions as, How is it possible for my thoughts to reach all the way to the sun or as far back in history as Julius Caesar? it is because we are imposing the wrong model of relations on the sentences that describe our intentional contents. Similarly, when we are puzzled about how we can have thoughts about things that do not exist at all, such as Santa Claus, it is because we are thinking of intentionality as if it were a relation like standing next to or hitting or sitting on top of. You cannot hit something that does not exist and you cannot sit on something that is 93 million miles away. But referring to or thinking about something is not at all like sitting on it or hitting it. It is rather a form of *representation* and the notion of representation does not require that the thing represented actually exist or that it exist in some immediate proximity to the representation of it. We ought to hear the question, How is it possible to think about Santa Claus if Santa Claus does not even exist? as like the question, How is it possible to make up a story about Santa Claus if Santa Claus does not even exist? There we have an easier problem because we see that it does not seem metaphysically difficult to make up fictional stories. When I say this I am not, of course, solving the problem because, strictly speaking, the intentionality of the story derives from the intentionality of the mental content. I am trying to remove a sense of mystery by showing how the apparently mysterious is like the obviously unmysterious. Our ability to have intentional contents about the nonexistent seems mysterious, but our ability to construct fictional stories seems much less mysterious.

However, there are a lot of other problems. For example, what is the relation between conscious and unconscious intentionality and how do intentional states get the content they have? I will have to work my way up to the point where I can answer these questions. At this point, it seems to me the best thing I can do is describe the formal structure of intentional states, because we will not get a grasp on how intentionality functions, until we see the structural features of intentional states, such as beliefs and desires, hopes and fears, perceptions, memories, and intentions.

II. THE STRUCTURE OF INTENTIONALITY

1. Propositional Content and Psychological Mode

Because intentional states are capable of referring to objects and states of affairs in the world beyond themselves, they must have some sort of *content* that determines this reference, and indeed we need to distinguish the content of the state from the type of state that it is. Thus I can believe that it will rain, hope that it will rain, fear that it will rain, or desire that it will rain. In each case there is the same content, that it will rain, but that content relates to the world in different psychological modes: belief, fear, hope, desire, etc. This distinction, by the way, exactly parallels the same distinction in language. Just as I can order you to leave the room, so I can predict that you will leave the room, and I can ask whether you will leave the room. In each case we have the same content, that you will leave the room, but it is presented in different sorts of speech acts. A good way to think of this is to think of the state as consisting in a psychological mode, such as belief or desire, with a propositional content, such as the proposition that it is raining. We can represent this as S(p), where the S stand for the mode or type of state and the p for the propositional content. Such states are often called "propositional attitudes."

Not all intentional states have an entire proposition as their content. One might just admire Eisenhower or love Marilyn, and in such cases the intentional state just refers to an object. Such states can be represented as S(n), where the n names or refers to an object.

Notice that intentional representations are always under certain aspects and not others. For example, I might intentionally represent an object as the Evening Star and not as the Morning Star even though one and the same object is both. The aspect "celestial body that shines near the horizon in the evening" is not the same aspect as "celestial body that shines near the horizon in the morning." *Intentional states always have aspectual shapes,* because all representation is under aspects. This is an important point, because any theory of intentionality must account for aspectual shape, and some materialist theories are unable to do so. I mentioned in chapter 3 that functionalism was unable to distinguish between the desire for water and the desire for H_2O and this is because the causal relations on which functionalism relies to analyze intentionality do not have the aspectual shapes characteristic of genuine intentionality. We will see in chapter 9, on the unconscious, that any theory of the unconscious needs to account for the presence of aspectual shape when an intentional state is unconscious.

2. Direction of Fit

Intentional states, again like speech acts, are related to the world in different ways. It is the aim of a belief to be true, and to the extent that the belief is true, it succeeds. To the extent that it is false, it fails. Desires, on the other hand, are not supposed to represent how the world is, but how we would like it to be. Thus, if I believe that it is raining, my belief will be true if and only if it is raining. But if I desire that it should rain, then my desire will be satisfied or fulfilled if and only if it rains. Though these look similar, there is a crucial distinction. In the case of the belief, the intentional state is supposed to represent how things are in the world. The belief is, so to speak *responsible for fitting the world*. But in the case of the desire, it is not the aim of the desire to represent how things are but rather how we would like them to be. In the case of the desire it is, so to speak, the *responsibility of the world to fit the content of the desire*. I am going to introduce a piece of jargon to describe this distinction. Where the mental state is responsible for fitting an independently existing reality, we can say that the mental state has the *"mind-to-world direction* of fit," or alternatively, it has the *"mind-to-world responsibility* of fit." The mental state fits or fails to fit how things really are in the world. Beliefs, convictions, hypotheses, etc., as well as perceptual experiences, all have this mind-to-world direction of fit. The most common expressions for appraising success in achieving the mind-to-world direction of fit are "true" and "false." Beliefs and convictions can be said to be true or false. Desires and intentions are not true or false the way beliefs are, because their aim is not to match an independently existing reality, but rather to get reality to match the content of the intentional state. For that reason I will say they have the *"world-to-mind direction* of fit" or the *"world-to-mind responsibility* for fit."

Some intentional states, though they have a propositional content, do not have a direction of fit because it is not their aim either to match reality (the mind-to-world direction of fit) or to get reality to match them (the world-to-mind direction of fit). Rather, they take it for granted that the fit already exists. Thus, if I am sorry that I stepped on your foot, or I am glad that the sun is shining, I take it for granted that I stepped on your foot and that the sun is shining. About such cases, I say that the intentional states have the *"null* direction of fit." They "presuppose" a fitting relation rather than assert it or try to bring it about. I find it convenient to represent the mind-to-world direction of fit with a downward arrow thus: ↓; the

world-to-mind fit with an upward arrow thus: ↑; and the null fit
with the null sign thus: Ø

3. Conditions of Satisfaction

Whenever we have an intentional state that has a non-null direction of fit, the fit will either be achieved or not: the belief will be
true, the desire will be fulfilled, the intention will be carried out or
not, as the case might be. In such cases, we can say that the belief,
desire, or intention is satisfied. What stands to the belief's being
true is what stands to the desire's being fulfilled, is what stands to
the intention's being carried out. I propose to describe this phenomenon by saying that every intentional state that has a non-null
direction of fit has *conditions of satisfaction*. We can think of mental
states as representations of their conditions of satisfaction. Indeed,
I will argue later on that the key to understanding intentionality is
conditions of satisfaction, but in order to say that, we need a few
more items in our apparatus.

4. Causal Self-Referentiality

The most biologically basic intentional phenomena, including perceptual experiences, intentions to do something, and memories,
have a peculiar logical feature in their conditions of satisfaction. It
is part of the conditions of satisfaction of, for example, my memory
that I went on a picnic yesterday, that if I really remember the event,
then the event itself must cause my memory of it. If we spell out the
conditions of satisfaction of the memory, they are not just that the
event occurred, but also that its occurrence caused the very memory that has the occurrence of the event as the rest of its conditions
of satisfaction. We can describe this by saying that memories, intentions, and perceptual experiences are all causally self-referential.
What this means is that the content of the state itself refers to the
state in making a causal requirement. The conditions of satisfaction
of the memory itself require that the memory be caused by the
event remembered. The conditions of satisfaction of the intention
require that the performance of the action represented in the content of the intention requires that that very intention should cause
that performance. And so on through other cases.

In this respect, intentions, memories, and perceptual experiences
are different from beliefs and desires. We can spell out the difference

as follows. If I believe that I went on a picnic yesterday, then the formal structure of my intentional state looks like this:

Believe (I went on a picnic yesterday).

But if I remember that I went on a picnic yesterday then the formal structure of my intentional state looks like this:

Remember (I went on a picnic yesterday, and my going on a picnic caused this memory).

For states that have the mind-to-world direction of fit we need to distinguish those that are causally self-referential, such as perceptions and memories, from those that are not, such as beliefs. Exactly parallel to this, for states that have the world-to-mind direction of fit we need to distinguish those that are causally self-referential, such as the intention that I have prior to doing something (what I call the "prior intention") and the intention I have while I am actually doing it (what I call the "intention-in-action") from those that are not causally self-referential, such as desires. Also every causally self-referential state with a direction of fit also has a direction of causation. In visual perception, for example, if I see that the cat is on the mat, I see how things really are (and thus achieve mind-to-world direction of fit) only if the cat's being on the mat causes me to see the situation that way (world-to-mind direction of causation). In intentional action, the arrows run the other way. I succeed in intentionally reaching the book on the top shelf (and thus achieve world-to-mind direction of fit) only if my trying, my intention-in-action, causes my success (mind-to-world direction of causation).

The resulting formal relations are so beautiful that I cannot resist setting them out in a chart, where I use the old-fashioned terminology of cognition and volition to name the two families:

	COGNITION			VOLITION		
	Perception	Memory	Belief	Intention in Action	Prior Intention	Desire
Causal Self-Reference	YES	YES	NO	YES	YES	NO
Direction of Fit	↓	↓	↓	↑	↑	↑
Direction of Causation	↑	↑	None	↓	↓	None

5. The Network of Intentionality and the Background of Preintentional Capacities

Intentional states do not in general come in isolated units. If I believe, for example, that it is raining, I cannot just have that belief in isolation. I must believe, for example, that rain consists of drops of water, that these fall out of the sky, that they generally go down and not up, that they make the ground wet, that they come out of clouds in the sky, and so on more or less indefinitely. Of course, someone might have the belief that it is raining and lack some of these other beliefs, but in general it seems that the belief that it is raining is only the belief that it is because of its position in a *"network"* of beliefs and other intentional states. And we can think of the totality of one's intentional states as forming an elaborate interacting network. We can even say that any intentional state only functions, that is it only determines its conditions of satisfaction, relative to the network of which it is a part. If I believe I own a car, I must also believe that cars are modes of transportation, that they are used on streets and highways, that they move about, that people can get in and out of cars, that cars are a kind of property that can be bought and sold, and so on.

If you follow out the threads in the network, you eventually reach a set of abilities, ways of coping with the world, dispositions, and capacities generally that I collectively call the "Background." For example, if I form the intention to go skiing I can do so only if I take for granted that I have the ability to ski, but the ability to ski is not itself an additional intention, belief, or desire. I hold the controversial thesis that intentional states in general require a background of nonintentional capacities in order to function all.

I have given a very brief sketch of the formal structure of intentionality. We can summarize it as follows. For any intentional state, there is a distinction between the type of state it is, and its content. Where the content is a whole proposition, it will represent states of affairs in the world and it will do this with one of the three directions of fit, mind-to-world, world-to-mind, or null. Intentional states that have a non-null direction of fit are thus representations of their conditions of satisfaction. And given the network of intentionality, even those states that have the null direction of fit, and even those that do not have a whole propositional content, are still largely constituted by states that do have a non-null direction of fit. Thus if I am sorry that I stepped on your foot, I must believe that I did so and wish I had not done so. And if I admire Jimmy Carter

I must have a set of beliefs and desires about Jimmy Carter. In general, *intentionality is representation of conditions of satisfaction*. The most biologically basic intentional states, those that relate animals directly to the environment, have a causally self-referential component in their conditions of satisfaction. Any intentional state can function, that is, it can determine conditions of satisfaction, only because of its position in a network of intentional states and against the background of pre-intentional capacities.

Later on, when I talk about the unconscious in chapter 9, we will see that the network of intentionality, when unconscious, is really a special case of background abilities, the ability to produce conscious intentional phenomena.

The formal structure of the intentionality that I have described is no trivial matter. This is in fact the structure of our conscious life. Indeed, it is the structure of our mental life, both conscious and unconscious. When we come to understand a social situation we are in, when we make up our minds to engage in some course of action, when we perceive the heavens on a starry night, when we suddenly have recollections of our childhood while eating a madeleine—all of these are manifestations of the formal structure that I have been describing. In order to understand our lives, we have to understand the structure of intentionality.

It is important to emphasize that none of this discussion is intended to be phenomenological. We are talking about the logical structure of intentionality. Phenomenology, for the most part, is unable to access this structure.

III. INTENTIONALITY-WITH-A-T AND INTENSIONALITY-WITH-AN-S

You will not understand the current philosophical literature on intentionality unless you see the difference between intentionality-with-a-t and intensionality-with-an-s.

These are often confused, even by professional philosophers. Intentionality-with-a-t, as we have seen, is that property of the mind by which it is directed at or about or of objects and states of affairs in the world independent of itself. Intensionality-with-an-s is opposed to *extensionality*. It is a property of certain sentences, statements, and other linguistic entities by which they fail to meet certain tests for extensionality. The connection between the two is that many sentences about intentional-with-a-t states are intensional-with-an-s sentences. There are several such tests for extensionality, but the two most famous are the substitution test (sometimes called Leibnitz's Law) and the test of existential inference. Let us consider each of these in order. The substitution test says that whenever two expressions refer to the same thing, you can substitute one for the other without changing the truth value of the statement in which you are making a substitution. Formally we can put this as follows:

1. $[(a=b) \& Fa] \to Fb$.
   If a is identical with b and a has property F, then b has property F.
   Thus from
2. Caesar crossed the Rubicon.
   and
3. Caesar is identical with Mark Anthony's best friend.
   we can infer
4. Mark Anthony's best friend crossed the Rubicon.
   For this reason, the occurrence of "Caesar" in 2 is said to be *extensional* with respect to substitutability. But there are sentences in which you cannot make the substitution. Thus from
5. Brutus believes that Caesar crossed the Rubicon.
   and the identity statement 3, we cannot validly infer
6. Brutus believes that Mark Anthony's best friend crossed the Rubicon,
   because Brutus might not believe that Caesar is Mark Anthony's best friend. Such a sentence is said to be *intensional* with respect to the occurrence of Caesar. It fails the test of substitutability.
   The principle of existential inference says that whenever a has the property F, you can validly infer that there exists an object that has the property F.
7. $Fa \to (\exists x)(Fx)$
   Thus from
8. John lives in Kansas City.
   we can validly infer
9. There is some x such that John lives in x.
   But there are sentences of this form where we cannot validly make the inference. Thus from
10. John is looking for the lost city of Atlantis
    It does not follow that
11. There is some x such that John is looking for x.
    Because the city he is looking for might not even exist.

Sentences such as 10 are said to be intensional, because they fail the test of existential inference.

Notice that both of these intensional sentences are about states that are intentional-with-a-t. This has led some philosophers to mistakenly suppose that there is something essentially intensional about intentionality. But that is a mistake. The reason that sentences about intentional-with-a-t states are often intensional-with-an-s is as follows: the states themselves are representations of their conditions of satisfaction. But sentences about those states are not representations of those conditions of satisfaction, rather they are representations of their representations. Hence the truth or falsity of such sentences does not depend on how things are in the real world as represented by the original intentional states, but how things are in the world of representations as it exists in the minds of the agents whose intentional states are being represented. Thus when I say Caesar crossed the Rubicon I am talking straight out about Caesar and the Rubicon. But when I say Brutus believed that Caesar crossed the Rubicon, I am talking about Brutus and what is going on inside his head. The truth of what I say depends not on the real world of Caesar and the Rubicon but on what is in Brutus' head that represents Caesar and the Rubicon. Thus I cannot make the substitution unless I have an extra premise to the effect that Brutus would accept it. Analogous remarks apply to the test of existential inference. If I talk about where John actually lives, then I am talking about an actual person and an actual place, but if I talk about what John is looking for, I am talking about an intentional state, trying to find something, whose conditions of satisfaction he is attempting to realize. But he might have that intentional state, he might be looking for something, even if the something he is looking for does not exist. Once again, the fact that the intensional-with-an-s sentence is a representation of a representation explains its intensionality.

The important thing to remember about the distinction between intentionality-with-a-t and intensionality-with-an-s is that there is nothing inherently intensional about intentionality. A statement to the effect that Brutus believes that Caesar crossed the Rubicon is indeed an intensional-with-an-s statement. But the belief itself, Brutus's actual belief, does not thereby become intensional-with-an-s. The belief itself is as extensional as it can get. It will be true only if both Caesar and the Rubicon exist (existential inference) and anything identical with Caesar crossed anything identical with the Rubicon (substitutability).

I do not want to give the impression that you understand all there is to understand about intensionality-with-an-s on the basis of the preceding paragraphs. There is much more be said. For more details see my book *Intentionality: An Essay in the Philosophy of Mind*.[2] All I want to do right now is give you enough tools so that you can follow arguments about intensionality-with-an-s and intentionality-with-a-t without making the mistakes that are common in contemporary philosophy.

IV. THE DETERMINATION OF INTENTIONAL CONTENT: TWO ARGUMENTS FOR EXTERNALISM

Most philosophers who write about these issues seem to think that there is a very general question, with an equally general answer, of the form, How is the content of our intentional states determined? The question is supposed to be interpreted as asking not, What is the account of how we came to have these intentional contents and not others? but rather, How are the intentional contents *constituted*? What fact about the intentional state as it exists here and now makes it a desire for water and not a desire for something else? Oddly enough, though these are quite distinct questions, the currently most influential view treats an answer to the first, What is the causal account for our having these intentional states? as providing the answer to the second, What is it about these intentional states that constitutes their having the content they do? This view, called "externalism," says that intentional content is in large part constituted by the (external) causal relations that the agent has to the external world and not by the (internal) features of the mind/brain.

The view that I have been tacitly assuming throughout this book is a form of internalism. According to internalism, so construed, our intentional contents are entirely a matter of what is inside our heads. Of course they refer to objects and states of affairs in the world. That is what intentionality is for—to relate us to the world by representing its various features. The content that enables an intentional state to refer to one object rather than another is entirely between the ears of the referring subject. Internalism, so construed, has in recent decades been challenged by a series of arguments for the view that mental contents themselves are not in the head, or at least not entirely in the head, but in large part reside in relations between what is going on in the head and the rest of the world. It is important to see that this externalist theory is not merely claiming that our inner mental contents are often caused by external events (both sides agree on that) but rather that the contents themselves are not truly inner but are, at best, a mixture of the inner and outer. If that sounds vague, I am afraid it is, because externalism is a rather vaguely stated thesis. I will now sketch the two best-known arguments for externalism, and this will help to make the doctrine seem less obscure. In order to explain these arguments I need to introduce the notion of indexicality. An indexical sentence or expression refers to some object by indicating the relations in which the object stands to the utterance of the expression itself. So if I say, "I am hungry" and you say "I am hungry" we utter the same sentence with the same meaning but the utterances have different conditions of satisfaction because of the occurrence of the indexical "I." "I" uttered by me refers to me. "I" uttered by you refers to you. There are lots of forms of indexicality in language: "I," "you," "here," "now," "this," "that," "yesterday," "tomorrow," and "over there," as well as tenses of verbs, are all examples of indexicals.

The First Argument for Externalism: Hilary Putnam and Twin Earth.[3]

You might think that "water" could be defined as a clear, colorless, tasteless liquid found in lakes and streams and coming out of the sky in the form of rain. But, says Hilary Putnam, that does not give the meaning of "water." To see this, imagine a galaxy just like ours, with a planet in it just like our planet, that we will call Twin Earth. On Twin Earth everything is exactly the same as it is on Earth, molecule for molecule, with one exception. What we on Earth call "water" is made of H_2O; what people on Twin Earth call "water" is not H_2O but has a very long chemical formula that we can abbreviate as "XYZ." Now, in 1750, before anybody knew anything about chemical composition, what was in the heads of the Twin Earth people when they used the word "water" was exactly the same as what was in the heads of the Earth people when they use the same word. But all the same, though the contents of the heads were the same, the meanings were different. Meanings cannot be in the head, because the same things are in their heads as are in our heads, but the meanings are different. "Water" on Earth refers to one kind of stuff; "water" on Twin Earth refers to another kind of stuff. The meaning on both Earth and Twin Earth, says Putnam, is determined by causal relations in which speakers stand to indexically presented substances. "Water" on Earth means whatever has the same structure as this indexically presented stuff. Ditto for Twin Earth. But since the stuffs are different, H_2O in one case, XYZ in the other, the meanings are different. Meanings, concludes Putnam, "just ain't in the head."[4]

What goes for meaning goes for mental content generally. Beliefs employing the expression "water" are different for the people on Twin Earth than for the people on Earth. But if so, it turns out that beliefs cannot be entirely in the head. What is in the head is exactly the same in the two cases, though the beliefs are different.

The Second Argument for Externalism: Tyler Burge and Arthritis[5]

Tyler Burge has a related argument to show that the contents of the mind are at least in part social. Here is how the argument goes. Imagine that Joe goes to see his doctor in Santa Monica. He says "Doctor, I have a pain in my thigh. I believe it is arthritis." We may suppose his doctor answers, "If it is a pain in your thigh, it can't be arthritis. Arthritis is an inflammation of the joints." Now let us keep the condition of Joe exactly the same but imagine that the community is different. Imagine that what is in Joe's head is exactly the same because he is the same person at the same time. But let us imagine that he is not in Santa Monica but in Twin Santa Monica. And imagine that in this community the word "arthritis" is used differently. It is used to name both muscle pains and joint inflammations. Now, in the second case, what is in Joe's brain is exactly the same as the first case, but it seems that his belief is different. In Santa Monica he holds a false belief that he has arthritis. In Twin Santa Monica he holds a true belief. We cannot report this belief by saying that he believes he has arthritis, because "arthritis" is a word of standard English. In Twin Santa Monica, they do not speak standard English, at least as far as this word is concerned. So we have to invent a word. We can say that in Twin Santa Monica he holds a true belief, the belief that he has tharthritis. Now, and this is the point of the thought experiment, though what is in his head in the two cases is exactly the same (it has to be the same because he is exactly the same person at the same time), all the same there are two different beliefs. There must be two different beliefs because one is true and the other is false, and the same belief cannot be both true and false.

The conclusion is like Putnam's. Just as Putnam showed that meanings are partly constituted by causal relations to the world, so

Burge's argument shows that mental contents are partly constituted by social relations with one's community. In both cases we
seem to have demonstrated that intentional contents are not internal to the head.

What are we to make of these arguments? I admire the philosophical acumen of their authors, but I think both arguments are
fallacious. The basic idea of internalism is that the mind—and by
"mind" here we mean what is inside the head—sets conditions
that an object must meet in order to be referred to by an expression
or other form of thought content. In a classic example, the expression "the Morning Star" sets a condition such that if an object satisfies that condition, the expression can be used literally to refer to
the object. Nothing in Putnam's account challenges this conception. For the traditional idea that a checklist of features is associated with each word—for example, with the word "water" are
associated such features as clear, colorless liquid, etc.—Putnam
substitutes an indexical definition: "Water is anything identical in
structure with what we are now seeing." On our account of the
causal self-referentiality of perceptual intentionality, that amounts
to saying that water is whatever is identical in structure with the
substance causing this very visual experience. But that definition
sets a condition that is entirely represented in the contents of the
mind. People on Earth are seeing a substance they call "water,"
and they set a condition that will be satisfied by anything else that
is relevantly similar to the stuff they have baptized as "water." For
people on Twin Earth we tell exactly the same story. They are seeing a substance they call "water," and they set a condition that will
be satisfied by anything else that is relevantly similar. The condition is entirely internal to the contents of the mind. Whether or not
a substance satisfies that condition is up to the world and not up to
the mind, in exactly the same way that for any other internally set
condition, such as being the Morning Star, whether or not an object
satisfies that condition is up to the world and not up to the mind.
Internalism is a theory about how the mind sets conditions. Objects
are referred to if they satisfy those conditions. What conditions are
set is up to the mind; whether an object satisfies those conditions is
up to the world. I have seen nothing in the externalist criticisms that
challenges this basic insight.

In the case of Burge's example, the only difference in Joe's mental
states in the two cases is an indexical difference. In both communities he believes:

1. I am having this very pain in my thigh. I believe it is arthritis.

But he also has a background presupposition that we can express as:

2. I take it for granted that my use of words matches that of my community and where there is a difference I will alter my usage to match the community.

But an application of 2 to the present case yields:

3. I take it for granted that in my community "arthritis" refers to pains like this and if not I will alter my usage to conform to the community.

There is thus an indexical component involved in any use of a public language. The difference between Joe in the first case and Joe in the second case is that the community is different. In the first case Joe is wrong about 3. Pains like that are not called "arthritis." In the second community he is right. Pains like that are called "arthritis." I cannot see that this example poses any problem whatever for even the most naïve versions of internalism. In response to this objection, Burge has told me (in conversation) that he simply wants to stipulate that Joe has no metalinguistic beliefs about how words are used. Quite so. We need not suppose he has thought about the matter at all. But it is a background assumption behind our social use of words that we share common meanings with other people in our community. When Joe finds that this background assumption is mistaken he does not alter in any way his conception of the nonlinguistic facts—he still has the same pain in the same place—but he alters his linguistic usage. I think Burge is right that we can reasonably suppose that Joe never had any explicit thoughts to the effect that his usage conforms to the community. But the presupposition of commonality of linguistic usage is a general background assumption, something that is prior to explicit beliefs and thoughts. Our use of language is presumed to conform to the other members of our community, otherwise we could not intend to communicate with them by using a common language.

V. HOW INTERNAL MENTAL CONTENT RELATES AGENTS TO THE WORLD

In order to explain in more depth what is wrong with these objections to internalism, I have to say a little bit about the nature of mental content and how it relates agents to the world. We have already seen that an intentional state sets conditions of satisfaction.

So for example, if I have the belief that Socrates drinks water then my belief will be true, and hence satisfied, if and only if Socrates drinks water. The questions we are asking now are, What features constitute the components of the thought that Socrates drinks water, and how do those component elements relate the agent to the total thought and to the external world? In this case let us concentrate our attention on "Socrates" and "water." (I will leave out a discussion of "drinks" because predication raises special problems that go beyond the issues of externalism and internalism.) Everybody agrees that each component, "Socrates" and "water," makes a contribution to the total truth condition of the thought. "Socrates" picks out Socrates and "water" refers to water. Just as associated with the whole sentence is the truth condition that Socrates drinks water, so associated with each of these two components is a condition, a condition that it contributes to the truth condition of the entire sentence. There are then two sets of questions about the components of the thought. First, how does each element relate to the condition that it determines and second, how does the agent relate to the determination of those conditions? Granted that "Socrates" refers to Socrates and "water" refers to water, how does the agent have to relate to these words in order that he can use them to determine the conditions of satisfaction of the whole thought? The traditional answer, and the answer given by common sense, is that each word sets the condition it does because of its *meaning* and the agent is able to use the words the way he does because he *knows* the meaning of each of the words. And knowing the meaning enables him to use the word in such a way as to introduce the corresponding condition into the truth conditions of the entire sentence.

We can now state the dispute between the internalists and the externalists with a little more precision: both sides agree that words make a contribution to the truth conditions of the entire sentence and both sides agree that there is some condition that the speaker himself must satisfy in order that he can use these words to set the truth conditions in question. The dispute is entirely about the nature of the condition satisfied by the speaker. The question is, Is the condition associated with the word something that is represented in the speaker's mind / brain, or is it something that is in part independent of the speaker's mind / brain? According to the internalist, the condition must be represented in the speaker's head. According to the externalist, the contents of the head are insufficient for successful reference. That is what Putnam meant when he said "Meanings just ain't in the head." The argument given by the externalists is in every case the same: two speakers could have type-identical contents in the heads and yet mean something different. But the answer given to this claim by the internalists is that in all cases where that is so, it is because there is some indexical component in the head that sets a different condition of satisfaction in the two cases, because it sets the condition relative to the head of the speaker in question. If we suppose, for example, that two identical twins who happen to be identical, as they say, "molecule for molecule," both think the thought "I am hungry" we may suppose that what it is in their heads is type-identical, but all the same they mean something different because twin A is referring to himself and twin B is referring to himself. Indexicality will enable type-identical thoughts in the head to determine different conditions of satisfaction because the conditions of satisfaction, being indexically determined, are fixed relative to the head in question. Thus in the Twin Earth case the people on both Earth and Twin Earth set conditions of satisfaction relative to themselves: What we call "water" is anything type-identical in structure with the stuff that *we* are seeing. But since the "we" in the two cases is different and since the people on Twin Earth are seeing something different from the people on Earth they will have different conditions of satisfaction even though the contents of the head are type-identical. There is nothing in this example to show that meanings are not in the head.

Analogous remarks can be made about Burge's example. Joe has exactly the same thought in the two communities. The thought is "I am having this very pain. I believe it is arthritis." And the Background presupposition is that pains like this are called "arthritis" in my community. But since the community is different in the two cases, the very same thought will determine different conditions of satisfaction relative to the two communities. In one case Joe has a true belief; in the other case he has a false belief.

Let us return to our original question. If we reject the externalist's claim that intentional content is determined by external causal chains, what then does determine intentional content? Causally speaking, I do not think there is any general answer to this question except to say that our intentional contents are determined by a combination of our life experiences and our innate biological capacities. I have already given a sketch of how an animal's feeling of thirst might be determined by neurobiological processes. If one were to change the example slightly so that I was not just thirsty in general but thirsty for a glass of draught Irish stout, or a 1953 Chateau Lafitte, then the story would become much more complicated. I would have to give an account of how my life experiences have led me to have certain sorts of taste experiences, that I was capable of recalling these in memory and capable of forming desires to repeat these experiences in the future. But if the story has to be more complicated to account for a specific desire, then it would become incredibly complicated if I tried to give an account of how one might have formed an intention with the content that I write the great American novel, marry a Republican, or explain intentionality in a single chapter.

But if we are talking not about the history of our intentional states, but about their *constitution,* for example, what fact about me makes it the case that I have the belief that Caesar crossed the Rubicon, then we have to appeal to the notion of conditions of satisfaction.

Before addressing that question directly, let us take stock of where we are. We began this chapter with three questions:

1. How is intentionality possible at all?
2. How are intentional contents determined?
3. How do intentional states work in detail?

We did not so much answer the first question as remove the need to ask it in that special philosophical tone of voice that makes any answer impossible. We brought it down to earth by transforming it into such questions as, How is it possible for an animal to be thirsty, or hungry, or frightened? Once those questions are answered, the first question is already answered insofar as it is a meaningful question. We postponed the second question until we had answered the third. In passing, I rejected the externalist answer to the second question. I now want to use our results in answering the third question to perform the same sort of maneuver on the second that we did on the first. The question, How is it possible for me to have a belief whose content is that Caesar crossed the Rubicon? is in principle no more difficult to answer than it is to answer the question, How was it possible for me to be thirsty for water? i.e., to have a desire whose content is that I drink water. In both cases the answer is provided by seeing the essential connection between intentionality and conditions of satisfaction. What makes my desire a desire to drink water is that it will be satisfied if and only if I drink water. That is not a psychological remark predicting what will make me feel good, but rather it is the definition of the relevant intentional content. In exactly the same way, what makes my belief have the content that Caesar crossed the Rubicon is the fact that it will be satisfied if and only if Caesar crossed the Rubicon. The content of the intentional state is exactly that which makes it have the conditions of satisfaction that it does. Those conditions of satisfaction are always represented under aspects. I represent a certain man as Caesar, for example, and not as Anthony's best friend, even though Caesar is identical with Antony's best friend.

But is not this answer to the second question circular? What makes an intentional state have the content it does? Answer: it has the conditions of satisfaction that it does. And what are those conditions of satisfaction? Those determined by the content of the intentional state. And that certainly looks circular. But that is precisely the sort of circularity I am seeking. We do not accept the question on its own terms, but rather reject it and substitute for it an account of how intentionality actually functions. It functions because of a set of very tight connections between intentional content, aspectual shape, and conditions of satisfaction. The next step in nailing this whole account down to the real world is to point to the central role of consciousness. To have an intentional state consciously, for example to think consciously that Caesar crossed the Rubicon, is to be consciously aware of the conditions of satisfaction. To have the same intentional state unconsciously is to have something that is in principle is at least capable of becoming conscious. I will discuss the relation of the conscious and unconscious in detail in chapter 9. For present purposes I want to say only the following. We reject the sense of the third question in which it does not admit of any answer and we substitute for that question an account of how intentional content actually functions. It actually functions because intentional agents have conscious thoughts where the very identity of the conscious thought is such as to determine that it has certain conditions of satisfaction and not others. Those conditions of satisfaction are represented under some aspects and not others. If you ask, How can a state of my brain have the content that Caesar crossed the Rubicon? it seems an impossibly difficult question. But if you ask, How can my conscious thought "Caesar crossed the Rubicon" have the content that Caesar crossed the Rubicon? then it is no longer impossible to answer. I know the meanings of the words, I know how they relate to objects and states of affairs in the world and in thinking the whole thought I am aware that it has precisely this condition of

satisfaction: Caesar crossed the Rubicon. Once we reject the metaphysical sense of the third question we demystify it by assimilat-
ing it to a general account of how intentionality actually functions.
And that is all that needs to be said about the constitution of intentional content in general. Beyond that, of course, we need to say a
great deal, much of which I have already said, about the network
and the background, about the direction of fit and causal self-
referentiality, psychological mode, and all the rest of it.

I will spell out the relations between consciousness and intentionality in chapter 9. For the moment, just this: one huge evolutionary advantage of human consciousness is that we can
coordinate a large amount of intentionality ("information") simultaneously in a single unified conscious field. Think of the amount
of coordinated intentionality ("information processing") when, for
example, you drive to work in the morning. Don't just think of the
coordination of perception and action. (For example, I am passing
the car on my right. There is a red light ahead.) Think also of the
constant accessing of unconscious intentionality. (For example, I
will be late for my 9:00 a.m. appointment. Where shall I have
lunch? I wonder how the meetings will go.) All of these are intentionalistic representations of the world, and we cope with the
world by way of these representations.

VI. CONCLUSION

I said at the beginning of this book that the worst thing we can do is
give the reader the impression that she understands something she
does not really understand. I do not wish you to get the impression
from reading this chapter that now you understand intentionality. I
have only scratched the surface of a very large subject. But I do want
you to have a certain overall conception of intentionality as representation and I do want you to be able to avoid mistakes that are
common in contemporary philosophy. Specifically, you should see
the distinction between intentionality-with-a-t and intensionality-
with-an-s. You should see the difficulties in the currently orthodox
externalist accounts of intentional content, and you should begin to
see the connection between intentionality and consciousness, a connection I will explain in detail in chapter 9. Most of all, you should
begin to get an idea of how intentionality works as a real feature of
the real world, and this understanding will, I hope, enable you to

avoid being intimidated into thinking there is some deep mystery about intrinsic or original intentionality that defies any natural explanation.

Suggestions for Further Reading

Burge, T., "Individualism and the Mental," in *Midwest Studies in Philosophy* 4, 1979.

Fodor, J., "Meaning and the World Order," in *Psychosemantics,* Cambridge, MA: MIT Press, chap. 4, 1988, reprinted in O'Connor, T., and D. Robb, eds., *Philosophy of Mind, Contemporary Readings,* London and New York: Routledge, 2003.

Putnam, H., "The Meaning of Meaning," in *Language, Mind, and Knowledge,* Gunderson, K., ed., *Minnesota Readings in the Philosophy of Science,* vol. 9, Minneapolis: University of Minnesota Press, 1975, 131–193.

Searle, J. R., *Intentionality, An Essay in the Philosophy of Mind,* Cambridge: Cambridge University Press, 1983.

CHAPTER 7

Mental Causation

One of the residual problems left to us from dualism is the problem of mental causation. Our first mind-body problem was, How can physical processes ever cause mental processes? But to many philosophers the other half of the question is even more pressing, How can anything as ethereal and insubstantial as mental processes ever have any physical effects in the real world? Surely the real physical world is "causally closed" in the sense that nothing from outside the physical world can ever have any causal effects inside the physical world.

By now, the reader will know that I do not think these are impossibly difficult questions, and that our acceptance of the Cartesian categories is what makes them seem difficult. However, there are a lot of fascinating problems that arise in the study of mental causation. Even if you accept my general account of mind-body relations, I think you will find some interesting issues about mental causation discussed in this chapter.

I. HUME'S ACCOUNT OF CAUSATION

We have to start with Hume. Just as when we talk about the mind in general there is no escaping Descartes, so when we talk about causation there is no escaping Hume. Hume's account of causation is by far his most original, powerful, and profound piece of philosophy, and I think most philosophers would agree with me that it is one of the most impressive pieces of philosophical prose ever written in the English language. Whatever else you learn from this book,

136

I would like you to learn something about Hume's skeptical account of causation. (Of course, what follows is not intended as a substitute for reading the real thing—Hume's Treatise, Book 1, Part 3—but what I will now tell you will give you a guide for making your way around the real territory.)[1] Here is how it goes:

Hume begins by asking what are the components of our reasoning considering cause and effect. In the twenty-first century we would put this in the form, What is the definition of "cause"? Hume says there are three components to our notion of causation:

Priority, by which he means the cause has to occur prior in time to the effect; causes cannot come after their effects.

Contiguity in space and time, by which he means the cause and effect have to be adjacent to each other. If I scratch my head in Berkeley and a building falls over in Paris, my scratching my head cannot be the cause of the building falling over unless there is a series of links in a "causal chain" between my head and the building in Paris.

Necessary connection, by which he means, in addition to priority and contiguity, the cause and effect must be necessarily connected in such a way that the cause actually *produces* the effect, the cause *makes the effect happen*, the cause *necessitates* the effect, or as Hume would summarize this, there is a *necessary connection* between cause and effect.

But, says Hume, when we begin to look at actual cases, we find that we cannot perceive any necessary connection. We observe that, for example, when I flip the light switch, the light goes on, and if I flip it again it goes off. I think there is a causal connection between flipping the switch A and the light going on B, but in fact all I can really observe is A followed by B. Hume presents the absence of necessary connection as if it were a sort of lamentable lack that we might overcome, as if by closer inspection we might discover a necessary connection. But he knows perfectly well that in the way that he has described the case, there could never be a necessary connection. For suppose I said that the necessary connection between flipping the switch and the light going on is the passage of electricity through the wire C, and I found some method of observing that, say through a metering device. But that would not help. For now I would have the flipping of the switch, the passage of the electricity, and the light going on, the sequence ACB. But I still would have no necessary connections between these three events. And if I found one, if I found apparent necessary connections between the switch A, the electricity C, and the light B, in the form of, let us say, the closing of the circuitry D, or the activation of the molecules in the tungsten filament E, these would still not be necessary connections. I would then have a sequence of five events, ADCEB, and these would require necessary connections between each. Hume's first skeptical result is there is no necessary connection between the so-called cause and the so-called effect.

At this point Hume really takes off. He says that we should examine the underlying principles of cause and effect, and he discovers two principles: the principle of causation and the principle of causality. The principle of causation says every event has a cause. The principle of causality says like causes have like effects. These, as he correctly sees, are not equivalent. For it might be the case that every event had a cause though there was no consistency in what sort of effects any particular cause might have, and no consistency in what sort of causes any effect might have. And it might be the case that when there were causes and effects, like causes had like effects, even though not every event had a cause. But, says Hume, if we examine these two principles, the principle of causation and the principle of causality, we find a peculiar feature. They do not seem to be provable. They are not true by definition. That is, they are not analytic truths. So they must be synthetic empirical truths. But now, and this is the real cruncher of Hume's argument, there is no way that we could establish them by empirical methods, because any attempt to establish anything by empirical methods presupposes exactly these two principles.

This is Hume's most celebrated result. It is called the problem of induction, and here is how it is stated. If you think of deductive arguments, such as the argument:

Socrates is a man.
All men are mortal.
Therefore Socrates is mortal.

You can see that the argument is valid because the conclusion is already contained implicitly in the premises. There is nothing in the conclusion that is not in the premises. We could represent this diagrammatically by saying we go from premise to conclusion, $P \rightarrow C$, where $P \geq C$. The premise always contains more information than the conclusion (or in a limiting case where we derive a proposition from itself, the premise is the same as the conclusion). Validity is guaranteed because there is nothing in the conclusion that is not already in the premises. But when we consider scientific or inductive arguments, such as an argument to prove our premise that all men are mortal, it seems we do not have this type of validity. For in the case of inductive arguments, we go from evidence E to hypothesis H. We say, for example, the evidence about the mortality of particular individual men provides evidence for, or supports, or establishes, the general hypothesis that all men are mortal. We go from evidence to hypothesis, E → H, but (and this is the difference from deduction) in the case of induction there is always more in the hypothesis than there was in the evidence. The hypothesis is always more than just a summary of the evidence. That is to say, E < H, E is less than H. In such a case, it might seem a shame that we ever used inductive arguments at all, but of course, they are absolutely essential, because how else would we establish the general propositions that form the premises of our deductive arguments? How would we ever establish that all men are mortal if we could not generalize from particular instances of mortal men, or from other sorts of evidence about particular cases, to the general conclusion that all men are mortal?

When we go from evidence to hypothesis, when we say the evidence supports the hypothesis, or establishes the hypothesis, or confirms the hypothesis, we do not do this in an arbitrary or unwarranted fashion. On the contrary, we have some principles or rules R by which we go from evidence to hypothesis, and you might think of these as the rules of scientific method. So we do not go in an arbitrary fashion E → H, but we go E → H on the basis of R. ER → H. But now, and this is Hume's decisive point, What is the ground for R? E, the evidence, we will suppose comes from actual observations. H is a generalization from the observations. But now, if we are to justify the move from E to H on the basis of R, what is the justification for R? And Hume's answer is: any attempt to justify R presupposes R. What is R exactly? (And here is where the connection with causation and causality comes in.) R can be stated in a variety of ways. The most obvious way to state it is just to say that every event has a cause and like causes have like effects. Other ways are to say that unobserved instances will resemble observed instances, that nature is uniform, that the future will resemble the past. All of these Hume takes as more-or-less equivalent for these purposes. Unless we presuppose some sort of uniformity of nature, the uniformity of nature guaranteed by causality and causation, we have no ground for inductive arguments. But, and this is the crucial point, there is no ground for the belief in the uniformity of nature, because any such a belief would have to be grounded in induction, which in turn would have to be grounded in the uniformity of nature; and thus the attempt to ground the belief in the uniformity of nature would be circular.

So far, Hume's results are almost entirely skeptical. There is no such thing as necessary connection in nature, and there is no such thing as a rational basis for induction. Typical of Hume's method, after he gets skeptical results, is that he then gives us reasons why we cannot accept these skeptical results and should just proceed as if skepticism had not been established. We are bound to continue with our old superstitions, and Hume is eager to explain to us exactly how.

When we were looking around for necessary connection, we did not find necessary connection in addition to priority and contiguity, but we did find another relation: the constant conjunction of resembling instances. We discovered that the thing we call the cause is always followed by the thing we call the effect. Just as a matter of fact about our living in the world, we discover that the things we call causes are always followed by the things we call effects. This constant repetition in our experience, this constant conjunction of resembling instances, gives rise to a certain expectation in our minds whereby when we perceive the thing we call the cause we automatically expect to perceive the thing we call the effect. It is this "felt determination of the mind" to pass from the perception of the causes to the lively expectations of the effect, and from the idea of the cause to the idea of the effect, that gives us the illusion that there is something in nature in addition to priority, contiguity, and constant conjunction. This felt determination of the mind gives us the conviction that there are necessary connections in nature. But that conviction is nothing but an illusion. The only reality is the reality of priority, contiguity, and constant conjunction. Causation on Hume's account is literally just one damn thing after another. The only point is that there is a regularity in the way one thing follows another, and this regularity gives us the illusion that there is something more. But the necessary connection we think exists in nature is entirely an illusion in the mind. The only reality is regularity.

The existence of the regularity in previously observed cases, however, is no ground whatever for supposing that the next case will resemble the preceding cases. It is in no way a solution of the problem of induction. It gives us the illusion that we can solve the problem of induction because we think that with the felt determination of the mind we have discovered a necessary connection. But the necessary connection is entirely in our mind, it is not in nature itself. In effect then, Hume copes with the problem of induction by showing how causality is prior to causation. The existence of regularities (causality) gives us the illusion of necessary connection, and the illusion of necessary connection gives us the conviction that every event has a cause (causation).

Hume's legacy about causation, then, involves at least two fundamental principles. First, there is no such thing as necessary connection in nature. And second, what we find in nature, in place of causal connections, are universal regularities. Hume's skepticism about necessary connection does not lead him to say there is no fact of the matter at all about causation. Rather, there is a fact of the matter, but it is not what we expected. We expected there to be a causal link between the cause and the effect, but what we in fact find is a sequence of events that instantiate universal laws. These two features have influenced the discussion of causation to this day. Most philosophers think that there are no causal connections in nature, and that any particular causal connection has to instantiate a universal law. Most of them are eager to point out that the terms in which the law is stated need not be the same as the terms that describe the incidents of the original causal relation. Thus, if I say, "The thing John did caused the phenomenon that Sally saw," and suppose John put the pot of water on the stove and turned the heat on, and Sally saw water boiling in the pot, then it would be true that the thing that John did caused the phenomenon that Sally saw, but there would be no law mentioning John and Sally or even putting and seeing. The scientific laws will be about such things as water pressure when water is heated in the Earth's atmosphere.

Hume's skepticism about induction has been less influential on contemporary philosophy than his regularity theory of causation. I think that most philosophers today think that Hume can be answered, and the standard textbook answer is that Hume mistakenly supposed that inductive arguments should meet deductive standards. He supposes there is something missing in an argument that proceeds by inductive methods on the basis of evidence to support a conclusion, because the premises do not entail the conclusion in the manner of the deductive argument. It is, on the view of contemporary philosophers, as if somebody said "My motorcycle is not a good motorcycle because it does not get good marks in a dog show." Motorcycles are not the same as dogs nor should they be judged by the standards by which we judge dogs. It is exactly the same sort of mistake to suppose that inductive arguments should be judged by deductive standards. By deductive standards there are valid deductive arguments, and by inductive standards there are valid inductive arguments. It is a mistake to confuse the one with the other.

Indeed, on one standard contemporary view, even this is conceding too much to Hume. The idea that there are even two styles of arguments, induction and deduction, is already a source of confusion. There are just deductive arguments, and one way to proceed in the sciences is called the hypothetico-deductive method. One forms a hypothesis, deduces a prediction, and then tests the hypothesis by testing to see if the prediction comes true. To the extent that the prediction comes true, we say that the original hypothesis is confirmed or supported. To the extent that it does not come true, we say that the hypothesis is disconfirmed or refuted. There is no flat opposition between induction and deduction. Rather, so-called induction is a matter of testing hypotheses by experiment and other sorts of evidence. And a typical way of testing a hypothesis is to deduce the consequences of the hypothesis and then see if those consequences can meet certain experimental tests. For example, the law of gravity would predict that a body would fall a certain distance within a certain time. Having made this deduction we then test the hypothesis by seeing whether objects do in fact fall this distance in that amount of time.

II. DO WE NEVER EXPERIENCE CAUSATION?

I said earlier that I have a great admiration for Hume's achievement in his analysis of necessary connection and his regularity theory of causal relations. But I also have to say that I think the theory is disastrously mistaken and that it has had a very bad effect on subsequent philosophy. I am not in this book going to undertake a general critique of Hume's account of causation and induction but shall just focus on those features that are essential for the philosophy of mind. Hume's chief negative result about necessary connection can be stated in one sentence: there is no impression of necessary connection; that is, there is no experience of force, efficacy, power, or causal relation. Is that right? Does that sound plausible to you? I have to confess that it does not seem at all plausible to me. I think that we perceive necessary connections pretty much throughout our waking life and I want to explain how.

When we have perceptual experiences, or when we engage in voluntary actions, as we saw in our discussion of intentionality, there is a causally self-referential condition in the conditions of satisfaction of the intentional phenomena. The intention in action is only satisfied if it causes the bodily movement, the perceptual experience is only satisfied if it is caused by the object perceived. But in both of these cases it is quite common, though of course not universally true, that we actually experience the causal connection between the experience, on the one hand, and objects and states of affairs in the world, on the other. If you have any doubts about this just raise your arm. Clearly there is a distinction between the experience of your raising your arm and your experience of someone else raising it. As I mentioned in chapter 5, the neurosurgeon, Wilder Penfield, found that he could cause his patient's arm to move by stimulating the neurons in the motor cortex with microelectrodes. Invariably the patients said something such as "I didn't do that, you did."[2] Now clearly this experience is different from actually voluntarily raising one's arm. In the normal case, where you raise your arm intentionally, you actually experience the causal efficacy of the conscious intention-in-action producing the bodily movement. Furthermore, if somebody bumps into you, you experience a certain perception, but you do not experience that perception as caused by you. You experience it as actually caused by the person's body banging into you. So in both of these cases, in both action and perception, it seems to me quite common, indeed normal, that we perceive a causal connection between objects and states of affairs in the world and our own conscious experiences. In the case of action we experience our conscious intentions-in-action causing bodily movements. In the case of perception we experience objects and states of affairs in the world causing perceptual experiences in us.

I think Hume was looking in the wrong place. He was looking in a detached way at objects and events outside of him and he discovered that there was no necessary connection between them. But if you think about the character of your actual experiences it seems to me quite common that you experience yourself making something happen (that is an intentional action), or you experience something making something happen to you (that is a perception). In both cases it is quite common to experience the causal connection.

Elizabeth Anscombe (in lectures) gave a good example of this. Suppose I am sitting here at my desk and a car backfires outside and it makes me jump. In this case I actually experience my involuntary movement as caused by the loud noise I heard. I do not have to wait for the conjunction of resembling instances. In this case I actually experience the causal nexus as part of my sequence of conscious experiences.

So far, these experiences would only give us a causal relation between our own experiences and the real world, but we want to be able to discover the same relation in the real world apart from our experiences. It seems to me not at all difficult to extend the conception of causation that we get from our own experiences to objects and states of affairs in the world that exist and interact with each other in ways that are totally independent of our experiences. The effect that I personally create when I cause the car to move by pushing it is an effect I can observe when I observe you pushing it. But the causal relation is the same whether I am pushing the car or I am observing you pushing the car. Furthermore, I can then extend this to the case where there are no agents involved at all. If I see one car pushing another car I see the physical force of the first as causing the second to move. So it seems that in addition to our actual experience of causation we can easily extend the notion of causation to sequences of events in the world that do not contain our experiences or for that matter anybody else's experiences. After all, causal relations involving human beings are only a tiny portion of causal relations in the universe. The point for the present discussion is that the same relation we experience when we make something happen or when something makes something happen to us, can be perceived to exist even when no experiences are involved in the causal relation.

There is nothing self-guaranteeing about our experience of causation. We could in any particular case be mistaken. But this possibility of error and illusion is built into any perceptual experience at all. The point for this discussion is that the experience of causation is no worse than any other perceptual experience.

III. MENTAL CAUSATION AND THE CAUSAL CLOSURE OF THE PHYSICAL

Let us suppose that I am right so far—that we do have the experience of causation as part of our normal waking consciousness, and that causation is a real relation in the real world. All the same, there seems to be a special problem about mental causation. Here is the problem: if consciousness is nonphysical, then how could it ever have a physical effect such as moving my body? Nonetheless, it seems in our experience that our consciousness does move our bodies. I consciously decide to raise my arm, and my arm goes up. Yet at the same time we know that there is another story to be told about the raising of the arm that has to do with neuron firings in the motor cortex, the secretion of acetylcholene at the axon end plates of my motor neurons, the stimulation of the ion channels, the attack on the cytoplasm of the muscle fiber, and eventually the arm rises. So if there is a story to be told about the effect of consciousness at the level of the mind, how does it fit with the story to be told about the chemistry and physiology at the level of the body? Worse yet, even supposing we did have a role for mental causation, that the mind did play a causal role in producing our bodily behavior, that seems to get us out of the frying pan and into the fire, because now it looks like we have too many causes. It looks like we have what philosophers call "causal overdetermination." It looks like there would be two separate sets of causes making my arm go up, one having to do with neurons, and the other one having to do with conscious intentionality.

We can now summarize the philosophical problem about mental causation with some precision: if mental states are real, nonphysical states, it is hard to see how they could have any effects on the physical world. But if they do have real effects on the physical world, then it looks like we will have causal overdetermination. Either way it seems we cannot make sense of the idea of mental causation. There are four propositions that taken together are inconsistent.

1. The mind-body distinction: the mental and the physical form distinct realms.
2. The causal closure of the physical: the physical realm is causally closed in the sense that nothing nonphysical can enter into it and act as a cause.
3. The causal exclusion principle: where the physical causes are sufficient for an event, there cannot be any other types of causes of that event.
4. Causal efficacy of the mental: mental states really do function causally.[3]

These four together are inconsistent. One way out is to give up 4, but this amounts to epiphenomenalism. As Jaegwon Kim writes, "If this be epiphenominalism let us make the most of it."[4]

In general, as we have seen over and over, when you have one of these impossible philosophical problems it usually turns out that you were making a false assumption. I believe that is the case in the present instance. The mistake is expressed in proposition 1, the traditional mind-body distinction. I said in chapter 4 that this mistake arises from supposing that if there is a level of description of brain processes at which they contain real and irreducible sequences of conscious states, and there is another level of description of brain processes at which they are purely biological phenomena, and the states of consciousness are not ontologically reducible to the neurobiological phenomena, then these two levels must be separate existences. We saw in chapter 4 that this is a mistake. The way out of this dilemma is to remind ourselves of a result we achieved in that chapter: the reality and irreducibility of consciousness do not imply that it is some separate type of entity or property "over and above" the brain system in which it is physically realized. The consciousness in the brain is not separate entity or property; it is just *the state that the brain is in.*

Our traditional vocabulary makes it almost impossible to state this point. If we say that the mental is irreducible to the physical then it looks like we are accepting dualism. But if we say that the mental just is physical at a higher level of description, then it looks like we are accepting materialism. The way out, to repeat a point I have made over and over, is to abandon the traditional vocabulary of mental and physical and just try to state all the facts. The relation of consciousness to brain processes is like the relation of the solidity of the piston to the molecular behavior of the metal alloys, or the liquidity of a body of water to the molecular behavior of the H_2O molecules, or the explosion in the car cylinder to the oxidization of the individual hydrocarbon molecules. In every case the higher-level causes, at the level of the entire system, are not something in addition to the causes at the microlevel of the components of the system. Rather, the causes at the level of the entire system are entirely accounted for, entirely causally reducible to, the causation of the microelements. That is as true of brain processes as it is of car engines, or of water circulating in washing machines. When I say that my conscious decision to raise my arm caused my arm to go up, I am not saying that some cause occurred *in addition* to the behavior of the neurons when they fire and produce all sorts of other neurobiological consequences, rather I am simply describing the whole neurobiological system at the level of the entire system and not at the level of particular microelements. The situation is exactly analogous to the explosion in the cylinder of the car engine. I can say either the explosion in the cylinder caused the piston to move, or I can say the oxidization of hydrocarbon molecules

released heat energy that exerted pressure on the molecular structure of the alloys. These are not two independent descriptions of
two independent sets of causes, but rather they are descriptions at
two different levels of one complete system. Of course, like all
analogies, this one only works up to a certain point. The disanalogy between the brain and the car engine lies in the fact that consciousness is not ontologically reducible in the way that the
explosion in the cylinder is ontologically reducible to the oxidization of the individual molecules. However, I have argued earlier
and will repeat the point here: the ontological irreducibility of consciousness comes not from the fact that it has some separate causal
role to play; rather, it comes from the fact that consciousness has a
first-person ontology and is thus not reducible to something that
has a third-person ontology, even though there is no causal efficacy
to consciousness that is not reducible to the causal efficacy of its
neuronal basis.

We can summarize the discussion of this section as follows. There
are supposed to be two problems about mental causation: First,
how can the mental, which is weightless and ethereal, ever affect
the physical world? And second, if the mental did function causally
would it not produce causal overdetermination? The way to
answer these questions is to abandon the assumptions that gave
rise to them in the first place. The basic assumption was that the
irreducibility of the mental implied that it was something over and
above the physical and not a part of the physical world. Once we
abandon this assumption, the answer to the two puzzles is first that
the mental is simply a feature (at the level of the system) of the
physical structure of the brain, and second, causally speaking, there
are not two independent phenomena, the conscious effort and the
unconscious neuron firings. There is just the brain system, which
has one level of description where neuron firings are occurring and
another level of description, the level of the system, where the system is conscious and indeed consciously trying to raise its arm.
Once we abandon the traditional Cartesian categories of the mental
and the physical, once we abandon the idea that there are two disconnected realms, then there really is no special problem about
mental causation. There are, of course, very difficult problems
about how it actually works in the neurobiology, and for the most
part we do not yet know the solutions to those problems.

One way to represent these relation is in the following sort of
diagram, where the top level shows the intention-in-action causing
a bodily movement and the bottom level shows how it works in

the neuronal and physiological plumbing. At each step the bottom level causes and realizes the top level:

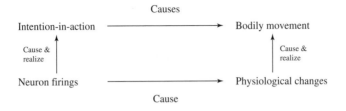

Such diagrams are useful pedagogically, but they are misleading if they suggest that the mental level is on top, like the frosting on the cake. Maybe a better diagram is one where the conscious intention is shown as existing throughout the system and not just on top. In this one the circles represent neurons and the shading represents the conscious state as spread through the system of neurons:

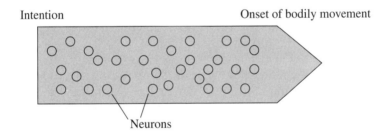

IV. MENTAL CAUSATION AND THE EXPLANATION OF HUMAN BEHAVIOR

Throughout this book we have seen that there are two somewhat different types of philosophical problems surrounding the issues in the philosophy of mind. On the one hand there are the traditional problems of the form, How is such a thing possible at all? How is it possible that brain states can cause consciousness, for example. But there are also questions of the form, How does it work in real life? What is the actual structure and function of human consciousness? In this chapter we have examined exactly this distinction between the, How is it possible that there can be mental causation at all? question and the, How does it function in real life? question. I want to conclude the chapter by saying at least a little bit about how mental causation functions in real life. Understanding the answer to this question is absolutely essential to understanding ourselves as human beings, for when we engage in voluntary human actions we typically engage on the basis of *reasons* and these reasons function causally in explaining our behavior, but the logical form of the explanation of human behavior in terms of reasons is radically different from standard forms of causation. I want now to explain some of these differences.

In a typical case of the ordinary nonmental causation we say such things as "The collapse of the freeway was caused by the earthquake." But if you contrast that with an explanation that we typically give of our own actions (and it is always a good idea to consider your own case so you see how intentional causation functions in your own life), we see that the logical structure of the explanation is radically different. Suppose I say, "I voted for Bush in the last election because I wanted a better educational policy."

If you look at the first explanation, the explanation of the collapse of the freeway, you see that it has several interesting logical features. First, the cause states a sufficient condition for the occurrence of the effect in that context. That is, in that particular context, given the structure of the freeway, and given the forces generated by the earthquake, once the earthquake occurred, the freeway had to collapse. Second, there are no purposes or goals involved, the earthquake and the collapse are just events that occur. Third, though the explanation, like any speech act, contains an intentional content, the intentional content itself does not function causally, rather, the intentional content "earthquake" or "there was an earthquake," simply describes a phenomenon but does not cause anything. Now, these three conditions are not present in the explanation of my voting behavior. In my case the explanation did not state sufficient conditions. Yes, I wanted an improvement in education; yes, I thought Bush would be better for education than Gore; but all the same, nothing forced me to vote the way I did. I could have voted for the other guy, all other conditions remaining the same. Second, you will not understand the explanation unless you see that it is stated in terms of the goals of the agent. The notions of goals, aims, purposes, teleology, etc., are essentially involved in this type of explanation. Indeed the actual explanation I gave is incomplete. We only understand the claim that an agent did A because he wanted to achieve B if we assume that the agent also *believed* that doing A would produce B, or at least make it more likely that B occur. And third, it is absolutely essential to these explanations in terms of intentional causation that we understand that the intentional content that occurs in the explanation, for example, I wanted a better educational policy, actually occurs in the very cause whose specification explains the behavior we are trying to explain.

All of these three features—the presupposition of freedom, the requirement that an explanation of action has to have the specification of a goal or other motivator, and the functioning of intentional causation as part of the explanatory mechanism—are quite unlike anything in standard explanations of natural phenomena such as earthquakes and forest fires. All three are parts of one much larger phenomenon, rationality. It is essential to see that the functioning of human intentionality requires rationality as a structural constitutive organizing principle of the entire system. I cannot exaggerate the importance of this phenomenon for understanding the differences between the naturalistic explanations we get in the natural sciences and the intentionalistic explanations we get in the social sciences. In the surface structure of the sentences the following explanations look very much alike:

1. I made a mark on the ballot paper because I wanted to vote for Bush.
2. I got a stomachache because I wanted to vote for Bush.

Though the surface structure is similar, the actual logical form is quite different. Number 2 just states that an event, my stomachache, was caused by an intentional state, my desire. But number 1 does not state a causally sufficient condition, and makes sense only within the context of a presupposed teleology.

Such explanations raise a host of philosophical problems. The most important of these is the problem of free will, and I turn to that in the next chapter.

Suggestions for Further Reading

Davidson, D., "Actions, Reasons and Causes," in *Essays on Actions and Events*, New York: Oxford University Press, 1980.

Heil, J., and A. Mele, eds., *Mental Causation*, Oxford: Clarendon Press, 1993.

Kim, J., *Mind in a Physical World: An Essay on the Mind-Body Problem and Causation*, Cambridge, MA: MIT Press, 1998.

Searle, J. R., *Intentionality: An Essay in the Philosophy of Mind*, Cambridge: Cambridge University Press, 1983.

CHAPTER 8

Free Will

Philosophical problems tend to hang together. In order to solve, or even address, one problem, you typically have to address a series of others. The problem of free will is an especially striking example of this general phenomenon. In order to address the problem of free will, we have to address the nature of consciousness, of causation, of scientific explanation, and of rationality. Worse yet, after we have examined all of these other issues and how they relate to the problem of free will, we will have clarified our problem but we still will not have a solution; or at least I am unable to see my way to a solution. All I can really hope to do in this chapter is explain what the issues are and what the possible solutions might be. The general conclusion that I reach is that we will need to know a great deal more about brain operations before we have a solution to the problem of free will that we can be at all confident is right.

I. WHY DO WE HAVE A PROBLEM ABOUT THE FREEDOM OF THE WILL?

There is a special problem about free will because we have two absolutely irreconcilable convictions, each of which seems to be completely correct and, indeed, inescapable. The first is that every event that occurs in the world has antecedently sufficient causes. The sufficient causes of an event are those that, in a particular context, are sufficient to determine that that event will occur. When we say the causes were sufficient we mean, given that those causes occurred, in that historical context, the event itself had to occur.

When we ask for an explanation of an event, we are not satisfied with explanations that just state that the event occurred as part of a sequence of events. We want to know what made the event happen. We want to know why that event occurred as opposed to some other events that might have occurred. The picture we have is that all events in the world are as determined as, for example, the fall of this pen is determined if I now release it. If I release the pen that I am now holding in my hand, in this context, it will fall to the table. Given the way the universe is structured, if I release it, it has to fall to the table because the forces acting on it are causally sufficient to determine that it will fall. Our conviction of determinism amounts to the view that what is true of the fall of the pen is true of every event that has ever occurred or will ever occur.

Our second conviction, that we do in fact have free will, is based on certain experiences of human freedom. We have the experience of making up our mind to do something and then doing it. It is part of our conscious experiences that we experience the causes of our decisions and actions, in the form of reasons for those decisions and actions, as not sufficient to force the actual decisions and actions. Think of what it is like to decide which candidate to vote for in an election, or even which item to choose from a menu in a restaurant, and you will see that there is a characteristic experience of making up your mind. And it is part of this experience that you have a sense of alternative choices open to you. There is, in short, a gap between the causes of your decisions and actions in the form of reasons, and the actual making of the decisions, and the performance of the actions. Voluntary decision making and acting contrast with perceiving in that, in the case of decision making and acting, there is a gap between the causes of the phenomenon, in the form of reasons for decision or action, and the actual occurrence of the decision or action; whereas in perception there is no such gap. This is why there is a problem of the "freedom of the will," but no problem of the "freedom of perception." If I look at my hand in front of my face, the causes, i.e., that the hand is right before my open eyes, that the light is good, and that my eyes are in good shape, are sufficient to produce the visual experience. There is no gap. In voluntary actions, by contrast, there are at least three gaps, or, to put it more precisely, at least three phases of a continuous gap. There is a gap between the awareness of the reasons for the action and the decision to perform the action. For example, in a typical case of voluntary decision making, where you are asked to choose between Smith and Jones, two candidates in an election, the set of reasons that you have for voting for Smith or Jones normally do not by themselves compel your decision. Second, there is a gap between the decision and the actual initiation of the action itself. For example, once you have made up your mind to vote for Jones your decision does not force the action itself. Once you get into the voting booth you still have to *act on* that decision. And third, for any extended series of actions, as for example if I am trying to learn Russian or to write a book about the philosophy of mind, there is a gap between the onset of the action and its continuation to completion. You cannot, so to speak, just give yourself a push and let your movements continue like a train moving on a railroad track. No, you have to make a constant effort to keep going with the action to its completion.

Now, having said all that, I immediately have to make some qualifications. Sometimes there is a gap in perception, as for example when we switch from seeing a sketched figure as a duck to seeing it as a rabbit. But this does not really count against the general point, because in these cases there is a voluntary element in the perception. It is up to us whether we see the figure as a duck or as a rabbit. And, of course, not all human actions contain an experience of the gap. Often we feel ourselves in the grip of some overpowering urge or emotion, and in those cases we do not have the sense of alternative possibilities. But this is precisely the contrast between free voluntary actions on the one hand and compulsive or addictive or obsessive actions on the other.

Our experience of the gap is the basis of our conviction that we have free will. But why should we set so much store by these experiences? After all, we have many experiences that we know are illusory. Why should we not simply accept that the experience of free will is an illusion, in the way that, as some philosophers claim, for example, color is an illusion? However, the experience of free will is not something that we can readily dismiss as a mere illusion. Whenever we make up our minds, we have to presuppose freedom. If, for example, I am in a restaurant and I am confronted with a menu and the waiter asks me what I would like, I cannot say "I'm a determinist, I'll just wait and see what happens," because even that utterance is only intelligible to me as an exercise of my free will. I cannot think of that utterance as something that just happened to me, like a sudden pain in the stomach. There is an oddity about the experience of free will in that we cannot get rid of the conviction that we are free even if we become philosophically convinced that the conviction is wrong. Whenever we decide or act voluntarily, which we do throughout the day, we have to decide or act on the presupposition of our own freedom. Our deciding and acting are unintelligible to us otherwise. We cannot think away our own free will.

So we seem to have, on the one hand, the deep conviction that every event that occurs must be explained by causally sufficient conditions, and on the other hand, experiences that give us the conviction of human freedom, a conviction we cannot abandon in practice, however much we may deny it in theory.

II. IS COMPATIBILISM A SOLUTION TO THE PROBLEM OF FREE WILL?

I think most philosophers today accept some version of the view that if we understand these notions correctly, we can see that the thesis of free will is actually compatible with the thesis of determinism. Determinism and free will are both true. This view is called, not surprisingly, compatibilism, and it was also originally baptized by William James as "soft determinism" to contrast it with "hard determinism," the thesis that free will and determinism are incompatible and that determinism is true and free will is false. According to the compatibilists, to say that an action is free is not to say that it does not have causally sufficient antecedent conditions; rather, it is to say that it has certain sorts of causal conditions. So for example, if I now decide to raise my right arm, and I do so, then under these conditions I raise my right arm of my own free will; and more grandly, if I decide to write the great American novel or vote for the Republican candidate, these again are decisions that I make and carry out of my own free will. Now of course, according to the compatibilists, they have causes like anything else. They are completely causally determined. The point, however, is that they are determined by my own inner convictions, rational processes, and reflections. So free actions are not undetermined actions; they are as determined as any other event that occurs in the world. But rather, their being free consists in their being determined by certain sorts of causes and not others. For example, if I decide to raise my arm in order to give a philosophical example, that is a free voluntary action. But if a man puts a gun to my head and says, "Raise your right arm!" then when I raise it, I am not acting freely. I am acting under threat, force, or compulsion. "Free," in short, is not contrasted with "caused," but is contrasted with "forced," "compelled," "under duress," and so forth.

It looks like on the compatibilist view we can have our cake and eat it too. We can say, yes, all actions are determined, but some actions are free because they are determined by certain sorts of inner psychological processes, forms of rationality, deliberation, etc.

Does compatibilism really give us a solution to the free-will problem? I said that I think most philosophers suppose that it does. And it certainly has a long and distinguished history. In different versions it was held by Thomas Hobbes, David Hume, John Stuart Mill, and in the twentieth century by A. J. Ayer and Charles Stevenson. Whether you think compatibilism gives a solution to the free-will problem depends on what you think the problem is. If the problem is about the ordinary use of words like "of my own free will," then it seems clear there is a use of these words where to say that I acted of my own free will leaves open the question of whether the antecedent causes were causally sufficient. There is indeed a use of the words that is consistent with compatibilism, but that is not the original free-will problem that bothered us. When people march in the street carrying signs demanding "Freedom Now," they are not usually thinking about the nature of causation; they just want the government to leave them alone, or some such. And that is, no doubt, an important use of the concept of freedom, but it is not the concept that is central to the problem of free will, at least not as I am construing that problem. Here is the problem: Are all of our decisions and actions preceded by causally sufficient conditions, conditions sufficient to determine that those decisions and actions will occur? Is the sequence of human and animal rational behavior determined in the way that the pen falling to the table is determined in its movement by the force of gravity and other forces acting upon it? That question is not answered by compatibilism.

Compatibilism makes a logical point about the concepts of "free" and "determined" and points out, correctly, that there is a use of these concepts according to which, to say that an action is free is not, so far, to raise any questions about whether or not it was determined, in the sense of having antecedently sufficient causal conditions. But once that logical point is accepted, there is still a factual, empirical question left over. *Is it the case that for every human action that ever occurred in the past, is occurring now, or ever will occur, the action was caused by antecedently sufficient conditions?* Are the causes of all of our actions sufficient causal conditions? Granted that there are causes of our actions, and granted that some actions, such as compulsive ones, are caused by antecedently sufficient conditions, is it the case that for every single action the causes of the action were sufficient to determine that that action, and nothing else, had to occur? Compatibilism does not answer or even address this problem of free will. The theory simply assumes that we are determined. But that question is still left open after we accept the compatibilist point about certain linguistic usages. Notice that the question of free will as I have stated it makes no essential use of notions like "freedom," "of my own free will," "voluntary," etc. It is just about causally sufficient conditions.

I think that another reason why many philosophers accept compatibilism is that they are not really very much interested in the problem of free will, as I have defined it. They are interested in the problem of "moral responsibility." They are anxious to insist that a person like Hitler does not escape moral responsibility for his actions even if we can show that his behavior was determined. In that sense they want to say moral responsibility is compatible with determinism; and because in at least one sense of "free" there seems to be a connection between moral responsibility and freedom, it looks like there must be a sense of "free" that is compatible with determinism. These are interesting issues, but they are not what concerns me in this book. My problem can be stated quite independently of all these disputes about determinism and moral responsibility. The question, to repeat, is whether for every human action (including the act of deciding) that has ever been performed or ever will be performed, the antecedent causes sufficient to determine that that action and no other action could have been performed.

So there remains a factual issue: Which is true, determinism or its negation (let's call it "libertarianism")? There are two aspects to this question: psychological and neurobiological. Let us consider each in turn.

III. IS PSYCHOLOGICAL DETERMINISM TRUE?

The question concerning psychological determinism is whether our psychological states are causally sufficient to determine all of our voluntary actions. Are our psychological states, in the forms of beliefs and desires, hopes and fears, as well as our awareness of our obligations and commitments, etc., causally sufficient to determine all of our decisions and actions? Note that I am treating this as a straightforward factual, empirical question. The first thing to notice is that our understanding of these concepts rests on an awareness of a contrast between the cases in which we are genuinely subject to psychological compulsions and those in which we are not. The drug addict, the alcoholic, and other types of compulsives do not have psychological freedom. Given the psychological situation they are in, they cannot help themselves. So the question is, Are all psychological causes like that? Is my deciding to vote for the Republican candidate exactly like the drug addict's compulsively taking heroin as a result of his addiction?

Well, let us make the case as strongly as we can for the determinist's claim. There are many experiments to show that often we are in a situation in which we think we are behaving in a free fashion psychologically, but in fact our behavior is determined. Perhaps the most impressive of these are the hypnosis cases. In a typical hypnosis experiment (and this one was actually performed), the subject was told that after he comes out of the hypnotic trance, when he hears the word "Germany," he will go to the window and open the window. In this experiment, as soon as the subject heard the word "Germany," he invented a perfectly rational-sounding reason for opening the window. He said something like, "It is awfully stuffy in here, we need some fresh air. Do you mind if I open the window?" To him, it seemed that his action was completely free. But we have good reason to think it was determined by causes of which he was unaware. So in this case, the gap has been an illusion. He had the illusion of engaging in free action, but in fact his behavior was completely determined. Our question now is, Does it seem reasonable to suppose that all actions are like that? Well, this is a factual claim, not to be settled by philosophical reflection. But it seems very unlikely that all of our actions are performed on the model of the drug addict or the person emerging from a hypnotic trance. I am not now under hypnosis and indeed I have never been under hypnosis. If I now decide what to have for lunch or where to spend the afternoon, the psychological causes operating on me are quite different from the psychological causes operating on the addict or the posthypnotic subject. I have described these two cases, hypnotism and addiction as if they were the same, but in fact, I think they are importantly different. The man under hypnosis is operating in the gap, but he is not aware of all of his motivations. He has an overriding motivation of which he is totally unconscious. He is in fact engaging in a free action, psychologically speaking, but his overriding motivation is unconscious. Full freedom requires an awareness of one's motivations, which in this case the agent lacks. This is unlike the addict who can be fully aware that he is in the grip of an addiction and nonetheless behave in an addictive fashion.

There are lots of experiments, similar to the hypnosis experiments, in which people experience the gap, but we have independent reasons to believe that they are not free. Many scientists think these experiments lend credence to the hypothesis that all of our actions are psychologically determined.[1] But I think they tend to support the reverse hypothesis. We understand all of these cases, of hypnosis, deception, confabulation, etc., by contrasting them with the standard case in which we do have free voluntary action. The cases in which the gap is an illusion are precisely cases that differ in certain important ways from the standard cases of voluntary actions. So I think they do not by themselves establish psychological determinism. But, to repeat, it is a factual empirical question, not to be settled by philosophical argument alone, whether or not our actions are all psychologically determined. The point I am making now is that the available evidence supports the view that we have psychological freedom. Even the cases where psychological freedom is absent are understood by contrast with the cases where it is present.

IV. IS NEUROBIOLOGICAL DETERMINISM TRUE?

For the purposes of this chapter, I am going to accept the conclusion that psychological freedom is real. The purely psychological causes of our actions are often not causally sufficient to determine the actions. However, that still leaves open the deep question, What about the underlying neurobiology? We might have free will at the psychological level in the sense that the psychology as such was not sufficient to fix our actions. But the underlying neurobiology, which also determines that psychology, might itself be causally sufficient to determine our actions. Throughout this book we have assumed that at any given instant the state of a person's consciousness was entirely causally determined by her neurobiology. Now we are arguing that the conscious states are typically not sufficient to determine decisions and actions. But that still leaves open the question, Is the neurobiology sufficient to determine the decisions and actions? Let us now turn to this, what I regard as the most serious form of the free-will problem.

We are now approaching the crux of the issue, and consequently it is a good idea to review how far we have come. In this and earlier chapters I have established, or at least advanced arguments to establish, the following claims:

1. Psychological libertarianism as I have defined it is probably true. The thesis says that our psychological states, beliefs,

desires, hopes, fears, etc., are not in every case causally sufficient to determine the subsequent action. As far as the psychological level is concerned, free actions do indeed exist,
though of course not all actions are free at the psychological
level. Sometimes, for example in the cases of compulsion,
rage, overpowering desire, etc., the agent is in the grip of psychologically sufficient conditions. But it is a claim of the
present discussion that not every case is like that. This is just
another way of saying that the gap is *psychologically* real, it is
not an illusion.

2. In earlier chapters I claimed that all of our psychological states
   without exception at any given instant are entirely determined
   by the state of the brain at that instant. Thus for example, at the
   present time all of my psychological states, conscious and
   unconscious, are determined by the activities going on in my
   brain. Any change in the psychological state would require a
   change in brain activity. It was this point that enabled us to
   solve the problem of epiphenomenalism. Our conscious states
   are higher-level or system features of the brain, and consequently there are not two separate sets of causes—the psychological and the neurobiological. The psychological is just the
   neurobiological described at a higher level.

But if the psychological freedom, the existence of the gap, is to
make a difference to the world, then it must somehow or other be
manifested in the neurobiology. How could it be? We have already
seen that the neurobiology is at any instant sufficient to fix the total
state of psychology at that instant, by bottom-up causation. So, the
absence of causally sufficient conditions at the psychological level,
the absence of sufficient conditions in psychological causation that,
so to speak, goes from left to right through time, will only make a
real difference if this absence at the psychological level is somehow
mirrored at the neurobiological level. *If freedom is real, then the gap
has to go all the way down to the level of the neurobiology.* But how
could it? There are no gaps in the brain.

V. CONSTRUCTING A TEST CASE

In order to examine this question, we will have to construct an
example where there is a clear factual difference between a free
action and a determined action. What exactly would the world be
like if determinism were true and how exactly does it contrast with

how the world would be if libertarianism were true? Let us now construct an example that will illustrate the difference. We will pick a famous example, even though it is mythological. The son of the King of Troy, Paris, was asked by Zeus to present a golden apple inscribed "to the fairest" to one of three goddesses, Aphrodite, Pallas Athena, and Hera. Contrary to a common misunderstanding represented in many famous paintings, Paris was not choosing which goddess was best looking, but rather which offered him the best bribe. Pallas Athena offered to make him ruler of Europe and Asia. Hera offered to enable him to lead the Trojans to a military victory over the Greeks, and Aphrodite offered him the most beautiful woman in the world. We all know that he chose Aphrodite with consequences that were nothing short of disastrous.

Now let us set up the case. We will suppose that at time t_1 Paris is presented with the choice. We will suppose that the total state of his brain at time t_1 included complete awareness of the choice as well as his reasons for any decision he might make. At time t_2, let us say ten seconds later, Paris decided to give the apple to Aphrodite and his arm moved out to give the apple to her. Let us suppose that there were absolutely no outside stimulus inputs coming into Paris's brain in the ten seconds between t_1 and t_2. We can suppose that he shut his eyes, that he heard nothing, and that no outside stimuli relevant to the decision reached his brain. Now the question about free will can be stated with some precision: if the total state of his brain at t_1 was causally sufficient to determine the total state of his brain at t_2, then at t_1 his decision was completely determined. Why? Because at t_2 he has made his decision and when the acetylcholene hits the axon end plates of his motor neurons, his arm begins to move toward Aphrodite by causal necessity. If the total state of the brain at t_1 is sufficient to fix the total state of the brain at t_2, in this case, and in all relevantly similar cases, then neither Paris nor any of us has free will. If that is how it works, so to speak in the plumbing, then free will is a massive illusion. If, on the other hand, the state of the brain at t1 is not causally sufficient to fix the state at t_2 then, *given certain crucial assumptions about the role of consciousness,* free will is a reality.

Let us explore each possibility in turn.

Hypothesis 1: Determinism and the Mechanical Brain

On the first hypothesis we have to assume that the brain is a machine in the traditional old-fashioned sense of car engines, steam engines, and electric generators. It is a completely deterministic system, and any appearance of indeterminism is an illusion based on our ignorance, so that this hypothesis fits well with what we tend to believe about nature and biology in general. The brain is an organ like any other, and it no more has free will than do the heart or the liver or the left thumb. This also fits in with a current conception in cognitive science, according to which we are supposed to think of the brain as the hardware implementing a digital computer program, and according to which the mind no more manifests free will than the program implemented in the hardware manifests free will. We might give the mind the illusion that it has free will by designing a program that had some randomizing or unpredictable elements, but all the same the whole system would remain deterministic.

Hypothesis 2: Indeterminism and the Quantum Brain

Hypothesis 1 is comforting in this respect—the brain turns out to be a machine like any other. But on Hypothesis 2 it is not at all clear what kind of a mechanism the brain will have to be in order for the system to be nondeterministic in the right way. But what exactly is the right way? We have to suppose that consciousness plays a causal role in determining our decisions and our free actions, but we also have to suppose that that causal role is not deterministic. That is, it is not a matter of sufficient conditions. Now the creation of consciousness at any given instance is a matter of sufficient conditions, so what we are supposing is that the left-right movements of neurobiological processes through time are not themselves causally sufficient. That is, each stage of the neurobiological process is not sufficient by itself to determine the next stage by way of causally sufficient conditions. Suppose that the explanation of each stage by the preceding stages depends on the fact that the whole system is conscious and has the peculiar kind of consciousness that manifests a gap, that is, voluntary consciousness. But what would any such system look like? We are assuming that the brain is, at the most basic level, nondeterministic; that is, that the gap that is real at the top level goes, so to speak, all the way down, down to the level of the neurons and subneuronal processes. Is there anything in nature that suggests even the possibility of such a non deterministic system? The only part of nature that we know for a fact today, at the time I write this, has a nondeterministic component is the quantum mechanical part. However, it is a bit misleading to call that a part because it is the most fundamental level of physics, the most basic level of the physical particles. At the quantum level the state of the system at t_1 is only causally responsible for the state of the system at t_2 in a statistical, nondeterministic manner. Predictions made at the quantum level are statistical because there is a random element.

It has always seemed to me in the past that the introduction of quantum mechanics into the discussion of free will was totally irrelevant, for the following reason: free will is not the same as randomness. Quantum mechanics gives us randomness but not freedom. That argument used to seem convincing to me, but now it seems to me that it commits the fallacy of composition. (The fallacy of composition is the fallacy of arguing from properties of the parts of a system to the whole system.) If we suppose that the creation of consciousness by the brain is a result of processes that are, at some level, quantum phenomena, and we suppose that the process of conscious deliberation inherits the absence of causal sufficiency of the quantum level, it does not thereby follow that it inherits randomness. It may well be that the evolutionary function of consciousness is at least in part to organize the brain in such a way that conscious decision making can proceed in the absence of causally sufficient conditions even though the effect of conscious rationality is precisely such as to avoid random decision making. In a word, the randomness of the microprocesses that cause the conscious phenomena at the macrolevel does not imply that the conscious phenomena are random. To suppose otherwise is to commit the fallacy of composition.

However, to say that free will is at least possible if there is a quantum mechanical explanation of consciousness is not to say that this is actually how it works or even that this is how it could work. It is only to say that, as far as we know, the only established nondeterministic element in nature is the quantum level, and if we are to suppose that consciousness is nondeterministic, that the gap is not only psychologically real but neurobiologically real, then, given the present state of physics and neurobiology, we have to suppose that there is a quantum mechanical component in the explanation of consciousness. I see no way to avoid this conclusion.

Of course, Hypothesis 2, the hypothesis that the random indeterminacy at the quantum level leads to an indeterminacy of a nonrandom kind at the conscious intentionalistic level, seems very unlikely and implausible. If we are given a choice between Hypothesis 1 and Hypothesis 2, but also given all that we know about nature, Hypothesis 1 seems much more plausible.

So let us now turn to explore the pros and cons of these two hypotheses. Hypothesis 1 seems much the more plausible and indeed it fits in with the way that the brain is described in standard textbooks of neurobiology. The brain is an organ like any other. It is composed of cells, and the processes by which the cells relate to each other is as deterministic as any other cellular process, even though, of course, the brain has a peculiar type of cell, the neuron, and inside the brain there are peculiar relations between the neurons. The neurons communicate by a remarkable process called the action potential that occurs at synapses. Is there anything to be said against Hypothesis 1? The only argument that I can think of against Hypothesis 1 is not that it runs counter to our experiences of freedom (after all, we have all kinds of illusory experiences), but rather, that it makes it seem an evolutionary fluke, a kind of meaningless evolutionary phenotype, that we should have the experience of the gap. The existence of the gap is not a minor phenotypical trait, like the existence of the appendix. That we should have these massive experiences of freedom if there is no biological cash value to the experience would seem an absurd result from an evolutionary point of view. The gap involves a major biological investment by such organisms as humans and higher animals. An enormous amount of the biological economy of the organism is devoted to conscious rational decision making. In the case of humans there is a huge diachronic as well as synchronic aspect of this. Across time we spend an enormous amount of time, effort, money, etc., in preparing ourselves and in training our young so that they can make better decisions rather than worse decisions. But if every detail of our supposedly free decisions and actions was already written in the book of history at the time of the Big Bang, if everything we do is entirely determined by causal forces operating on us, if the whole experience of free rational decision making is an illusion, then why is it such a pervasive part of our biological life history? And why is it so unlike anything else we know in evolution? This it seems to me is the only solid argument that I can think of against Hypothesis 1. It runs counter to what we know about evolution.

It is rather easy to mount arguments against Hypothesis 2. In fact, Hypothesis 2 looks so strange on its face that it immediately has an air of implausibility. It denies that the brain is an organ like any other and it assigns a special role to free, conscious decision making. Now we have seen that there is nothing dualistic about the fact that consciousness can play a causal role in the determination of our behavior. We are forced to neither dualism nor epiphenomenalism, but all the same, even though we avoid those two mistakes, it still leaves us with a very strange account of consciousness. I said in the introduction to this book that I would emphasize areas of human ignorance as well as areas of understanding. This seems to me a massive case of human ignorance. We really do not know how free will exists in the brain, if it exists at all. We do not know why or how evolution has given us the unshakeable conviction of free will. We do not, in short, know how it could possibly work. But we also know that the conviction of our own freedom is inescapable. We cannot act except under the presupposition of freedom.

VI. CONCLUSION

The problem of free will is going to be with us for a long time. The various efforts to evade it, such as compatibilism, merely enable it to resurface in another form. Even after we have resolved the most fundamental questions addressed in this book, questions such as, What is the nature of the mind? How does it relate to the rest of the physical world? How can there be such a thing as mental causation? and How can our minds have intentionality? there is still the question of whether or not we really do have freedom.

Suggestions for Further Reading

A collection of articles on free will is contained in Watson, G., ed., *Free Will*, 2nd ed., Oxford: Oxford University Press, 2003.

Some recent books are:

Kane, R., *The Significance of Free Will*, Oxford: Oxford University Press, 1996.
Slimansky, S., *Free Will and Illusion*, Oxford: Oxford University Press, 2002.
Wolf, S., *Freedom within Reason*, Oxford: Oxford University Press, 1994.
Wegner, D. N., *The Illusion of Conscious Will*, Cambridge, MA: MIT Press, 2003.
Searle, J. R., *Rationality in Action*, Cambridge, MA: MIT Press, 2001.

CHAPTER 9

The Unconscious and the Explanation of Behavior

One of my main aims in this book is to explain how mental phenomena—consciousness, intentionality, mental causation, and all of the other features of our mental life—fit into the rest of the universe. How, for example, does consciousness exist in a universe that consists entirely of physical particles in fields of force? How can mental states function causally in such a universe? So far, most of our investigation has been about conscious mental phenomena. In this chapter we will begin a serious exploration of the nature and mode of existence of *unconscious* mental states.

I. FOUR TYPES OF THE UNCONSCIOUS

Let us begin by asking, naïvely, Do unconscious mental states really exist? How can there be a state that is literally mental and at the same time totally unconscious? Such states would lack qualitativeness and subjectivity and would not be part of the unified field of consciousness. So in what sense, if any, would they be *mental* states? And if such things do exist, how can they function causally as mental states while they are unconscious? We have become so used to talking about the unconscious, so comfortable with the idea that there are unconscious mental states in addition to conscious mental states, that we have forgotten just how puzzling the notion of the unconscious really is. For Descartes, the answer to the question, Do unconscious mental states exist? is obvious. The idea of an unconscious mental state is a self contradiction. Mind is defined for Descartes as *res cogitans* (thinking being) and "thinking" for Descartes is just another name for consciousness. So the idea of an unconscious mental state would be the idea of an unconscious consciousness, a plain self-contradiction. For a long time the Cartesian idea that there is a necessary connection between the mental and consciousness was extremely influential. It is only in the past century or so that the idea and importance of unconscious mental states has come to be generally accepted. Freud is usually given most of the credit for this acceptance, but his ideas were certainly anticipated by Nietzsche and by several literary figures, of whom Dostoyevsky is probably the most important.

So what exactly is an unconscious mental state, such as an unconscious belief or desire? I think many people, including some extremely sophisticated authors such as Freud, have the following rather simplistic picture. An unconscious mental state is exactly like a conscious mental state only minus the consciousness. The problem with this picture is that it is very hard to make any sense of it. To see this try it out: think to yourself consciously, "George Washington was the first president of the United States." Now do exactly the same thing, only unconsciously. Subtract the consciousness. I have no idea what it would be like to do that, or what the instruction is supposed to mean. Yet the notion of the unconscious seems to be one we cannot do without, so we had better try to explain it.

My strategy in this chapter, as in earlier chapters, will be to begin with simple and unproblematic cases and then build the more difficult and puzzling cases on top of them. Let us start with some unproblematic cases of attributions of mental states to people where the attribution is not of a state that is conscious then and there. To take an obvious sort of case, it can be truly said of me, even when I am sound asleep, that I believe that George Washington was the first president of the United States. Now what fact corresponds to this claim? What fact about me makes it true that I have this belief even when I am not conscious? Notice furthermore that we can even say of a person who is wide awake, and who happens to be thinking about something else entirely, that he believes that George Washington was the first president of the United States. So again, what fact corresponds to these claims? Notice that neither of these is a puzzling or controversial attribution of unconsciousness. Descartes himself could have agreed to the truth of either of these claims. In both cases the fact that corresponds to the claims is that there is in him a structure that is capable of producing the state in a conscious form. If when the man is awake you ask him, for example, who was the first president, he is capable of giving the correct answer because he is capable of producing the conscious thought in question. Notice that in this case, we have identified a structure not in virtue of its intrinsic structural features but in virtue of what it is capable of causing. This sort of attribution is very common in all sorts of real-life unproblematic cases. We say of a substance in a bottle that it is a cleanser or bleach or poison without identifying the chemical structure any further. We just identify it by what it does, not by what structure enables it to do it; and I am suggesting that when we say the man has the unconscious belief that George Washington was the first president of the United States we are identifying a structure in him, not in virtue of its intrinsic neurobiological features, but in virtue of what it does, in virtue of the conscious state that it is capable of causing.

In these cases we have identified one type of unconscious mental state, an unproblematic type that Freud described as "preconscious."

A second type of unconscious mental state is more problematic. It often happens that an agent has mental states that function causally in her behavior, where she is totally unaware of the functioning of the mental state and may even sincerely deny it. Some of these cases are of the sort that Freud described as repression. But more generally, we can characterize these, again using the Freudian vocabulary, as the dynamic unconscious. These are cases where the unconscious mental state functions causally, even when unconscious. A Freudian style example is the case of Dora, who develops a cough because of her unconscious sexual desire for Herr K.[1] Freudian examples are often problematic and much of his clinical work, I think, was scientifically inadequate. But let us take some cases where there really is little doubt about the scientific accuracy of the description. We considered in chapter 8 an example of hypnosis where the agent clearly acts out of a motive of which he is unaware and would presumably deny if he were challenged. In the hypnosis case the man has the desire to obey the order, "Open the window when you hear the word 'Germany'" even though he is unaware that he has been given any such order and is unaware of any desire to carry out the order. These second types of cases we will call, following Freud, cases of repressed unconscious mental states.

A third type of unconscious mental state is also very commonly discussed in the cognitive science literature. These are the cases where the agent not only cannot bring the mental state to consciousness in fact, but could not bring it to consciousness even in principle, because it is not the sort of thing that can form the content of a conscious intentional state. So, for example, in cognitive science it is commonly said that a child learns a language by "unconsciously" applying many computational rules of universal grammar, or that the child is able to perceive visually by performing "unconscious" computational operations over the input that comes into the child's retina. In both of these kinds of cases, both in the acquisition of language and the forming of perceptions, the computational rules are not the kinds of things that could ever be consciously thought. Ultimately they reduce entirely to massive sequences of zeros and ones, and whatever the child can do when he or she thinks, he or she cannot think in zeros and ones, and indeed the zeros and ones are just a manner of speaking. The zeros and ones exist in the mind of the observer and form a manner of description of what is going on unconsciously in the child's mind. Let us call these cases, where the agent operates with rules that are not only unconscious in fact, but not even the sort of thing that could be conscious, the "deep unconscious."

In addition to these three types, there is a fourth form of neurobiological phenomenon that is not conscious. There are all sorts of things going on in the brain, many of which function crucially in controlling our mental lives but that are not cases of mental phenomena at all. So, for example, the secretion of serotonin at the synaptic cleft is simply not a mental phenomenon. Seretonin is important for several kinds of mental phenomena, and indeed some important drugs, such as Prozac, are used specifically to influence serotonin, but there is no mental reality to the behavior of serotonin as such. Let us call these sorts of cases the "nonconscious." There are other examples of the nonconscious that are more problematic. So, for example, when I am totally unconscious, the medulla will still control my breathing. This is why I do not die when I am unconscious or in a sound sleep. But there is no mental reality to the events in the medulla that keep me breathing even when unconscious. I am not unconsciously following the rule "Keep breathing"; rather, the medulla is just functioning in a nonmental fashion, in the same way that the stomach functions in a nonmental fashion when I am digesting food.

To summarize then, we have identified four types of unconscious phenomena: the preconscious, the repressed unconscious, the deep unconscious, and the nonconscious. The first and the fourth seem to me to be unproblematic. What about the second and the third? In the sections that follow, I will argue that the way to understand the repressed cases is on the model of the first, the preconscious; and the way to understand the third, the deep unconscious cases, is on the model of the fourth, the nonconscious cases.

II. THE CONNECTION PRINCIPLE

I turn now to the cases of repression. Our question is this, How can a repressed mental state exist and function as a mental state when it is completely unconscious? Well, we already saw the answer to that in the case of the preconscious. To ascribe a mental state to a person at a time when the state is unconscious is just to ascribe to that person a structure, the details of which may be completely unknown, that is capable of producing that state in a conscious form. There is really no difficulty in saying of someone who is asleep that he believes that George Washington was the first president and there is no difficulty in attributing all sorts of beliefs to a conscious person even though he is not thinking about those beliefs at the time of the attribution. Now this method, it seems to me, works just as well for the second class of cases, the repression cases. If I say that Sam acts out of a repressed hostility to his brother or that Wolfgang acts out of an unconscious desire to fulfill the command he was given during the hypnosis, in both cases I am attributing a neurobiological structure capable of causing a mental state in a conscious form.

But now that leaves us with what seems to be the most difficult problem. How can these unconscious states, when unconscious, succeed in causing actual human behavior? How do we account for the "dynamic unconscious"? It seems to me that when we attribute these unconscious mental states to an agent, we are attributing neurobiological features capable of causing consciousness. Not only are they capable of causing conscious states, but they are capable of causing conscious, or indeed unconscious, behavior. But the question is how can the state function causally as a mental state at a time when it is nothing but an unconscious neurobiological structure? The way to answer that question, as we have done with earlier difficult questions, is to work up to it by taking the simple and more obvious cases first.

I once had a fractured wrist. This injury caused me a fair amount of pain during the day and the pain increased if I was not careful about the movements I made with my arm. I noticed an interesting thing in sleep. I would be totally sound asleep, so that I felt no pain whatever, and yet, my body would move during the night in such a way as to protect the injury. How should we describe such a case? Should we say that during sleep I had an unconscious pain and my unconscious pain caused me to behave in such a way as to avoid aggravating the pain? Or should we say, on the other hand, that while I was sound asleep I had no pain whatever, but rather the underlying neurobiology that was capable of causing the pain in a conscious form acted on me causally in such a way as to prevent any pain stimulation? It seems to me that the facts are the same in both cases. We do not normally talk about unconscious pains; but we easily could, and cases like this would give us the motivation for talking about unconscious pains. Notice in this case the neurobiology is capable of causing the pain in a conscious form, even though when I am sound asleep I do not consciously feel any pain. But, and this is the crucial point for this part of the discussion, the neurobiology that is capable of causing the pain in a conscious form is also capable of causing behavior appropriate to avoiding the pain even at a time when I do not feel the pain. Now that seems to me exactly right for describing the cases of the dynamic repressed unconscious. The agent is not conscious of any motivation when the dynamic unconscious is active. Nonetheless, there is a neurobiological structure that is capable both of causing the motivation to occur as part of his conscious thoughts and capable of causing behavior appropriate to having that motivation. The only disanalogy between this case and the pain case is that the agent may have extra reasons for not wanting to admit the motivation to himself. But—and this is the answer that I am proposing to the question—the mode of existence, the ontology, of the unconscious motivation, when unconscious, is that of a neurobiological structure capable of causing the motivation in a conscious form and capable of causing behavior that is appropriate to having that motivation. This, incidentally, is why the Freudians were so anxious to bring the unconscious to consciousness. As long as it remains unconscious, it is not in our control. We cannot reflect on it, or appraise it, or evaluate it, or subject it to rationality, in a way we normally can with motivations that exist as part of our conscious rational thought processes in the gap.

So far, then, in this chapter I have suggested that there are completely unproblematic cases of the unconscious, the cases we called the preconscious. These are the cases that even someone like Descartes could accept. But I have also, more controversially, maintained that these provide the appropriate model for considering the repressed cases, the cases where the "dynamic unconscious" is in operation. I am suggesting that the same sort of neurobiological processes that can cause a conscious state can also cause behavior appropriate to having that conscious state. So we have assimilated the first two types of cases of unconsciousness to what we already know about the brain and how it works, as well as what we know about our conscious mental life. No metaphysical mystery remains about the notion of the unconscious, at least for these sorts of cases.

But now let us turn to our third class of cases, the deep unconscious, and here the thesis I want to maintain can be stated quite simply. There are no such cases. There is no such thing as a deep unconscious mental state. There are *non*conscious neurobiological processes that we can describe *as if* they were intentional, and there are neurobiological processes capable of producing states in the conscious form; but to the extent that the mental state is not even the kind of thing that could become the content of a conscious state, it is not a genuine mental state. We have been discussing these cases as if the neurobiology were intentional, as if it were mental, as if it were following rules; but that is not the case. The thesis I am putting forward is that we understand an unconscious mental state only as a state that, though not conscious then and there, is capable of becoming conscious; and when we attribute such a state to an agent, we are describing a brain mechanism, not in terms of its neural biological properties, but in terms of its capacity to cause conscious states and behavior. I call this view the "Connection Principle," because it claims that our notion of the unconscious is logically connected to the notion of consciousness. An unconscious mental state must be the kind of thing that could be a conscious mental state.[2]

What is the argument for this apparently startling conclusion? We saw in our explanation of intentionality (chapter 6) that all intentional phenomena have *aspectual shapes*. But in the case of the deep unconscious there is no aspectual shape. There is no form of the intentional states that determines one intentional content rather than another. The argument that I am making here is that we should assimilate the third type of unconscious, the deep unconscious, to the fourth kind, the nonconscious, because the deep unconscious cases do not have the essential feature of intentionalistic phenomena, the aspectual shape of the intentional state that enables it to function in mental causation and therefore to justify the mentalistic forms of causal explanations. There are no deep unconscious mental states. There are, rather, neurobiological features that behave as if they had intentionality.

What is wrong with just saying of the processes in the brain that they are unconscious intentional states occurring right then and there as unconscious intentional states? Why do we have to go through this elaborate dispositional analysis where we say that the attribution of unconscious intentionality is like describing something as poison or bleach? The answer is that the neurobiology as such has no aspectual shape. We can see this if we consider examples. Imagine a man who wants to drink water. Now he may have a desire for water but not a desire for H_2O, simply because he does not know that water is H_2O. But the external behavior will be exactly the same in the two cases: the case of desiring water and the case of desiring H_2O. In each case he will seek to drink the same sort of stuff. But the two desires are different. How is this difference to be captured at the level of the neurophysiology? The neurophysiology, described in terms of synaptic strength and action potentials, knows nothing of aspectual shape. Yet we do want to be able to say that the man who has an unconscious desire for water is in a different intentional state from the man who has an unconscious desire for H_2O, even though the manifestation of this desire in the form of behavior would be exactly the same in the two cases. The answer that I am proposing, and indeed the only answer that I can think of that would make any sense at all, is that we are describing the neurobiological structure in terms of its capacity to cause conscious thoughts and conscious behavior. For the person who does not know that water is H_2O, the neurobiology that corresponds to the desire "I want water" is different from the neurobiology that corresponds to the desire "I want H_2O." But all the same, at the level of the neurobiology, these different aspectual shapes do not exist as aspectual shapes, but, for example, as differences in neuronal structure. So we can give a legitimate sense to the notion of the unconscious, provided we describe it in terms of the causal capacities of the brain to cause consciousness.

But this has an interesting consequence. It means that we have no notion of the unconscious except in terms of the conscious. Something that is not even the sort of thing that could be brought to consciousness cannot be an intentional state because it cannot have aspectual shape. For that reason there are no deep unconscious mental states. There are neurobiological structures capable of causing conscious states and capable of causing behavior appropriate to those mental states, and these cover both the preconscious and

repressed unconscious states, and there are neurobiological structures capable of causing behavior that is *as if* it were intentionally
motivated, but where the sort of motivation could not be a
conscious intentional content and therefore has no psychological
reality.

I have given a dispositional analysis of unconscious mental states.
An unconscious mental state, when unconscious, consists in a
capacity of the brain to produce that state in a conscious form and to
produce behavior appropriate to that state. But this result has an
unexpected consequence for our earlier analysis of intentionality. I
made a distinction between the network of intentional states and the
background of capacities that enables these states to function. But
what are the elements of the network when they are unconscious?
What, for example, is the status of my belief that George Washington was the first president when I am sound asleep? On the dispositional analysis I just gave, it consists of a brain capacity. But then, the
background also consists of such capacities. So it turns out that the
network of intentionality, when unconscious, is a subclass of background capacities; it is the special capacity to produce certain forms
of conscious thoughts and behavior.

III. UNCONSCIOUS REASONS FOR ACTION

The topic of the unconscious differs from most of the other topics
we have discussed in this book in that it is not immediately experienced but rather is something we have found it necessary to postulate for some other purpose. Why is it so important to us? Why
does it matter to us that we give an account of the unconscious,
when the unconscious is by definition not even experienced?

The answer is that the unconscious has come to figure hugely in
our explanation of human behavior. It is because we want to
explain our behavior that we postulate the unconscious at all. I
have heard philosophers claim that the reason we say that people
have beliefs and desires is so that we can explain their behavior.
Frankly, I think that is about as unintelligent as saying the reason
we say that people have feet is so that we can explain their walking
behavior. No, the reason we say they have feet is because they
have feet, and the reason we say they have beliefs and desires is
because they have beliefs and desires. But the postulation of the
unconscious really is part of an explanatory need. The reason we
say that people have unconscious motivations is that we have

found no other way to explain some forms of their behavior. The postulation of unconscious mental states, unlike the "postulation" of feet, or beliefs and desires, really *is* done for an extraneous purpose: the explanation of human behavior. That is why we had a special problem about the ontology of the unconscious and that is why it is worth going through the effort to get an account of the unconscious that is consistent with our overall conception of the physical world and the role of the mental in that world.

But if we require the notion of unconscious mental states in order to explain human behavior, then we need a prior conception of human behavior and its explanation before we can know how to apply the concept of the unconscious. I have, in a preliminary fashion at least, given an account of the structure of human action in chapter 6, Intentionality. That chapter has certain implications for the explanation of human actions, and I now want to spell some of those out.

The key notion for the explanation of a human action is the notion of a reason. We saw in our discussion of mental causation that the content of the explanation has to match the content in the mind of the agent whose behavior is being explained. This is a point of stunning importance for such disciplines as history and the social sciences. It is disguised from us by the enormous complexity of actual explanations. So we say, for example, that the rise in American interest rates caused a rise in the value of the dollar. And on the surface that looks very simple, like saying that the rise in temperature caused a rise in pressure. But in fact the explanation in terms of interest rates is immensely complicated. To spell it all out, we would have to explain how the perception of higher interest rates in the United States led investors to desire to invest in American securities so that they could make a higher level of profit because of the higher interest rates and how that desire in turn led to a desire to buy more dollars with which to make these investments. So when I say that the intentional content in the explanation has to match the intentional content in the minds of the agents whose behavior is being explained, I do not mean there is any simple one to one matching in the actual surface of the explanation.

What then is a reason for an action? That looks like a very simple question but the answer to it is immensely complicated, and to spell it out in detail would take us beyond the scope of this book. I have in fact written a book about it (*Rationality in Action*, MIT Press, 2000), so you can look up the details. Let me just say the following: if you ask yourself how you explain your own behavior, for example, why did you vote for the candidate you did in fact vote for in the last election, you will find that your answers fall into two categories. Either you will give some sort of motivation, for example, "I wanted lower taxes," or you will give some fact that you believed is related to the motivation, for example, "I believed the Republicans would lower taxes." Taken together, this complex forms what I call a "total reason." Reasons are always propositional in form and something is a reason only if it is part of a total reason. The key point for the discussion of the unconscious is this. There are some forms of human behavior that make sense only if we postulate a reason for action of which the agent himself is unconscious.

A special subcategory of reasons for action are rules governing human behavior, and a special form of intentional causation occurs in rule-governed behavior. The agent does what he does at least in part because he is following a rule. But what does it mean to follow a rule?

IV. UNCONSCIOUS RULE FOLLOWING

The explanatory power of the postulation of unconscious mental processes largely depends on the assumption that these processes are cases of unconscious *rule following*. The idea is that our intelligent behavior is explained by a lot of unconscious mental processes that consist in our following rules of which we are not aware and could not become aware. But if we are going to understand the notion of unconscious rule following then we have to understand the notion of rule following in the first place; and that would seem to require that we understand conscious rule following. What is it exactly that one does when one performs an action by way of following a rule? The answer to that question is by no means obvious. In order to explore it, we will have to specify some of the features of rule following. The first distinction we need to make, and it is crucial for everything that follows, is that between *rule-governed* behavior and *rule-described* behavior. Rule-governed, or rule-guided, behavior is such that the agent who is following the rule is causally influenced in his behavior by the rule. The rule functions causally in producing the very behavior that constitutes following it. So, for example, if I follow the rule "Drive on the right-hand side of the road" then the content of that rule must function causally in producing my behavior. This is not to say that the behavior is entirely determined by the rule. No one goes out driving just for the sake of following that rule, but all the same the content of the rule must function causally or it is not the case that one is following the rule. In this respect rule-following behavior differs from rule-described behavior. So, the ball rolling down the inclined plane can be described by the rules of Newtonian mechanics, but it does not follow that the ball is in any sense following those rules. The behavior of the ball rolling down the inclined plane is rule described but is not rule following.

What, then, are some of the features of rule-following behavior? Let us list them.

1. As we just stated, the content of the rule must function causally in producing the behavior.

2. Because of feature 1, rules have the logical properties that are common to volitional intentional states and directive speech acts. This is why the analogy is often made between following a rule and obeying an order. Specifically, the conditions of satisfaction of the rule have the world-to-rule direction of fit. The behavior must change so as to match the content of the rule. The rule also has the causal self-referentiality that we saw earlier was characteristic of prior intentions and intentions-in-action. The rule is followed only if the rule itself causes the behavior that constitutes following it.

3. It follows from 1 and 2 that every rule must have an intentional content that determines a certain aspectual shape. So you might have extensionally equivalent rules that were not at all equivalent in the conditions under which they are followed. The rule, for example, "Drive on the right-hand side of the road" in my car would give the same result as "Drive in such a way that the steering wheel is near the center line of the road, and the passenger seat is near the curb." Given the structure of American cars this rule will produce exactly the same result as the initial rule, but the two rules, though extensionally equivalent, are not the same rule because they have different aspectual shapes.

4. Rule following is typically voluntary. In order that the rule should be able to guide behavior it has to be the kind of thing that the agent can follow voluntarily. The gap, in short, is present in rule-governed behavior. This is why, for example, the "rules" according to which I digest carbohydrates are not cases of rule following, but cases of rule-described behavior. This is because it is not up to me. In short, it is a feature of rule following that the rule can either be followed or broken. But where the rule cannot be broken, it cannot be followed either.

5. Rules, like any other intentional contents, are always subject to different interpretations. It is always possible to offer another interpretation of the rule. So, for example, most rules of human behavior are what are sometimes called "other-things-being-equal" or *ceteris paribus* rules. And this is because the rule is subject to interpretations. So, for example, I do indeed follow the rule "Drive on the right-hand side of the road," but when I follow this rule I do not simply stop when confronted with an obstruction blocking the right hand side of the road; I swerve around it onto the left side of the road. I *interpret* the rule in such a way as to allow me to do things that are not specified in the content of the rule.

This feature of rule following, that it is always subject to different interpretations, has led to a certain form of skepticism. On one interpretation of Wittgenstein's famous private-language argument, Wittgenstein is arguing that any behavior at all can be made consistent with a rule so long as we allow ourselves liberty of interpreting the rule.[3] And his answer to that, according to some interpretations, is to say that our following of the rule is a social practice and that society makes it possible to achieve agreement about what constitutes following the rule. For this reason, Wittgenstein is supposed to have shown that a "private language" would be impossible because there would be no public check on the interpretations of the rule.

6. Human conscious rule following goes on in real time. When I follow the rule, "Drive on the right-hand side of the road," the rule functions causally in my real psychological time to determine conditions of satisfaction. As far as this ordinary sense of rule following is concerned, it is impossible that there should be, for example, thousands of computational rules that I follow more or less instantaneously in a way that a commercial digital computer does. Rule following takes a certain amount of time and it goes on in real time.

These are the paradigmatic features of conscious rule following. But when we postulate unconscious rule following (and such postulations are all too common), how many of these features can we keep? If we are talking literally about rule following, these are the features we need to preserve. If talk about unconscious rule following is to be taken literally, then such rule following has to have these features: the rule functions causally with the world-to-rule direction of fit and at the rule-to-world direction of causation. The rules have to have an aspectual shape, be followed voluntarily, be followed in a way that is subject to different interpretations; and they have to be followed in real time. Some postulations of unconscious rule following, such as rule following in the performance of speech acts, meet these conditions. But many postulations of unconscious rule following, as in the cognitive science accounts of visual perception and language acquisition, do not meet these conditions.

V. CONCLUSION

The conclusion of this chapter is somewhat depressing. The notion of the unconscious is one of the most confused and ill-thought-out conceptions of modern intellectual life. Yet it seems we cannot get on without it. What we need to do, then, is to try to develop a coherent notion of the unconscious, which we can fit into what we know about the rest of reality, including what we know about how the brain works. The result is the Connection Principle. Most of the people who work in these fields object to my account of the Connection Principle, but I have not seen them present any alternative coherent conception of the unconscious. The upshot is that we can continue to use the notion of the unconscious legitimately, but we have to recognize that we are using it as a dispositional notion. To say of an agent that he has such-and-such an unconscious intentional state, and that that state is functioning actively in causing his behavior, is to say that he has a brain state that is capable of causing that state in a conscious form, even though in a particular instance it may be incapable of causing it in a conscious form because of brain damage, repression, etc. I am not entirely satisfied with this conclusion, but I cannot think of an alternative conclusion that is superior to it.

Suggestions for Further Reading

Freud, S., 1912, "A Note on The Unconscious in Psychoanalysis," in *Collected Papers*, vol. 4, J. Riviere, trans., New York: Basic Books, 1959, 22–29.
Freud, S., 1915, "The Unconscious," in *Collected Papers*, vol. 4, J. Riviere, trans., New York: Basic Books, 1959, 98–136.
Searle, J. R., *The Rediscovery of the Mind*, Cambridge, MA: MIT Press, 1992, chap. 7.
Searle, J. R., *Rationality in Action*, Cambridge, MA: MIT Press, 2001.

CHAPTER 10

Perception

One of the chief functions of the mind, both in our day-to-day living and over the long evolutionary haul, is to relate us to the rest of the world, especially by way of perception and action. To put the point in the simplest possible terms, by perception we take in information about the world, we then coordinate this information both consciously and unconsciously, and make decisions or otherwise form intentions, which result in actions by way of which we cope with the world. In this chapter we will consider the relations between perception and the world that exists apart from our perceptions, what philosophers like to call, misleadingly, the "external world."

Why is there supposed to be a problem? If I extend my arm forward, I see my hand in front of my face. What could be easier than that? There is a tripartite distinction between me, the hand, and the actual conscious experience of perceiving by way of which I perceive the hand. There is, of course, a complex neurobiological story to be told about how the reflection of light off of the hand attacks the visual system and sets up a series of neuronal processes that eventually result in the conscious experience of seeing the hand. Furthermore, there are some philosophical niceties, as we saw in our discussion of intentionality, about the form of the causal self-referentiality involved in the conditions of satisfaction of the visual experience. But so far it does not seem very difficult. However, I have to tell you that there are few problems in the history of philosophy that have given more trouble than the problem of perception.

I. ARGUMENTS FOR THE SENSE-DATUM THEORY

The view of perception that I have just adumbrated is a form of perceptual realism and is sometimes called "direct realism" and sometimes even "naïve realism." Most of the great philosophers in the history of the subject are convinced that it is false. They believe (and by "they" I mean such great philosophers as Descartes, Locke, Berkeley, Hume, and Kant) that we do not see the real world. We do not see independently existing objects and states of affairs in the world. All that we ever actually perceive directly—that is, perceive without the mediation of any inferential processes—are our own inner experiences. In the past century philosophers usually put this point by saying "We do not perceive material objects, we perceive only sense data." Some of the earlier terminology used for sense data were "ideas" (Locke), "impressions" (Hume), and "representations" (Kant). But if asked, "What is the direct object of a perceptual verb, taken literally, strictly, and philosophically?" the tradition has almost always been to say that the direct objects of perceptual verbs are not expressions naming independently existing material objects but expressions naming our own inner experiences, our sense data.

What are the arguments for this apparently counterintuitive view? There are two famous families of arguments, the argument from science and the argument from illusion. I will consider each in turn.

The Argument from Science

The scientific account of perception shows how the peripheral nerve endings are stimulated by objects in the world, and how the stimulation of the nerve endings eventually sends signals into the central nervous system and finally to the brain, and how in the brain the whole set of neurobiological processes causes a perceptual experience. But the only actual object of our awareness is that experience in the brain. There is no way we could ever have direct access to the external world. All we can ever have direct access to is the effect that the external world has on our nervous system.

This argument seems to presuppose that we were talking about the actual perception of the real world when we described how objects in the world cause the stimulation of our nerve endings; but in fact the argument concludes that such a perception is impossible. Bertrand Russell once ironically stated this apparent paradox by saying: "Naïve realism leads to physics, and physics, if true, shows that naïve realism is false. Therefore naïve realism, if true, is false; therefore it is false."[1]

The point that I take it Russell is making is that naïve realism seems somehow self-defeating. If you try to take seriously the idea that we are in direct perceptual contact with the external world, and do science on that basis, science will give you the result that we cannot be in direct perceptual contact with the external world.

I think the argument most likely to convince most people in the history of this subject is the argument from science. But in the history of philosophy the argument that has been more influential among philosophers is called the argument from illusion.

The Argument from Illusion[2]

If we try to take naïve realism seriously it seems to lead to some sort of inconsistency and self-contradiction. Here is how. Suppose I now hold a knife in my hand and I see the knife. But Macbeth, in a much more dramatic situation, also had the experience of seeing a knife, specifically a dagger. However, Macbeth was having a hallucination. He did not see a real dagger, but only a hallucinatory dagger. So in Macbeth's case we cannot say that he saw a material object. But he definitely saw something. We might say he saw the "appearance of a dagger" or a "hallucinatory dagger." But now, and this is a crucial step, if we are going to say in Macbeth's case that he only saw the appearance of a dagger, then we should say it in every case, because there is no qualitative difference between the character of the experience in the veridical cases and in the hallucinatory cases. That is why Macbeth was deceived: there was no difference between the experience he had and the experience of actually seeing a dagger. But if we say that in every case we only see an appearance and not the object itself, we should surely get a name for these appearances. Let us call them "sense data." Conclusion: we never see material objects, but only sense data. And now the question arises, What is the relationship between the sense data we do see and the material objects that apparently we do not see?

This form of argument has been run on a wide variety of different sorts of examples. Here is another one. When I hold a finger up in front of my face and focus my eyes on the wall at the far side of the room, a phenomenon occurs known as double vision. I see my finger double. But now, when I see my finger double, I do not see two fingers. There is only one finger there. But I obviously do see two of something. What do I see two of? Well let us call these somethings that I see, the appearances of a finger—and I do indeed see two appearances of a finger. But now—and again this is a crucial step—there is no qualitative difference between seeing the appearances of a finger and seeing the real finger. I can prove this to myself by refocusing my eyes so that the two appearances coalesce into a single appearance. Where I was previously seeing two appearances I am now seeing only one appearance. So if we are going to say in the double vision case that I only see appearances and not material objects, we should say it in every case. Let us get a name for these appearances; let us call them "sense data."

Here is a third argument. If I put a straight stick in a glass of water, because of the refractive properties of light, the stick looks bent. But now, the stick is not really bent; it just looks bent. Still, when I see the stick I am directly seeing something bent. What is it? I am directly seeing the appearance of a stick and the stick does indeed present a bent appearance. But the stick is not itself bent; the appearance is bent. But then what I directly see is bent, so what I am seeing is the appearance and not the stick. And by now you will recognize what the next step is going to be: if I am going to say in this case that I do not see the stick but only the appearance, I should say it in every case because there is no qualitative difference between the cases. We need a term to describe these appearances. Guess what? We will call them "sense data." Conclusion: I never see material objects but only sense data.

I could keep going all day with these examples, but just a couple of more to give you the full flavor of the style of argument. Suppose I get up from my chair and walk around the table, while keeping my eyes on the table. As I walk around, something is changing; furthermore, something I directly perceive is changing. The table is not changing. The table remains absolutely unchanged throughout my walk. But what does change? Obviously, it is the appearance of the table. The table presents to me a different appearance from different points of view. But now, since what I see is changing and the table is not changing, and what I see is the appearance, it seems that I am seeing only appearances and not the table. Furthermore, since there is no qualitative distinction between this experience and any other, I seem forced to the conclusion that I never see anything but appearances. We need a technical term to name these appearances. We will call them "sense data."

Here is another example, also famous. I take from my pocket a coin and hold it up. As I look at it straight on it looks round. But if I turn it slightly at an angle it no longer looks round; it looks elliptical. But now we know one thing for certain: the coin itself is not elliptical. It has not changed its shape as I turned it on an angle. But we also know that I am directly perceiving something elliptical. There is no question that right here now in my visual field there is something elliptical; I directly see it. But it seems then that what I am seeing is not the coin, for the coin is round. What I am directly seeing, what I am seeing without any inferential process at all, is the elliptical appearance of the coin. And if I am going to say in this case I only see appearances, I should say it in every case for there is no qualitative change when I turn the coin directly upright so that it now presents a round rather than an elliptical appearance. The conclusion is obvious: we should say in every case that I see appearances, not material objects, and these appearances can be called "sense data."

Nearly all of the famous philosophers of the past 350 years, and most of the respectable philosophers until about the middle of the twentieth-century, accepted some sort of sense-datum theory. Hume, indeed, thought that naïve realism was so obviously false that he hardly bothered to refute it. At one point he says that if you are tempted to naïve realism you can refute it by just pushing one eyeball. When you push one eyeball you see everything double and, according to Hume, the naïve realist would have to conclude that the universe simply doubled in the number of objects that it contains. But since it obviously did not double, Hume thinks it follows that we are not seeing material objects.[3]

The argument from illusion has a logical structure that is common to all of these examples. Here is how it goes:

1. Naïve realists assume that, in the typical case at least, we see material objects and that we see them as they really are.
2. But there are lots of cases, as even the naïve realist would admit, where we do not see material objects (for example, in the hallucination cases), or do not see them as they really are (as for example, in the bent stick case and the elliptical coin case).
3. But even in theses cases we do see something and we do see it as it really is. In the cases where there is no material object there at all, as for example in the Macbeth dagger case, Macbeth did see something. There was something directly present in his visual field. And in the cases where there is a material object there but we do not see it as it really is, as in the examples of the

elliptical coin and the bent stick, we do see something elliptical and we do see something bent. Both the elliptical entity and the bent entity are directly present to us in our visual field.

4. In these cases we directly see appearances, etc. (sense data) and not material objects.

5. These cases are not qualitatively different from the standard case, hence if we are going to say in these cases that we see sense data and not material objects we should say the same thing in every case.

II. CONSEQUENCES OF THE SENSE-DATUM THEORY

Direct realism is the view that we, at least typically, directly perceive objects and states of affairs in the world. Direct realism is denied when we say that we never perceive objects and states of affairs but only our own experiences, our own sense data. But once we make that move we have a very serious question: What is the relationship between the sense data that we do perceive and the objects that we apparently do not perceive? There are a number of answers to this question in the history of philosophy but I believe that basically they boil down to two families. One family, the most immediately appealing, is to say we do not perceive objects themselves, but we do perceive *representations* of objects. The sense datum that we do perceive is a kind of a picture of the object, and so we can find out about the object by inferring the presence and features of the object from the characteristics of the sense data. The actual object in the real world resembles the sense data at least in certain respects. Some philosophers, perhaps most importantly Locke, made a distinction between those features of the sense data that have corresponding resembling elements in the real world and those features that do not. The features of the real world that actually resemble sense data were called "primary qualities" and they consisted of shape, size, number, movement, and solidity. (Locke's list is "solidity, extension, figure, motion or rest, and number.")[4] But there are other sense data for which there is no corresponding resembling feature in the real object. Locke misleadingly called such features of objects "secondary qualities." This is misleading because strictly speaking there are no such qualities of objects. Rather, as Locke points out, the secondary qualities are just the powers that the primary qualities have to cause in us certain experiences. These secondary qualities are color, smell, taste, and sound. Our experiences of both primary and secondary qualities are caused by real features of the object; but the object itself does not have the features corresponding to our experiences of the secondary qualities.

This doctrine is called the representative theory of perception and it was worked out in some detail, especially by Locke. According to the representative theory of perception, we spend our conscious lives as if we were inside a movie theater. We can see pictures of the real world on the screen of the movie theater, but we can never go beyond the inside of the movie theater to see the real world itself, because the movie theater is entirely in our mind. All we ever see are more pictures, more representations. The representative theory was attacked, I think very effectively, by both Berkeley and Hume. There are a number of forms of the attack, but the basic argument, the one to which there does not appear to be an answer, is this: if we say that our sense data resemble objects and thus represent them in the way that a movie of a scene represents the actual scene, then the problem is that we have given no clear meaning to the notion of "resemblance," and consequently no clear meaning to "representation." How can we say that the sense data we do see resemble the object that we do not see if the object is by hypothesis totally invisible? It is as if I said I had two cars in my garage and they both looked exactly alike, but one was totally invisible. It makes no sense at all to say that there is a perceptual resemblance relation between something that has perceptual features and something that has no perceptual features.

When Berkeley saw this point he did not, as one might have hoped, go back to naïve realism and say he must have made a mistake when he moved from the naïve realist theory of perception to the sense-datum theory. Rather, Berkeley says the only things that exist are minds and ideas. The real world consists entirely of sense data. There are no such things as material objects in addition to our actual and possible experiences. Hume, though in a more complex fashion, adopted a similar conclusion. This view has various names but perhaps the most common name for it is phenomenalism. Material objects consist in collections of sense data; there are no material objects over and above, or in addition to mental phenomena.

Phenomenalism was intended as a logical thesis and thus can be most clearly stated as a logical thesis about language. Instead of saying objects consist of sense data, which makes it look as if we are disagreeing with the view that objects consist of molecules, what we should really say is that statements about objects, and indeed empirical statements in general, can be translated without loss of meaning into statements about sense data. The same verificationist impulse that led to behaviorism in the philosophy of mind led to phenomenalism in the philosophy of perception. Just as the only evidence we have for other minds is behavior, so it seems the only evidence we have for material objects is sense data. A truly scientific conception of minds must therefore be behavioristic, and analogously a truly scientific conception of the material world must be phenomenalistic.

III. REFUTATION OF THE SENSE-DATUM THEORY

I believe this whole way of thinking about perception is hopelessly misconceived. As I said earlier I believe it is the most disastrous theory in the history of philosophy over the past four centuries. Why? Because it makes it impossible to give a true account of how human beings and other animals relate to the real world. It leads almost inevitably from Descartes and Locke to Berkeley and Hume, and from there to Kant. And then things get really bad as the tradition leads to Hegel and absolute idealism. The whole thought of attacking it once again depresses me enormously, but I will not have done the job I promised you I would do in this book if I did not to attempt answer it point by point. So here goes.

The arguments for the sense datum-thesis are, without exception, fallacious. Let us consider them in order.

The Argument from Science

Science does not refute naïve realism. To say that because we can give a causal account of how it comes about that we see the real world, it follows that we do not see the real world, is to commit a famous fallacy. It is called the genetic fallacy. It is the fallacy of assuming that a causal account that explains the genesis of a belief, that explains how the belief was acquired, thereby shows the belief to be false.

The genetic fallacy is usually about beliefs, but the form of the fallacy can be generalized. The idea is that if you can show that the causes of a belief or other intentional content are insufficient to prove its truth, then you have somehow refuted the belief or other intentional state.

In my intellectual childhood, the most common forms of the genetic fallacy were in Freudianism and Marxism. You doubt the truth of Marxism? That only shows that you are misled by your bourgeois class background. You doubt the truth of Freud's teachings? That only proves you are a victim of your own repressions. Nowadays, one does not hear the genetic fallacy much except from postmodernists. I used to wonder why the fallacy was so common in postmodernism until I read an account that explains why the postmodernists really have no other form of argument available to them.[5]

Anyway, the form of the genetic fallacy in the theory of perception goes as follows. We can show that when you apparently see your hand in front of your face, what is actually happening is that light reflected from the hand is causing you to have a visual experience, which you take to be a visual experience of your hand. Because we can explain why you think you are seeing a hand, we can show that you did not really see a hand in front of your face but only the visual experience, which was the effect of the neurobiological processes.

So stated, I hope it is obvious that this is a fallacy. The causal account of how I come to see my hand in front of my face does not show that I do not really see my hand in front of my face.

The Argument from Illusion

Replying to the argument from illusion is trickier. I will borrow both the ideas and the techniques of my teacher in philosophy, J. L. Austin in order to refute this argument.[6]

Notice that in every one of the arguments I gave, the linguistic strategy is to get a noun that will be the direct object of verbs of perception but that does not name a material object. So, in the case of Macbeth's dagger, we were told that we did not see a real dagger but only a hallucinatory dagger. But the difficulty with this is that in the sense of "see," I really see a knife in my hand; in the case of the hallucination, I do not see anything. Expressions like "hallucinatory dagger" cannot name a species of dagger. To put it in words of one syllable, when Macbeth had a hallucination, he did not see anything. At least not anything in the dagger line of business. No doubt he saw his hands. So from the fact that Macbeth had a hallucination that was phenomenologically indistinguishable from a real experience it does not follow that he saw a special kind of object or entity that is common to both veridical and illusory experiences.

Similar objections can be made to the double-vision cases. One should never accept the question uncritically. The question was, When I see my finger double what do I see two of? The answer to this is: when you see your finger double you do not see two of anything. You see one finger and you see it double.

In both the double-finger and the bent-stick examples, the notion of appearance is introduced to provide a direct object of the verbs of perception. The idea is that you do not see the object itself but only its appearance. But if you think about this, there is something self-contradictory about the idea that I might see the appearance of an object and not see the object. To see the appearance of an object is just to see the way it looks. And there is no way you can see the way something looks without seeing that something. Consideration of examples will make this completely clear. Suppose I ask you, "Did you see the way Sally looked at the party?" It makes no sense for you to say, "Yes I saw the way she looked but unfortunately I couldn't see her. I could only see her appearance."

Let us apply these considerations to the example of the table. I get up and walk around the table. The appearance of the table changes, because I see it from different points of view, but the table does not change; therefore it seems that I see the appearance and not the table. I hope it is obvious that this is a fallacy. Of course the table looks different from different points of view. But the changes in my visual experiences, which are themselves brought about by the fact that I am changing my position and therefore my point of view, do not show that I fail to see the table, but only something that, so to speak, gets between me and the table, its appearance. On the contrary, the whole discussion presupposes that I am actually seeing the table throughout, for there is no way that the table could continue to present to me different appearances from different points of view if I were not actually seeing the table.

The crucial false step in the argument structure I summarized was step 3: in every case you perceive something and perceive it as it really is. This is not true. In the hallucination cases you perceive nothing and in the other cases—the bent stick, elliptical coin, etc.—you do perceive the object but under conditions that may be more or less misleading. From the fact that the stick looks (sort of) bent it does not follow that you are really seeing a bent entity, the look. No, you are really seeing a stick, an independently existing material object, which under those conditions looks bent.

It is an amazing fact about the history of philosophy that these arguments have had the influence they have had. I do not believe they will bear a moment's scrutiny and I leave it to the reader, as a five-finger exercise, to see how we could apply these lessons to show the fallacy in the argument about the elliptical coin.

IV. A TRANSCENDENTAL ARGUMENT FOR DIRECT REALISM

But, one might say, refuting the arguments against naïve realism is not sufficient to show that naïve realism is true. This is a correct objection. We need some argument to show that on at least some occasions we do actually perceive material objects and states of affairs in the world. What could such an argument possibly be?

The problem we are confronting here is a variation of traditional skepticism. The skeptic's argument is always the same: you could have all the evidence you do have, indeed you could have all possible evidence, and still be mistaken. So prove, for example, that you really are seeing the table in front of you and not just having a hallucination, dreaming, being deceived by an evil demon, etc. There is no way that I can answer the skeptic directly about my present visual experience of the table. The whole point of the skeptic is that I could be having exactly this experience and still be mistaken. And if I could be mistaken in this case, why not in every case?

I do not believe it is philosophically astute to try to answer this argument directly. I do not believe that I can prove to the skeptic that I am now really seeing the table as opposed to having a hallucination, dreaming, etc. What I can do instead, is to show that a certain style of discourse, the one in which the skeptic is currently engaged, presupposes the truth of some version of direct realism. (I like to think of my version as "naïve" but it does not matter whether it is naïve or sophisticated.) The realism in question has to contain the view that we have at least on some occasions perceptual access to publicly observable phenomena. These are commonly thought of as "material objects," but again that designation is not crucial. What is crucial is that different people can at least on some occasions perceive the same publicly observable phenomena— chairs, tables, trees, mountains, clouds, etc. The argument that I am about to present is a "transcendental" argument in one of Kant's many senses of that term. In a transcendental argument in this sense, we assume a certain proposition p to be true and then show that a condition of the possibility of the truth of p is that another proposition q should also be true. In this case we assume that there is an intelligible discourse shared publicly by different speakers / hearers. We assume that people actually communicate with each other in a public language about public objects and states of affairs in the world. We then show that a condition of the possibility of such communication is some form of direct realism. The key to the argument is to see that the sense-datum hypothesis has, without explicitly revealing it, reduced the *publicly* available world of material objects to a *private* world of sense data. Only I can experience my sense data. Only you can experience your sense data. But how, then, can we ever talk about the same object in a public language? How, in short, can we ever succeeded in communicating with each other about public objects? If material objects are reducible to sense data, and the only sense data I have access to are my own sense data, then I could never communicate with you about a public material object.

Here are the steps of the argument:

1. We assume that we successfully communicate with other human beings at least some of the time.
2. The form of the communication in question is of publicly available meanings in a public language. Specifically, when I say such things as, "This table is made of wood," I assume you will understand the words in the same way that I do. Otherwise we are not succeeding in communicating.
3. But in order to succeed in communicating in a public language, we have to assume common, publicly available objects of reference. So, for example, when I use the expression "this table" I have to assume that you understand the expression in the same way that I intend it. I have to assume we are both referring to the same table, and when you understand me in my utterance of "this table" you take it as referring to the same object you refer to in this context in your utterance of "this table."
4. That implies that you and I share a perceptual access to one and the same object. And that is just another way of saying that I have to presuppose that you and I are both seeing or otherwise perceiving the same public object. A public language presupposes a public world. But that public availability of that public world is precisely the direct realism that I am here attempting to defend. The problem with the sense-datum hypothesis, as with phenomenalism in general, is that it ignores the privacy of the sense data. Once you claim that we do not see publicly available objects but only sense data, then it looks like solipsism is going

to follow rather swiftly. If I can only talk meaningfully about objects that are in principle epistemically available to me, and the only epistemically available objects are private sense data, then there is no way that I can succeed in communicating in a public language, because there is no way that I can share the same object of reference with other speakers. That is what I meant when I said that a public language presupposes a public world. But the presupposition of that public world is precisely the naïve realism that I have been defending. We do not prove the truth of naïve realism; rather, we prove the unintelligibility of its denial in a public language.

Suggestions for Further Reading

The classic attack on realist theories of perception is in Berkeley's *Principles of Human Knowledge*, Dancy, J., ed., Oxford: Oxford University Press, 1998. See also, Berkeley, G., *Three Dialogues between Hylas and Philonous*, Turbayne, C., ed., Indianapolis: Bobbs-Merrill Educational Publishing, 1985.

For a modern statement of the sense-datum theories, see Ayer, A. J., *The Foundations of Empirical Knowledge,* London: Macmillan, 1953.

For a criticism of the sense-datum theories, see Austin, J. L., *Sense and Sensibilia*, Warnock, G. J., ed., Oxford: Clarendon Press, 1962.

For an account of the intentionality of perception, see Searle, J. R., *Intentionality: An Essay in the Philosophy of Mind,* Cambridge: Cambridge University Press, 1983, chap. 2.

CHAPTER 11

The Self

In Descartes' famous slogan, "I think therefore I am," what does the "I" refer to? For Descartes it definitely does not refer to my body; rather, it refers to my mind, the mental substance that constitutes the essential me. We have now seen good reason to suppose that Cartesian dualism is not a philosophically acceptable account of the nature of the mind. But for those of us who reject dualism there is still a serious question left over: What exactly is the self? What fact about me makes me me? Many contemporary philosophers, including myself until fairly recently, think that Hume had more or less the last word on this issue. In addition to the sequence of experiences, and the body in which these experiences occur, there is no such thing as the self. Hume says, when I turn my attention inward and try to discover some entity that constitutes the essential me, all I discover are particular experiences; there is no such thing as the self in addition to these experiences.

There are several more-or-less separate questions about the self, and I will now distinguish, for the purposes of this chapter, three different families.

I. THREE PROBLEMS OF THE SELF

1. What Are the Criteria of Personal Identity?

A persistent traditional question in philosophy has been, What fact about a person makes that person the same person through the various changes that he or she undergoes in the course of a lifetime?

In my own case, for example, I have undergone a rather large number of changes over the past decades. My body looks somewhat different, I have learned some new things and forgotten some old ones, my abilities and tastes have changed in various ways, but all the same there is no question that I remain exactly the same person through these changes. I am identical with the person who bore my name and lived in my house decades ago. But what fact about the sequence of events and changes that I have been describing makes it the case that they are all events in the life of one and the same person?

2. What Exactly Is the Subject of Our Attribution of Psychological Properties?

In addition to the sequence of psychological events that constitute perception, action, reflection, and so forth, and the body in which these psychological events occur, do we have to postulate something in addition to the body and its sequence of psychological events?

I have not stated this question very precisely and I will try to make it more precise later. The point for present purposes is to pose a general question, In addition to the sequence of my actual thoughts and feelings and the body in which they occur, do we need to postulate a thing, an entity, an "I" that is the subject of all of these events? Let us suppose that we can all agree, as I have been assuming throughout this book, that I am constituted at least in part by a physical body, and that this body contains a sequence of mental phenomena—conscious states and unconscious brain processes capable of producing conscious states. The question is, Is there anything else we have to postulate? And if so, what is it? As far as I can tell, most contemporary philosophers follow Hume in thinking that we do not have to postulate anything more; but I have been reluctantly forced to the conclusion that we do, and I will explain why in the course of this chapter.

3. What Exactly Makes Me the Person I Am?

This question is often thought of in contemporary life as a matter of the social, psychological, cultural, and biological forces that shape my particular personality and make me the sort of person that I am. There is, in popular speech, a use of the notion of "identity" in such expressions as "identity politics" or "cultural identity," which concerns the sources, both cultural and biological, that shape one's personality. I think that this is a different sense of the notion of personal identity from those expressed in questions 1 and 2. It has more to do with character and personality than it does with the metaphysical problem of the existence and identity of a self across time.

This chapter will be concerned with the family of questions that surround questions 1 and 2 above. We will see that they give us enough difficulty without going into questions of personality.

II. WHY IS THERE A SPECIAL PROBLEM ABOUT PERSONAL IDENTITY?

Questions about identity are as old as philosophy, but there does seem to be a special problem about the identity of persons. Probably the most famous puzzle about identity in the history of the subject is the example of the "Ship of Theseus." A ship made of wood is entirely rebuilt gradually over a period of time. It continues to function, it has a crew that sails it around the Mediterranean, but one by one the boards that constitute it are gradually replaced until finally there is not a single board left from the original construction. Now, is it still the same ship? Well, I think most of us would feel that it is the same ship, that the spatial and temporal continuity of functioning was sufficient to guarantee its identity as a ship, because the notion of a ship is, after all, a functional notion. But now suppose somebody gathers up all the discarded boards and constructs a ship out of them that contains all and only the parts of the ship that was originally launched, so that every single board in the second ship is identical with a board that was in the ship as originally launched. Which is the ship we originally started with? Is it the one that has the continuity of function or is it the one that has the continuity of parts? The mistake in these discussions, as is so often the case in philosophy, is to suppose that there must be some additional fact of the matter about identity beyond all of the facts that I have just told you. It seems to me there isn't any further fact of the matter. It is up to us to say which is the original ship. This might be a matter of some importance, for example, who owns which ship? Who is responsible for the taxes? Which ship has docking rights? But there is no additional factual question left over as to which ship is identical with the original ship beyond all of the facts that I just told you.

Some of the questions about personal identity are like the example of the Ship of Theseus, but in the case of personal identity, we feel there is a special problem that is not present in these traditional examples. We tend to feel that each of us is presented to himself or herself in a special way, and that these first-person experiences are essential to our identity in a way that the third-person phenomena are more or less incidental. We feel, for example, that we all understand what it would mean to say that we might wake up one morning to find ourselves in a different body. Like Gregor Samsa in the story by Franz Kafka, our physical external appearance would have changed totally, yet we feel somehow that we would know, even if no one else could be convinced, that we were the same person who before occupied a different body. To make this example seem more concrete, let us suppose that brain transplants become possible and that my brain is transplanted into the body of Jones and Jones's brain is transplanted into my body. It seems to me there is no question from my point of view that I will now think that I am exactly the same person as before, but my brain (and hence I) now occupy a different body. I might have trouble convincing other people of this, but we feel, at least from the first-person point of view, there would be no question that I would think of myself as the same person as the person who once occupied a different body and who now occupies Jones's body.

A more puzzling case is this: imagine that all of my mental capacities are equally realized on each side of my brain. Now imagine a case of brain bisection where the two halves of my brain are transplanted each into a different body. The original body, we will suppose, is discarded and now there are two halves of my brain in two different bodies. Which of the resulting characters, if I may so describe them, is me? This case seems to me like the Ship of Theseus in that there is no fact of the matter beyond what I have just told you. That is, it seems to me that we have equal reason for saying that I am number one or that I am number two or, I think what we would be more likely to say is that there are now two people where there was previously only one. This case is like fission cases, where one amoeba splits into two. Yet even in this case, from the first-person point of view, one feels there must be a fact of the matter. If I now am one of the offspring of this fission, I am likely to feel, "I am still me, the same unique individual I always was. I don't care what anybody else says." The problem is that my twin will have exactly the same conviction with the same justification and we can't both be right.

It is typical of our concepts that their application to the real world presupposes certain sorts of regularities. This is as much true of the concepts of a ship, or house or tree or car or dog, as it is of such fancy concepts as personal identity. We normally are able to apply the concept of personal identity because the first-person criteria and the third-person criteria tend to come together. They do not come apart in radical ways. But it is easy to imagine science-fiction worlds in which they come apart radically. Suppose that fusion and fission became common, that is, suppose that it was quite common when several people were walking down the street that suddenly they would coalesce into one body. Or, to take the fission case, imagine that a single person might branch out into five identical people as a result of the fission of her original body. If such cases became common, then we would have very serious problems with our notion of personal identity. It seems to me that it would probably no longer apply.

III. THE CRITERIA OF PERSONAL IDENTITY

If we actually look at the criteria that people employ in ordinary speech for deciding which person today is identical with which person in the past we find that there are at least four conditions that constitute our notion of personal identity. Two of these are from the third-person point of view, one is from the first-person point of view, and one is mixed. Let us review them.

1. Spatio-temporal Continuity of Body

My body is continuous in space and time with an infant born seven decades ago. It is this spatio-temporal continuity more than anything else that the public relies on in regarding me as the same person. Notice that the spatio-temporal continuity of my body does not imply the spatio-temporal continuity of the micro parts of which the body is composed. At the molecular level, the parts of my body are constantly being replaced. The molecules that compose my body are now totally different from the molecules with which I began life, but all the same, yes, it is still the same body, in large part because it is spatio-temporally continuous with the original body of the infant.

2. Relative Temporal Continuity of Structure

Though my structure changes over the decades—I grow bigger and I grow older—all the same, I am recognizably a human being. If, like Gregor Samsa, I woke up one morning metamorphosed into the body of a large insect, or if I should suddenly turn into an elephant or a giraffe, it is not at all clear that other people would be willing to say that it is still JRS. So, in addition to the sheer brute continuity of a continuum through space and time, it seems we need also to acknowledge certain sorts of structural regularities in the changes that this spatio-temporal object undergoes.

The reason there is a special problem about personal identity is that these two conditions do not seem to be enough for my first-person point of view. Even if other people refuse to recognize a certain object as me, all the same, I have a confidence that I would know from my insider's first-person point of view who I was, even if I were in the body of an elephant or a giraffe or even if I had shrunk to the size of my thumb, all the same, I feel confident I would be able to identify myself. But what are these criteria supposed to amount to?

The next criterion is a first-person criterion.

3. Memory

From my inner point of view, it seems that there is a continuous sequence of conscious states bound together by my capacity at any given point to remember conscious experiences occurring in the past. To many philosophers, most famously Locke, it has seemed that this is the essential element of personal identity. The reason we need this in addition to bodily identity is that it seems easy to imagine cases where I might wake up in a different body, but from my point of view there is no question that it would still be me. I still have my experiences as part of the sequence. It includes memory experiences of past conscious states. Locke claimed this was the essential feature of personal identity. He called it "consciousness," but the standard interpretation is that he meant memory. Reid and Hume thought they could refute it by pointing out that the memory relations were intransitive. That is, the old general might remember events that occurred when he was a young lieutenant and the young lieutenant might remember events that occurred in his childhood, but the old general might have forgotten the childhood. They were surely right about this, but the fact that one forgets things does not seem to count seriously against the claim that from the first-person point of view, the sequence of my conscious states, bound together by memory, is essential to my sense of my existence as a specific individual.

4. Continuity of Personality

This is perhaps less important than the other three, but nonetheless there is a certain relative continuity of my personality and my dispositions. If I woke up tomorrow morning feeling and behaving exactly like Princess Diana shortly before her death then we might wonder if I was "really the same person." Or to take a case from real life, in the famous clinical example of Phineas Gage, Gage's brain was damaged when he was working on a railway construction crew and a steel bar went entirely through his skull. Miraculously, Gage survived but his personality was totally changed. Whereas before he had been a cheerful and pleasant person he became mean, suspicious, vicious, and nasty. In some sense we might feel that Gage was "a different person." Notice, however, that in describing these cases, we continue to use the same proper name as before. For practical purposes there is no question that it is still Phineas Gage that we are discussing. The sense in which he is a different person is not one that we regard as essential for practical purposes, such as figuring out who owes his income tax or owns his house. Still, his friends and family might feel that he is "not the same person."

As I remarked earlier, it is typical of our concepts that we often have a variety of criteria that enable a concept to function and the tacit background presupposition is that all of these go together. And in the cases we are familiar with in normal life, these do go together. All the same, there are some puzzles that arise.

IV. IDENTITY AND MEMORY

I have said that memory plays an essential role in our first-person conception of personal identity. Here is how. I now have conscious memories of earlier conscious experiences in my life, and I have a capacity to call up a very large number of other conscious memories of earlier conscious experiences in my life. My sense that I am exactly the same person over time, from my first-person point of view, is in a large part a matter of my ability to produce conscious memories of earlier conscious events in my life.

I think this is what Locke meant when he said that consciousness functions essentially in our conception of personal identity, but regardless of whether or not Locke meant this, continuity of memory is at least an important part of our concept of personal identity. Leibnitz made a similar point: imagine that you become Emperor of China, but that you lose every trace of every kind of memory of your past. There is no difference, says Leibnitz, between imagining this and imagining that you cease to exist and a new Emperor of China comes into existence.

There is a stock objection to Locke's account, which many people think is decisive and that I now want to state and answer. Here is how it goes. The account is circular. We can truly say of an agent that he can remember events in his earlier life only on the presupposition that he is identical with the person to whom those events occurred in the earlier life. But we cannot therefore explain personal identity in terms of memory, because the memory in question presupposes the very identity that we are trying to explain. We can put this more formally as follows:

A person P_2 at time T_2 is identical to an earlier person P_1 at time T_1 if and only if P_2 at T_2 remembers events occurring to P_1 at T_1, where the events in question are conscious experiences and the experience of remembering is itself a conscious experience.

The claim that this is circular is justified as follows: in order that P_2 at T_2 should really remember an event occurring to P_1 at T_1, as opposed to just thinking that he remembers it, P_2 has to be identical with P_1. But if that is true, then we cannot use the memory to justify the claim of identity or the criterion of identity, because we require identity as a necessary condition on the validity of the memory.

We can illustrate these points with examples. Suppose I now say, sincerely, I remember writing *The Critique of Pure Reason*. This does not in any way establish or tend to support the view that I am identical with Immanuel Kant, because we know that I could not have written *The Critique of Pure Reason*, since I am not identical with Immanuel Kant, and he wrote *The Critique of Pure Reason*. But by exactly the same token, if I say I now remember writing *Speech Acts*, this does not by itself go any way toward establishing that I am identical with John Searle, the author of *Speech Acts*, because we would have to know that I am John Searle before we could know that I correctly remember writing *Speech Acts*. The two cases are exactly parallel. Is this argument decisive against the theory that memory is an essential part of personal identity? I think the answer depends on which question we take the theory as trying to answer. If we take it as answering the question, What are the criteria of personal identity such that if those criteria are satisfied, then person P$_2$ at T$_2$ would be identical with person P$_1$ at an earlier time T$_1$? then the criterion fails. No matter how many of Kant's putative memories I have, I am still not Kant. However, there is a different question, which it seems to me this theory answers, and that is the first-person question: What is it about me, about my personal experiences, that makes me sense myself as a continuing entity through time, which is in addition to the continuity of my body? And to this question, it seems to me that the continuity of my memory experiences is an essential part of my sense of myself as a continuing self. Someone who is not me might have type-identical personal experiences that give him a sense of himself which is type identical to my sense of myself. All the same, we are not identical, and yet each of us has a sense of himself as a continuing self.

V. AN ARGUMENT FOR THE EXISTENCE OF A NON-HUMEAN SELF

All of these discussions leave open the question of whether or not we need the notion of a self in addition to the notion of particular psychological states and dispositions at all. I think most philosophers agree with Hume in his criticisms of both Locke and Descartes that there is no self or personal identity beyond the sequence of our actual experiences. Hume's skepticism about the self is like his skepticism about necessary connection and causation. He looks around to see if he can find some unifying impression that unites all of his various perceptions together and, not surprisingly, he fails to find any such unifying impression. When I turn my attention inward, he tells us, what I find are specific experiences. I find this or that desire for a drink of water, or a slight headache, or feeling of the pressure of the shoes against my feet, but there is no experience of the self in addition to these particular experiences. Consequently, any identity that I might attribute to myself must be a result of the sequence of particular experiences. It is an illusion, Hume tells us, to suppose that there is something over and above the specific experiences that constitute my self. As with necessary connection, Hume talks as if it were some lamentable failure on our part that we fail to find the experience of the self, just as we fail to find the experience of necessary connection. But, as in the earlier case, Hume is making a logical point, not a psychological point about the absence of a certain kind of experience. The point is, nothing could count as an experience of the self, because any experience we have, even an experience that lasted an entire lifetime, would simply be just another experience. Suppose I had a continuous yellow spot in my visual field that was with me my entire conscious life, always present. Would that be a self? No, it would just be a yellow spot. Nothing could satisfy the conditions necessary for something to be an experience of the self, that is, an experience that bound all of our other experience together. I think that Hume's arguments at the level they are directed at are quite convincing; and I believe that many, perhaps most, philosophers agree with me about the power of Hume's argument.

But I have reluctantly come to the conclusion that Hume left something out; and this leads to our second set of questions: Do we need to postulate something in addition to our bodies and the sequence of our experiences? I have come to the conclusion that, yes, we absolutely must postulate a self in addition to the sequence of experiences and I will now give you an argument for this postulation.

Let us go back to our original supposition that I consist of a body and a sequence of experiences. This sequence will include such things as the taste of coffee, the sight of the color red, the view of the San Francisco Bay from my window, etc. Is anything left out? I think there is. The first thing to notice is something I have remarked on earlier. We do not just have disordered experiences; rather, all of the experiences I have at any instant are experienced as part of a single, unified conscious field. Furthermore, the continuation of that conscious field throughout time is experienced by the possessor of that conscious field as a continuation of his or her own consciousness. That is, I do not experience my consciousness of five minutes ago or even five years ago as disconnected from my present consciousness; rather, I have the experience of a continuous consciousness interrupted by phases of sleep. (It is a fascinating fact, insufficiently appreciated in philosophical discussions, that one maintains a sense of the passage of time even during sleep, in at least this sense: when one wakes up, one has a sense of greater or lesser time having passed while one was asleep. This apparently is not true of people who have been knocked unconscious or have had a general anesthetic.)

The arguments that convinced me that we need to postulate at least a formal notion of the self (and I will say later what I mean by "formal") have to do with the notions of rationality, free choice, decision making, and reasons for action. We noticed in chapter 7 that intentionalistic explanations of rational human decision making and acting have a peculiar logical form that differs from the

standard form of causal explanations. The contrast is between saying, for example:

1. I made an X on the ballot paper because I wanted to vote for
   Bush
   and
2. I got a stomachache because I wanted to vote for Bush.

Now we will suppose, for the sake of the argument, that both of
these are true, and that both give adequate explanations. All the
same, their logical form is quite different. On a standard interpretation, number 2 states causally sufficient conditions. In that context, my desire to vote for Bush was sufficient to produce in me a
stomachache. But on a standard interpretation, number 1 does not
state causally sufficient conditions. Yes, I did make an X on the ballot paper for that reason, but all the same, I might not have. I might
have decided not to vote for Bush after all, or to leave the room, or
do any number of other things. But now we seem to have a puzzle.
How can the explanation of my behavior in terms of reasons be an
adequate explanation if it does not give causally sufficient conditions? Without such conditions, it does not explain why I did what
I did, rather than any number of other things that I could equally
well have done, all other conditions remaining the same. It seems
that if the explanation does not state causally sufficient conditions,
then it does not adequately explain the phenomenon that it was
supposed to explain. But the decisive answer to that point is that
the explanation is perfectly adequate from my point of view. It is
my behavior that I am explaining, and I can explain why I did
what I did by giving my reasons for doing what I did, without in
any way being committed to the view that the reasons state causally sufficient conditions. Indeed, I may be perfectly well aware
that they do not state causally sufficient conditions.

But how, then, are we to interpret statements of form 1, indeed,
how are we to interpret any statement that gives an explanation
of my free voluntary behavior by giving my reasons for acting?
And the answer, I believe, is that we have to suppose that in
addition to the "bundle of perceptions," as described by Hume,
there are certain formal constraints on the entity that makes the
decisions and carries out the actions. We have to postulate a
rational self or agent that is capable of acting freely and capable
of assuming responsibility for actions. It is the complex of the
notions of free action, explanation, responsibility, and reason that
give us the motivation for postulating something in addition to

the sequence of experiences and the body in which they occur. To be more precise, in order to account for free, rational actions, we have to suppose there is a single entity X such that X is conscious (with all that consciousness implies), X persists through time, X formulates and reflects on reasons for action under the constraints of rationality, X is capable of deciding, initiating, and carrying out actions under the presupposition of freedom, and (already implicit in what I have said), X is responsible for at least some of its actions.

Hume thought he had a decisive objection against any such postulation. I have no experience of this self, this X. If I turn my attention inward and examine all the experiences I am now having, none of them would I call my "self." I feel the shirt on my back, the aftertaste of coffee in my mouth, a slight hangover headache from last night, and the sight of the trees outside my window, but none of these is a self, and none of them would count as a self. So what then is this self? I think Hume is absolutely right; there is no experience of this entity, but that does not mean that we do not have to postulate some such entity or formal principle, and I will now explore further what sorts of reasons compel us to that and what sort of entity the self in question might be.

One way to think of these issues is to think of them as engineering problems. If you were designing a conscious robot, and you wanted a robot that would duplicate the full range of human rational capacities, that is, it would be able to reflect on reasons for action, make decisions, and act under the presupposition of its own freedom, then what would you have to put into the robot?

The first and obvious requirement of any such robot would have to be that it is conscious. Furthermore, the form of its consciousness would have to be cognitive, in the sense that it would have to take in perceptual inputs, consciously process the information derived from perception, and reason on the basis of that information toward action.

The second feature that it would have to have would be the capacity to initiate action, a capacity sometimes called "agency." This is a capacity additional to conscious perceptions. It is a peculiar capacity that humans and many animals have. It is a feature of certain sorts of consciousness, but not of all. The third step is, I believe, the crucial one. The conscious rational agent that we have created must be able to engage in something that in English we call *acting on* reasons. Now, this is important because the notion of acting on a reason is different from the notion of having something happen to one causally. That was the point of the illustration I gave earlier about the difference between the claim that I got a stomachache because I wanted to vote for Bush, and the claim that I performed a free action, I acted on my desire to vote for Bush. The notion of "acting on" presupposes the gap of free will that I have described earlier. So far then, we have put into our robot consciousness, with conscious perceptual experiences and other intentional states, the capacity to reflect on its intentional states and rational agency, which is the peculiar capacity to undertake actions on the presupposition of freedom. But if we have done that much, we already have a self. The self as I am describing it is a purely formal notion; it does not involve having a particular type of reason or a particular type of perception. Rather, it is a formal notion involving the capacity to organize its intentionality under constraints of rationality in such a way as to undertake voluntary, intentional actions, where the reasons are not causally sufficient to fix the action.

Why is such a notion of the self "formal" rather than "substantive"? To answer that question, I want to draw an analogy between the self and another formal notion. In order to understand my visual perceptions, I have to understand them as occurring *from a point of view,* but the point of view itself is not something that I see or otherwise perceive. The point of view is a purely formal requirement necessary to render intelligible the character of my experiences. The point of view itself has no substantive features other than this one formal constraint, namely, it has to be that point from which my experiences take place. Now, similarly, the notion of a self that I am postulating is a purely formal notion, but it is more complex. It has to be an entity, such that one and the same entity has consciousness, perception, rationality, the capacity to engage in action, and the capacity to organize perceptions and reasons, so as to perform voluntary actions on the presupposition of freedom. If you have got all of that, you have a self.

Now we can account for a whole lot of other features, of which two in particular are central for our notion of the human self. One is responsibility. When I engage in actions I undertake responsibility, and thus such questions as desert, blame, reward, justice, praise, and condemnation make a kind of sense that they would not make otherwise. Second, we are now able to account for the peculiar relations that rational animals have toward time. I can organize time, I can plan for the future, because one and the same self that makes the plans will exist in the future to execute those plans.

VI. CONCLUSION

In this chapter I have been mostly concerned with two issues, first the criteria of personal identity, or in other words, what fact about a person makes that person the same person across time and change. And second, I have tried to provide an argument to the effect that though Hume was right that there is no self as the object of our experiences, nonetheless there is a formal or logical requirement that we postulate a self as something in addition to the experiences in order that we can make sense of the character of our experiences. As far as the argument goes, I am not dissatisfied with it. But I am very dissatisfied by the fact that it does not seem to me to go far enough, and I do not really know how to complete it. I have two related worries. First, the underlying difficulty with Hume was his atomistic conception of experience. He thought that experiences always came to us in discrete units that he called "impressions" and "ideas." But we know that that is wrong. We know, as I have tried to emphasize, that we have a total, unified, conscious field and that in this conscious field our experiences are organized both at any given point and across time into quite orderly and complex structures. The Gestalt psychologists gave us a lot of evidence for this nonatomistic but rather holistic character of our perceptual experiences. A second worry that I have is that I do not know how to account for the fact that an important feature of our experiences is what one might call a "sense of self." One way to put this is to say that there is definitely something that it feels like to be me. And one way to get yourself to see that there is something that it feels like to be you is to try to imagine what it must feel like to be someone totally different. Imagine what it felt like to have been Adolf Hitler or Napoleon or George Washington. And it is important when you do this imaginative exercise that you not cheat and imagine yourself in the situation of Adolf Hitler, etc.; rather, you have to imagine not yourself playing the role of Adolf Hitler, but what it is like to be Adolf Hitler. If you do that I think you see that you imagine an experience that is quite different from the experience where you normally have a sense of your self as this self and not some other self. But of course the existence of the sense of self does not solve the problem of personal identity. Granted that there is something that it feels like to be me, that is not sufficient to guarantee that anybody who has that experience must be identical with me, because it is quite possible that any number of other people might have this same type-identical experience that I call the "sense of what it is to be me." My sense of self definitely exists, but it does not solve the problem of personal identity, and it does not yet so far flesh out the purely formal requirement that I said was necessary to supplement Hume's account in order to account for the possibility of free rational action. So, though this chapter is a beginning of a discussion of the self, it is not more than a beginning.

Suggestions for Further Reading

The classic statement of skepticism about the self is in Hume's *Treatise of Human Nature*, Selby-Bigge, L. A., ed., Oxford: Clarendon Press, 1951, Book I, Part IV, section VI, of personal identity, 251–263, as well as the Appendix, 623–939.

Locke's conception is to be found in his *Essay Concerning Human Understanding*, London: Routledge, 1894, especially chap. 27, "Of Identity and Diversity."

Other works about issues raised in this chapter are:

Parfit, D., *Reasons and Persons*, Oxford: Oxford University Press, 1986.
Searle, J. R., *Rationality in Action*, Cambridge, MA: MIT Press, 2001, especially chap. 3.

The following is a collection of essays:

Perry, J., ed., *Personal Identity*, Berkeley and Los Angeles: University of California Press, 1975.

EPILOGUE

Philosophy and the
Scientific World-View

I have now completed the task I have set for myself in the first chapter. I have tried to give an account of the mind that will situate mental phenomena as part of the natural world. Our account of the mind in all of its aspects—consciousness, intentionality, free will, mental causation, perception, intentional action, etc.—is naturalistic in this sense: first, it treats mental phenomena as just a part of nature. We should think of consciousness and intentionality as just as much a part of the natural world as photosynthesis or digestion. Second, the explanatory apparatus that we use to give a causal account of mental phenomena is an apparatus that we need to account for nature generally. The level at which we attempt to account for mental phenomena is biological rather than, say, at the level of subatomic physics. The reason for this is that consciousness and other mental phenomena are biological phenomena; they are created by biological processes and are specific to certain sorts of biological organisms. Of course, this is not to deny that our individual minds are shaped by our culture. But culture is not something in opposition to biology; rather, culture is the form that biology takes in different communities. One culture may differ from another culture, but there are limits to the differences. Each must be an expression of the underlying biological commonality of the human species. There could not be a long-term conflict between nature and culture, for if there were, nature would always win; culture would always lose.

People sometimes speak of the "scientific world-view" as if it were one view of how things are among others, as if there might be all sorts of world-views and "science" gave us one of them. In one way this is right; but in another way this is misleading and indeed suggests something false. It is possible to look at the same reality with different interests in mind. There is an economic point of view, an aesthetic point of view, a political point of view, etc., and the point of view of scientific investigation, in this sense, is one point of view among others. However, there is a way of interpreting this conception where it suggests that science names a specific kind of ontology, as if there were a scientific reality that is different from, for example, the reality of common sense. I think that is profoundly mistaken. The view implicit in this book, which I now want to make explicit, is that science does not name an ontological domain; it names rather a set of methods for finding out about anything at all that admits of systematic investigation. The fact that hydrogen atoms have one electron, for example, was discovered by something called the "scientific method," but that fact, once discovered, is not the property of science; it is entirely public property. It is a fact like any other. So if we are interested in reality and truth, there is really no such thing as "scientific reality" or "scientific truth." There are just the facts that we know. I cannot tell you how much confusion in philosophy has been generated by the failure to perceive these points. So, for example, there are frequently debates about the reality of the entities postulated by science. But either these entities exist or they do not. The view that I have of the matter is this: The fact that hydrogen atoms have one electron is a fact like the fact that I have one nose. The only difference is that for quite accidental reasons of evolution, I do not need any professional assistance to discover that I only have one nose, whereas given our structure and given the structure of hydrogen atoms, it takes a good deal of professional expertise to discover how many electrons are in a hydrogen atom.

There is no such thing as the scientific world. There is, rather, just the world, and what we are trying to do is describe how it works and describe our situation in it. As far as we know, its most fundamental principles are given by atomic physics, and, for that little corner of it that most concerns us, evolutionary biology. The two basic principles on which any such investigation as the one I have been engaging in depends on are, first, the notion that the most fundamental entities in reality are those described by atomic physics; and, second, that we, as biological beasts, are the products of long periods of evolution, perhaps as long as five billion years. Now, once you accept these points, and they are not points just about science but about how the world works, then some of the questions about the human mind admit of rather simple philosophical answers, though that does not imply that they admit of simple neurobiological answers.

We do not live in several different, or even two different, worlds, a mental world and a physical world, a scientific world and a world of common sense. Rather, there is just one world; it is the world we all live in, and we need to account for how we exist as a part of it.

Notes

WHY I WROTE THIS BOOK

1. J. R. Searle, *The Rediscovery of the Mind* (Cambridge, MA: MIT Press, 1992).

1. A DOZEN PROBLEMS
IN THE PHILOSOPHY OF MIND

1. I do not wish to suggest that mine is the only reasonable interpretation of Descartes. My claim is rather that the interpretation presented here has been the most influential in the history of the subject.
2. G. Ryle, *The Concept of Mind* (London: Hutchinson, 1949).

2. THE TURN TO MATERIALISM

1. K. Popper and J. C. Eccles, *The Self and Its Brain* (Berlin: Springer, 1977).
2. J. C. Eccles, *How the Self Controls Its Brain* (Berlin: Springer-Verlag, 1994), 5.
3. Eccles, *How the Self Controls Its Brain*, 69.
4. H. Stapp, *The Mindful Universe*, forthcoming.
5. The classical statement of idealism is in George Berkeley, *A Treatise Concerning the Principles of Human Knowledge*, ed. J. Dancy (Oxford: Oxford University Press, 1998).
6. H. Feigl, "The 'Mental' and the 'Physical'" in H. Feigl, M. Scriven and G. Maxwell, eds., *Minnesota Studies in the Philosophy of Science*, vol. 2 (Minneapolis: University of Minnesota Press, 1958).
7. D. Chalmers, *The Conscious Mind: In Search of a Fundamental Theory* (Oxford: Oxford University Press, 1996).
8. Some famous logical behaviorists were G. Ryle, see his *The Concept of Mind* (London: Hutchinson, 1949), and C. Hempel, "The Logical Analysis of

Psychology" in N. Block, ed., *Readings in Philosophy of Psychology*, vol. 1 (Cambridge, MA: Harvard University Press, 1980).

9. I cannot find the exact source of this quote. I think it is an adaptation of Ogden and Richards' characterization of Watson as "affecting general anesthesia." C. K. Ogden and I. A. Richards, *The Meaning of Meaning* (1926, London: Harcourt Brace and Company, 1949), 23.

10. Three classic statements of the identity theory are in U. T. Place, "Is consciousness a brain process?" *British Journal of Psychology*, vol. 47, no. 1 (1956): 44–50; J. J. C. Smart, "Sensations and Brain Processes," in D. Rosenthal, ed., *The Nature of Mind* (New York: Oxford University Press, 1991), 169–176; H. Feigl, "The 'mental' and the 'physical,'" in Feigl, *Minnesota Studies in the Philosophy of Science*.

11. This objection and the ones which follow are discussed in Smart, "Sensations and Brain Processes," in Rosenthal, *The Nature of Mind*.

12. This objection was presented by, among other people, J. T. Stevenson, "Sensations and Brain Processes: A reply to J. J. C. Smart" in C. V. Borst, ed., *The Mind-Brain Identity Theory* (New York: St. Martin's Press, 1970), 87–92.

13. G. Maxwell, "Unity of Consciousness and Mind-Brain Identity" in J. C. Eccles, ed., *Mind and Brain: The Many Faceted Problems* (Washington: Paragon House, 1974), 233–237.

14. This objection was discussed in Smart's original article, and also in J. J. C. Smart, "Further Remarks on Sensations and Brain Processes," in Borst, *The Mind-Brain Identity Theory*, 93–94.

15. J. R. Searle, *The Rediscovery of the Mind* (Cambridge, MA: MIT Press, 1992).

16. N. Block, "Troubles with Functionalism," in C. Wade Savage, ed., *Minnesota Studies in the Philosophy of Science*, vol. 9 (Minneapolis: University of Minnesota Press, 1978), 261–325.

17. Among the early proponents of functionalism were H. Putnam, D. Lewis, and D. Armstrong. See H. Putnam, "The Nature of Mental States," in Block, *Readings in Philosophy of Psychology*, 223–231; D. Lewis, "Psychophysical and Theoretical Identifications," in Block, *Readings in Philosophy of Psychology*, and D. Lewis, "Mad Pain and Martian Pain," in Block, *Readings in Philosophy of Psychology*, 207–222; D. Armstrong, *A Materialist Theory of the Mind* (London: Routledge, 1993).

18. P. Johnson-Laird, *The Computer and the Mind* (Cambridge, MA: Harvard University Press, 1988), and *Mental Models, Toward a Cognitive Science of Language, Inference and Consciousness* (Cambridge, MA: Harvard University Press, 1983).

19. Eliminativism was originally stated by R. Rorty and P. Feyerabend. A recent advocate is Paul Churchland. See P. Feyerabend, "Mental Events and the Brain," *Journal of Philosophy* (1963): 295–296; R. Rorty, "Mind-Body Identity, Privacy and Categories," in D. Rosenthal, ed., *Materialism, and the Mind-Body Problem* (Englewood Cliffs, NJ: Prentice Hall, 1971), 174–199; P. M. Churchland, "Eliminative Materialism and the Propositional Attitudes," in Rosenthal, *The Nature of Mind*.

20. D. Davidson, "Mental Events," reprinted in D. Davidson, *Essays on Actions and Events* (Oxford: Oxford University Press, 1980), 207–227.

21. P. M. Churchland., "Eliminative Materialism and the Propositional Attitudes," in Rosenthal, *The Nature of Mind*, 603.

3. ARGUMENTS AGAINST MATERIALISM

1. T. Nagel "What Is It Like to Be a Bat?" *Philosophical Review,* vol. 83 (1974): 435–450, reprinted in David Chalmers, ed., *The Philosophy of Mind: Classical and Contemporary Readings* (New York: Oxford University Press, 2002).
2. F. Jackson, "What Mary Didn't Know," *Journal of Philosophy,* vol: 83 (1982): 291–295, reprinted in T. O'Connor and D. Robb, eds., *Philosophy of Mind* (New York: Routledge 2003); F. Jackson, "Epiphenomenal Qualia," *Philosophical Quarterly,* vol. 32 (1986): 127–136, reprinted in Chalmers, *The Philosophy of the Mind.*
3. N. Block, "Troubles with Functionalism," *Minnesota Studies in the Philosophy of Science*, vol. 9 (Minneapolis: Minnesota University Press, 1978), 261–325, reprinted in N. Block (ed.), *Readings in Philosophy of Psychology* (Cambridge, MA: Harvard University Press, 1980), 268–305.
4. S. A. Kripke, *Naming and Necessity* (Cambridge, MA: Harvard University Press, 1980), relevant portion reprinted in Chalmers, *The Philosophy of Mind,* 329–332.
5. J. R. Searle, "Minds, Brains and Programs," *Behavioral and Brain Sciences,* 3 (1980): 417–424, reprinted in many publications, including O'Connor and Robb, *Philosophy of Mind,* 332–352.
6. H. Dreyfus, *What Computers Can't Do,* rev. ed. (New York: Harper & Row, 1979).
7. J. R. Searle, *The Rediscovery of the Mind* (Cambridge, MA: MIT Press, 1992).
8. T. Nagel, "Armstrong on the Mind," in Block, *Readings in Philosophy of Psychology,* 205.
9. The insufficiency of behavior to discriminate discriminable meanings was shown by W. V. O. Quine, *Word and Object* (Cambridge, MA: Harvard University Press, 1962). He did not see that the argument was a *reductio ad absurdum* of behaviorist accounts of meaning. For a criticism of Quine's views, see, J. R. Searle, "Indeterminacy, Empiricism, and the First Person," *Journal of Philosophy,* vol. 84, no. 3 (March, 1987): 123–147; reprinted in J. R. Searle, *Consciousness and Language* (Cambridge: Cambridge University Press, 2002).
10. C. McGinn, "Anomalous Monism and Kripke's Cartesian Intuitions," in Block, *Readings in the Philosophy of Psychology,* 156–158.
11. D. Dennett, "Back from the Drawing Board," in D. Dahlbom, *Dennett and His Critics* (Cambridge, MA: Routledge, 1993), 211.

4. CONSCIOUSNESS PART I

1. D. Chalmers, *The Conscious Mind: In Search of a Theory of Conscious Experience* (New York: Oxford University Press, 1996), 115–121.
2. T. Huxley, "On the Hypothesis that Animals Are Automata and Its History," in D. M. Armstrong, *The Mind-Body Problem: An Opinionated Introduction* (Boulder: Westview Press, 1999), 148.
3. J. Kim, *Mind in a Physical World* (Cambridge, MA: MIT Press, 1998), 44.
4. For an earlier version of this list see H. Feigl, "The 'Mental' and the 'Physical'," *Minnesota Studies in the Philosophy of Science,* vol. 2, eds. H. Fiegl, M. Scriven, and G. Maxwell (Minneapolis: University of Minnesota Press, 1958).
5. J. Kim, *The Philosophy of Mind* (Boulder: Westview Press, 1998), 59.

5. CONSCIOUSNESS PART II

1. See, for example, the chapter on pain and temperature (chapter 5) in C. R. Noback and R. J. Demarest, *The Nervous System: Introduction and Review* (New York: McGraw-Hill, 1977).
2. M. S. Gazzaniga, *The Social Brain: Discovering the Networks of the Mind* (New York: Basic Books, 1985).
3. W. Penfield, *The Mystery of the Mind: A Critical Study of Consciousness and the Human Brain* (Princeton: Princeton University Press, 1975), 76.
4. D. Dennett, *Consciousness Explained* (Boston: Little, Brown, 1991). Specifically, he says consciousness is a virtual von Neumann machine implemented in a connectionist architecture.
5. T. Nagel, *The View from Nowhere* (Oxford: Oxford University Press, 1986).
6. C. McGinn, "Can We Solve the Mind-Body Problem?" *Mind*, vol. 98 (1989): 349–356.
7. J. Kim, "Epiphenomenal and Supervenient Causation," *Midwest Studies in Philosophy* vol. 9 (1984): 257–270.
8. D. Chalmers, *The Conscious Mind: In Search of a Fundamental Theory* (Oxford: Oxford University Press, 1986).
9. C. Koch, *The Quest for Consciousness: A Neurobiological Approach* (Englewood, CO: Roberts and Co., 2004).

6. INTENTIONALITY

1. D. Dennett, "The Intentional Stance," in *Brainstorms: Philosophical Essays on Mind and Psychology* (Montgomery, VT: Bradford Books, 1978).
2. J. R. Searle, *Intentionality: An Essay in the Philosophy of the Mind* (Cambridge: Cambridge University Press, 1983).
3. H. Putnam, "Meaning of 'Meaning,'" in K. Gunderson, ed., *Language, Mind, and Knowledge* (Minneapolis: University of Minnesota Press, 1975), 131–193, excerpt reprinted in D. Chalmers, ed., *The Philosophy of Mind: Classical and Contemporary Readings* (New York: Oxford University Press, 2002).
4. In Chalmers, *Philosophy of Mind*, 587.
5. T. Burge, "Individualism and the Mental," *Midwest Studies in Philosophy*, vol. 4 (1979), excerpt reprinted in Chalmers, *Philosophy of Mind*.

7. MENTAL CAUSATION

1. D. Hume, *A Treatise of Human Nature*, ed. L. A. Selby-Bigge (Oxford: Clarendon Press, 1951).
2. W. Penfield, *The Mystery of the Mind* (Princeton: Princeton University Press, 1975), 76.
3. J. Kim, *Mind in a Physical World: An Essay on the Mind-Body Problem and Mental Causation* (Cambridge, MA: MIT Press, 1998).
4. J. Kim, "Causality, Identity and Supervenience in the Mind-Body Problem," *Midwest Studies in Philosophy*, vol. 4 (1979): 47.

8. FREE WILL

1. D. N. Wegner, *The Illusion of Conscious Will* (Cambridge, MA: MIT Press, 2003).

9. THE UNCONSCIOUS
AND THE EXPLANATION OF BEHAVIOR

1. S. Freud, "Fragment of an Analysis of a Case of Hysteria," in *Collected Papers*, vol. 3 (New York: Basic Books, 1959), 13–146, esp. 49ff.
2. J. R. Searle, *The Rediscovery of the Mind* (Cambridge, MA: MIT Press, 1992).
3. L. Wittgenstein, *Philosophical Investigations* (New York: Macmillan, 1958); cf. S. Kripke, *Wittgenstein on Rules and Private Language* (Cambridge, MA: Harvard University Press, 1982).

10. PERCEPTION

1. B. Russell, *An Inquiry into Meaning and Truth* (London: Allen and Unwin, 1940), 15.
2. For a statement of several different versions of the argument from illusion, cf. A. J. Ayer, *The Foundations of Empirical Knowledge* (London: Macmillan, 1953).
3. D. Hume, *A Treatise of Human Nature*, ed., L. A. Selby-Bigge (Oxford: Clarendon Press, 1951), 210–211.
4. J. Locke, *An Essay Concerning Human Understanding*, ed. A. S. Pringle-Pattison (Oxford: Clarendon Press, 1924), 67.
5. M. Bauerlein, *Literary Criticism: An Autopsy* (Philadelphia: University of Pennsylvania Press, 1997).
6. J. L. Austin, *Sense and Sensibilia* (Oxford: Oxford University Press, 1962).

Index

deep, 168
dispositional analysis of, 172–173
as dynamic, 171
as nonconscious, 168
as preconscious, 167
as repressed, 167
as rule-described, 175–178
and rule following,
175–178

as rule-governed,
175–178

Weak Artificial Intelligence, 46

zombies, 64, 71
and zagnets, 71

Name Index

Anscombe, E., 143
Aristotle, 53
Austin, J. L., 187
Ayer, A. J., 195

Berkeley, G., 34, 180, 185, 186
Block, N., 61
Bradley, F., 34
Burge, T., 127–128

Chalmers, D., 33, 104
Chomsky, N., 37
Church, A., 47
Churchland, P., 55

Davidson, D., 52–53
Dennett, D., 71, 115
Descartes, R., 8–11, 15, 16,
    22–23, 38, 110, 165–166, 180,
    186, 192
Ding, H., ix

Eccles, J. C., 23, 29–30
Eddington, 33

Freud, S., 167

Gazzaniga, M., 96

Hegel, G., 34
Hobbes, T., 155
Hudin, J., ix
Hume, D., 25, 36, 37, 103,
    143, 155, 180, 183, 185–186,
    192, 197, 200

Jackson, F., 60–61, 66–68
James, W., 154

Kant, I., 180, 199
Kim, J., 87, 103, 145
Kripke, S., 61–62, 68–69, 87

Leibniz, G., 39
Locke, J., 180, 184, 185, 186, 198

Maxwell, G., 40
McGinn, C., 102